Ben Dirs writes on sport for the BBC, covering everything from Olympic Games, Ashes series and Rugby World Cups, to Snooker World Championships, Wimbledon and boxing. He has been ringside for many of the biggest bouts involving British boxers over the last ten years, including Ricky Hatton's Las Vegas super-fights against Floyd Mayweather and Manny Pacquiao, Joe Calzaghe's defeats of American legends Roy Jones Jr and Bernard Hopkins, David Haye's heavyweight clashes against Nikolay Valuev and Wladimir Klitschko and Carl Froch's thrill____ ____ ____ ____ Mikkel Kessler. This is his fourth bo___

Praise for *The H*___

'The compelling story behind two classic rivals who inspired a generation of fans and fighters' Ron Lewis, *The Times*

'A tremendous account of one of sport's most intense rivalries and a golden age in British boxing' *Boxing News*

'The rivalry between Nigel Benn and Chris Eubank was so hot even hardcore American fans took notice. If young boxing fans want to know what a real rivalry between real champions looks and *feels* like, we strongly recommend they read *The Hate Game*' *The Ring*

'Lovers of quality boxing writing will relish this intriguing insight. Dirs speaks to all the main protagonists behind the scenes – trainers, promoters, TV executives – and captures the essence of the simmering animosity that spawned one of the most brutal rivalries ever' *Metro*

'Framed by a list of impeccable sources, Dirs digs deep behind the scenes to uncover fresh anecdotes and is particularly good at exposing the myths which helped the Benn–Eubank story evolve into a position where it could so powerfully polarise public opinion. A fine, fresh insight into one of British boxing's most compelling eras' *Press Association*

THE HATE GAME

Benn, Eubank and boxing's bitterest rivalry

Ben Dirs

**SIMON &
SCHUSTER**

London · New York · Sydney · Toronto · New Delhi

A CBS COMPANY

First published in Great Britain by Simon & Schuster UK Ltd, 2013
This paperback edition published by Simon and Schuster UK Ltd, 2014
A CBS COMPANY

1 3 5 7 9 10 8 6 4 2

Simon & Schuster UK Ltd
1st Floor
222 Gray's Inn Road
London WC1X 8HB

www.simonandschuster.co.uk

Simon & Schuster Australia,
Sydney

Simon & Schuster India,
New Delhi

A CIP catalogue record for this book is available from the British Library

Paperback ISBN: 978-1-47112-904-9
eBook ISBN: 978-1-47112-905-6

Typeset by Hewer Text UK Ltd, Edinburgh
Printed in the UK by CPI Group (UK) Ltd, Croydon, CR0 4YY

CONTENTS

Foreword

When mates and acquaintances of mine insist boxing ain't like it used to be, the names of Benn and Eubank are usually included in the first sentence of the lament. They were the Coe and Ovett of the ring, everyone took sides, no one preferred not to comment. Such was the clamour at the time that much of the rest of their sport was reduced to a sideshow. The rivalry became a reference point, a gauge for all showdowns to be measured against in time to come.

As the 1980s disappeared over the horizon, boxing should have been in mourning. The three Americans and one Panamanian who now trade as the Four Kings – Sugar Ray Leonard, Tommy Hearns, Marvin Hagler and Roberto Duran – were done rivalling. On the British scene, Barry McGuigan had retired and we wondered who could regenerate his ridiculous TV viewing figures. It is a measure of the appeal of Benn and Eubank that the transition was seamless.

The story of each man has been told often and in various forms. Here, for the first time, Ben Dirs brings together all the duckers and divers and dreamers and schemers whose input, from the centre to the periphery, created and then exaggerated the antagonism that captivated a nation. The American promoter Bob Arum once said that the hardest men in boxing are not the ones wearing gloves and a gumshield but those sporting suits and a briefcase. This book serves as an X-ray of the underbelly of a business masquerading as a sport. Bending the ears of boxers, promoters, managers, trainers and writers, Dirs takes us on a journey through the mire of ruthless self-interest which underpinned but somehow rarely undermined one of the great duels in British boxing history. Remarkably, the urge to revise history is resisted by his sources, as wounds left to fester for two decades are reopened. Benn and Eubank provided plenty of memories in the ring but the accounts of the deal-makers and the contemporaries are invaluable to our wider understanding of such an important era.

At the heart of the story are two men who could fight. All boxers are brave but some are prepared to give more than others when they lace up gloves. Benn and Eubank engaged not in fights but events. That we saw them in the same ring only twice remains a frustration for boxing fans of overlapping generations. But at least we saw them. Today, they might well have been kept apart, with factional infighting steering them along parallel career paths, never to converge and combust. Maybe it was different back then. Maybe my pals have a point.

Mike Costello, BBC boxing commentator
Thursday 30 May 2013

Author's note

Any lisping in this book was suggested by the interviewees and not the author.

PROLOGUE
Parliamentary procedure

Chris Eubank is sweating under the lights but still full of running. Fresh from a 20-second knockout of Reginaldo dos Santos, already consumed by Nigel Benn. 'This is why I shall take you out on the night of eighteenth of November,' Eubank, nostrils twitching wildly, spits down the camera lens. 'You are mine, you belong to me, I am the man.' Cut to the television studio. Benn, looking fine in a bottle-green zoot suit with shoulders you could set a meal for five on, raises an eyebrow before swivelling to face the camera.

'Nigel Benn, he's talking to you,' says presenter Nick Owen. Stoking the ire, fuelling the hate.

'Tell him to face me,' says Benn, flickering into flames. 'Thing about him, he's all hype. He's *all* hype. And I can't wait to give him a good, good hiding.'

The camera pulls back to reveal Eubank, his back to Benn, head bowed as if in contemplation. Eubank, looking sharp as always in a charcoal suit, raises his chin, narrows his eyes and peers into the middle distance: a study in disdain.

'You know,' Benn goes on, 'he went out there and done the job on the guy. Who was it? Another road sweeper? Hey, I've done that before. Now I'm with the big boys. I'm there. I'm there already. He's got to prove himself, not me.'

Eubank breaks into a half-smile and for a second it looks like he might start corpsing. 'Will you prove yourself, Chris?' says Owen. And, just like that, Eubank is back on script, giving the performance of a lifetime.

'On the particular night in question I will show that I have what it takes,' says Eubank. 'He's the real hype. I've come up the hard way . . .'

'I'm gonna prove myself, boy,' says Benn, his words rolling in like dark plumes over Eubank's shoulder.

'You've had your time,' says Eubank, deigning to face Benn at last. 'Let's have some parliamentary procedure here. Right?' Benn turns away and laughs. A 'what have we got here?' kind of laugh. An 'I'm not sure I know how to deal with this man' kind of laugh. Off camera, Benn's manager, Ambrose Mendy, lets out an exasperated 'Oh God . . .' Eubank has got them. Hook, line and sinker.

'But what makes you think you can beat Nigel Benn?' says Owen.

'Because he's just a puncher,' says Eubank, 'he's only got a puncher's chance. I'm a skillster, I'm a fighter, I can punch as hard as he can. I can box, I can slug. Everything is loaded in my favour for this fight . . .' Benn swivels menacingly from side to side and leers. Every word from Eubank another log for the flames.

'Do you go along with that, Ambrose Mendy?' asks Owen.

'Not at all, not at all,' replies Mendy, also resplendent in green. 'Chris Eubank tries to talk as if he came out of some silver-spoon society. He's a kid off the street the same as us and we're gonna find out on the night just who's fooling who. And with regards to Chris saying boxing is a mug's game, we've got something to show you, it's a piece of our own artwork . . .' Benn and Mendy unfurl home-made posters of

Eubank's head transposed on a mug. Seconds later, Mendy is quoting from *King Lear*. It is beguiling, disorientating stuff.

'A Shakespearean quote for you, young man, to learn: "How much sharper than the serpent's tooth it is to have a thankless child." And that's from all the professional boxers in this country.' Henry Cooper might have put it differently but he would have agreed with the sentiment. If he only knew what it was.

'Barry Hearn, why is this boxer the man they all love to hate?' says Owen.

'Well, I don't think they do,' says Hearn, Eubank's manager and promoter. 'I think that's an image that's been afforded to him by some of the journalists in Fleet Street. It takes a bit of time to appreciate Chris Eubank . . .' Eubank raises his chin still higher and fans his hand across his chest: simultaneously doing his best to look unappreciated while demonstrating why he takes time to appreciate.

'But why is it so important to beat this particular man?' says Owen.

'This is the business,' says Eubank. 'This is the business . . .'

Boxing is sporting offal: blood, guts, brains, hearts, spleens, marrow encased in splintered bone. The bits most people are too squeamish to consume. Because they smell too real, taste too real, feel too real. It is why you rarely find accidental boxing writers, in the same way you find football or cricket writers who stumbled across their sport: you need a cast-iron stomach to cover a game that is as likely to leave you retching in the gutter as it is to have you purring over its pungent deliciousness. And just as eating offal is considered absurd by many – why innards and entrails when you could have steak? – so you require a keen sense of the absurd to cover boxing. Consciously or subconsciously the absurdity offsets the brutality and the tragedy. This has always been the case, stretching back to the days when men fought with bare knuckles on waterfronts and heaths. Take William 'Bendigo' Thompson, also known as 'The Nottingham Jester' because of his penchant for defaming opponents' wives and mothers and pulling faces during fights. In 1839, Thompson beat one James 'Deaf ' Burke to be crowned Champion Prize Fighter of All England. On his return to Nottingham, Thompson somersaulted into the crowd and broke a kneecap, meaning he was unable to defend his title for two years. He made up for it, winning a third match against arch rival Ben Caunt in 1845. After 96 rounds. Five years later he was lured out of retirement when someone dared to call him a coward. That someone being his 82-year-old mother.

For Benn and Eubank the brutality and the tragedy could wait. This was some of the absurd stuff: a black boxer talking like a toff; a black boxing manager quoting Shakespeare. If it was disorientating for the British public it was scarcely less so for boxing insiders who knew the black boxer talking like a toff had an impoverished childhood in England before learning his trade in New York's burnt-out South Bronx; and that the black boxing manager quoting Shakespeare learned his schtick in prison and held court in a restaurant in Stratford. East London, that is. As the *Guardian* boxing writer Kevin Mitchell observes: 'Let's face it, these are pretty weird circles we move in.'

Mendy and Hearn knew better than most that the absurd stuff mattered. The flim-flam, the nonsense, the set-up. But even these two masters of boxing's dark arts could not have imagined that Benn and Eubank's first joint public appearance would be an almost perfect distillation of what would become the greatest rivalry in British boxing. They played their parts to perfection and the British public got it. Even if it wasn't exactly sure what it was it was getting.

'You won't even face him, why won't you face him tonight?' says Owen. Stoking the ire, fuelling the hate.

'I have nothing to say to Nigel,' says Eubank. 'I find the man intolerable. In fact he's so wild, I have no time for such people. He has no class as far as I see it.' Even Benn is grinning now. A grin that says: 'I hate to admit it but this guy is good.' Eubank continues: 'About Nigel Benn I would say this: the man is a powerful puncher, a very powerful puncher. For this I would like his autograph because after I've finished with him, he isn't going to be anybody.'

'It seems that this one is working you up more than any other fight,' says Owen to Benn. Stoking the ire, fuelling the hate.

'Yeah, more than anyone else,' says Benn. 'I think the public is demanding this. I walk down the street and they say, "Hey, give this boy a hiding . . ."'

'I have to say, there seems a genuine element of hate between these two,' says Owen. Stoking the ire, fuelling the hate.

'For sure,' says Benn.

'I don't hate the man,' says Eubank, 'I just want his WBO title. I pray that I have enough dignity not to hate the man. Hate doesn't come into it for me. Hate destroys the game and makes it look brutal, and that's why a lot of people don't take to it. I intend to prove I am a better fighter than the man. Which I am.'

'I personally do hate him,' says Benn. 'I personally do hate him . . .'

And it is time to sign the contracts. To translate all that ire and hate – real and imagined – into gospel. Forever and ever, Amen.

CHAPTER ONE
Having a good whack

Cast a rod into the vast sea of boxing history and you will not always come up with the correct information. Because for every straight talker in boxing there is a bullshit merchant; for every realist there is a fantasist; for every man who tells it like it was there is a man who tells it like he would have liked it to have been. Stir in fading memories, old loyalties and festering beefs and you invariably end up with more than one version of the same story. And sometimes in boxing you get two versions of the same story that diverge so wildly you wonder whether either of the storytellers was there at all.

'After the Michael Watson fight it felt like that old soul classic by Teddy Pendergrass, "The Whole Town's Laughing at Me",' says Benn's former manager Ambrose Mendy. 'We were there to take on everybody, were proclaiming Nigel to be the greatest and he had been masterly schooled in the ring. After the fight I chucked everybody out of the changing room. Nigel was tearful with his head in his hands, saying, "It's all gone now." And by that he meant the gold and the jewellery and the cars. Then he said: "What are we gonna do?" And I said: "Oh, it's *we* now is it? Before the fight it was *I*." But I also said to Nigel: "Do you still believe you can be middleweight champion of the world?" And he gave me this eerie look and said: "Of course I fucking can." I was like, "Well get up, we're going back in." And we did the complete ring entrance all over again. It was really elaborate, involving more than 50 people, with Michael Jackson lookalikes and God knows what else. When we were heading towards the ring no one had a clue what was going on, everyone was in a state of astonishment. And to be honest, I didn't have a clue what we were doing either. I just knew it was inspired and the right thing to do. And that was Nigel reborn.'

'You take it from me,' says Brian Lynch, Benn's trainer for the Watson fight, 'that's a lot of bollocks. Nigel had disappeared before anybody got back to the van where we were changing. All his clothes were on the floor and he'd gone. He run away and I didn't see him no more. He thought he was going to walk through Watson and he didn't. He knew he'd done it all wrong.'

Whatever the truth – and even Benn is hazy on the details – all signs point to desolation. Benn's ascent through the ranks was as thrilling to Brits as Mike Tyson's was to Americans, each vanquished opponent another kill to notch on his impressive fuselage. But Watson shot Benn down, rendering him a mangled, smoking wreckage. 'There was complete devastation after the Michael Watson fight,' says Benn. 'That was the worst defeat ever. Ever. I cried my eyes out. Everyone had been telling me: "Nige, you're the best", and I was loving all that adoration, all that adulation. People were paying me ten grand to have their picture taken with me at their bar mitzvah, people were throwing BMWs and Bentleys at me. I was thinking: "Hello? Not too long ago I was signing on and getting £36.40 every two weeks." But after the Watson fight everything we'd built was gone.'

★ ★ ★

Lynch spotted Benn's potential as an unpolished talent fighting out of West Ham Amateur Boxing Club. Rough-hewn but already dark and destructive. 'The first things that impressed me about him were his discipline and his aggression,' says Lynch. 'When I weighed him up, my opinion was that he didn't have much skill, he didn't have much technique but he had that raw aggression, like Rocky Marciano and Mike Tyson. So when lots of people were saying he wasn't going to make it I thought he had a long way to go. Contrary to what some people say now, he didn't have a bad chin and he didn't get hit much because he was quick, with very fast hands – in and out, gone. He used to take a few shots to give them but he was so confident in his own power he wasn't really worried about that: once he'd hit them they got knocked out, got stopped or swallowed it. Rod Douglas beat him in the ABAs in 1985, before I started training him, but when they both moved up to middleweight a year later Nigel bashed him up and went on to win the ABA finals.'

Benn considered quitting boxing after his defeat to Douglas in 1985, an early sign that he found it difficult to reconcile the sense of entitlement that came with the ownership of two wrecking-ball fists. But the determination that had been instilled in him during his time with the Royal Regiment of Fusiliers served him well on Civvy Street. 'When I was on the streets of Northern Ireland during The Troubles, the rain and snow would just bounce off my chest,' says Benn. 'I was determined, nothing stopped me. It gave me that little bit extra as a boxer.' And so Benn was naturally drawn to Lynch, a former Thames lighterman and no stranger to hard graft. With Lynch cracking the whip, Benn cut a swathe through the amateur ranks, culminating in glory at the 1986 ABA finals, which should have led to a spot at the Commonwealth Games. But when Benn, whose girlfriend Sharron had recently given birth to his first child, missed England's first training session he was jettisoned from the squad. Worse, Rod Douglas replaced him and went on to win gold in Edinburgh.

Stung by what he saw as his humiliation at the hands of grey fools in blazers, Benn threw off his vest, resigned his job as a store detective and waded into the shark-infested unpaid waters. Safe in the knowledge that punchers have people believing pretty much anything is possible, he wasn't short of suitors. Quickest to draw his cheque book was Burt McCarthy, cousin of former British featherweight champion and East End legend Sammy and who had guided the career of Errol Christie, another hugely gifted amateur star who won a record 11 titles by the age of 18. It was written of Christie that 'his chin sets questions his heart cannot answer' and there are few better examples of how an amateur's skills are not necessarily transferable to the professional ranks. Irresistible in a vest, Christie found the rough and tumble of professional boxing less to his liking. His days as a prospect were effectively brought to an end when Mark Kaylor, another product of West Ham ABC, knocked him out in a British title eliminator at Wembley Arena in 1985. Christie was only 22 and destined never to fight for a professional title. But scratch a boxing manager and you'll discover an inveterate gambler underneath and it is a measure of the gambling instincts of McCarthy that he was willing to take the same risk with Benn.

Benn made his pro debut against Graeme Ahmed at Fairfield Hall, Croydon, on 28 January 1987. It is modern boxing convention to stick a former amateur starlet in with a bona fide tomato can for his first paid fight, but Ahmed was a 26-fight veteran with 16 wins on his record. Knocked out only twice previously, Benn had him down three times in the second round before the referee called a halt to proceedings. Five knockouts followed in the next six months before Benn was matched with Manchester's Eddie Smith. Smith had a win over future British and European middleweight champion Tony Sibson on his record and had also been in with Kaylor. Benn took him out in one round.

But the fight that first brought Benn wider media and public attention was his 16-second knockout of Liverpool's Ian Chantler, ranked number seven in Britain at the time. 'I get worried when a guy goes down,' said Benn after the fight. 'In case he doesn't get up for me to hit him again.' It was a win that moved McCarthy to say: 'Nigel will need three guys just to count his money – or weigh it.' McCarthy wouldn't be one of them. Christie's career having ground to a virtual standstill after a fourth defeat in November 1987, McCarthy declared himself 'disenchanted with the business of boxing' and there-fore unable to take Benn any further. Enter Frank Warren, who as a young, thrusting manager and promoter had succeeded in blowing open a cartel that had ruled British boxing for years, chief among it Mickey Duff. Where McCarthy was disenchanted with the business of boxing, Warren was high on it and looking for his next fix. A few sniffs of the intoxicating Benn, who was voted 1987 Young Boxer of the Year by the Boxing Writers' Club of Great Britain after 12 straight knockouts, and Warren was hooked.

Under Warren's guidance, Benn continued to fight with a regularity that would make most modern boxers come out in hives and needed only seven rounds to dispose of four oppo-nents in the space of 46 days at the start of 1988. But Benn was growing impatient, warning after his two-round demolition of Venezuelan trial horse Fermin Chirino in January of that year: 'I don't want to fight any more Mexican roadsweepers.'

Benn's geography might have been out but the message to Warren was clear. So Warren threw his slobbering attack dog some live meat, matching Benn with Ghana's Abdul Umaru Sanda for the Commonwealth middleweight title in April at the Alexandra Pavilion in Muswell Hill. Sanda had lost a close points decision to then British and European title-holder Sibson only two years earlier and, although a late replacement, was expected to provide a stern test: 'Benn's slam-bang tactics might not succeed against Sanda as they have done against his other 16 opponents, who had to go home early,' was how *The Times* saw it. Benn had Sanda down twice before stopping him in the second round.

But after only one more fight for Warren, a second-round stoppage of American Tim Williams, Benn joined forces with Ambrose Mendy, a frighteningly ambitious and somewhat wayward former Warren employee. 'I was invited to a meeting at Browns nightclub in Hackney and, lo and behold, Nigel was there,' says Mendy. 'He poured out his concerns over his relationship with Frank Warren. One of his disenchantments was that Warren wasn't getting him any real opponents. He was adamant that if he had to go back to Frank he would quit boxing and go back to being a store detective. That said to me that he knew exactly what he wanted. That counted for a lot. So when he asked if I would represent him, I said I'd be happy to.'

'When Nigel left it was bad news and quite annoying,' concedes Warren, who once admitted he was 'in the business of creating monsters'. 'Ambrose Mendy did with Nigel Benn what he does with a lot of people: blew down his ear, promised him the world, told him everything he wanted to hear. And then didn't deliver. Nigel believed what he said and it all turned to tears. What does Ambrose Mendy know about boxing? I know what he knows about boxing: nothing. And it's not just him, there's a lot of people who come into the sport who think they know better than everyone else, think there's a new way of doing things. But I'd already been doing it for years when I signed Nigel Benn. I lived and breathed boxing, and still do.'

Even before their bust-up over Benn, Warren and Mendy's relationship had been somewhat complicated, even by boxing's dysfunctional standards. Mendy had worked as a marketing man for Warren for a short time, while Warren had been best man at Mendy's wedding. So far, so cosy. 'He was working in our office at the time on sponsorship,' says Warren. 'And he asked me to be his best man. I got married about three months before him and he wasn't even invited. Anyway, it drifted on and on and suddenly I had to be up the church and I was thinking: "What on earth have I let myself in for?" My good friend Ernie Fossey [Warren's long-time matchmaker and right-hand man] said, "You're being stupid, you shouldn't do this." Fossey was right: a week after Mendy's wedding, Warren sacked him. Then came Mendy's sweet revenge.

After Benn's defection, Warren and Mendy exchanged writs before Benn was eventually cleared to box again, ostensibly under his own management. Mendy was announced as Benn's 'commercial representative' and at other times described as his agent. It was a measure of their bond that even when the British Boxing Board of Control refused Mendy a manager's licence and threatened to strip Benn of his own licence and Commonwealth belt if he continued the relationship, Benn stood firm. 'We never had a contract,' says Mendy. 'I took Nigel to the cemetery where my mum was buried and made a commitment with a handshake over her grave. That's the kind of relationship we had.' 'I loved him more than any other person,' says Benn.

Benn's enforced sabbatical from the ring – after 18 fights in 16 months since turning pro, he didn't fight for five months after the Tim Williams encounter – did little to dull his savagery. 'He was a raw, physical threat in the ring,' recalls Kevin Mitchell of the *Guardian*. 'There was never much subtlety involved, it was all or nothing. Every night he got in the ring there was an electricity that ran through the place, even early in his career, that's why he had such an amazing following. I saw him against Anthony Logan at the Royal Albert Hall [in October 1988] and when he was taking that beating in the second round I remember thinking: "He's got to be gone." But he withstood it and knocked Logan out with a left hand that started somewhere down by his knees. Nigel fought like he did because he lived life to the full in everything he did. He was an emotional man, fully committed.'

Indeed, the Logan fight was further proof that Benn's emotional incontinence, so easily set flowing, was to the detriment of his boxing. 'When Nigel fought Anthony Logan, Logan hit him about 20 times without answer before Nigel knocked him out with one punch that nearly killed him,' says Mendy. 'And the reason they fought at such a luna-tic pace was because Logan had made "small island" insults to Nigel – Logan was from Jamaica and Nigel's parents were Barbadian. They had to be separated at a pre-fight press conference because Logan called him a Jamaican bus driver. Nigel dragged Lloyd Honeyghan into a toilet after that press conference because Lloyd, who was born in Jamaica, was getting very pally with Logan. Lloyd was world welterweight champion at the time but he emerged from the toilet looking sheepish, while Nigel looked pretty satisfied that he'd cleared up the situation.'

After the Logan fight Benn resolved never again to ignore the instructions of his trainer, who was so disgusted with Benn's performance he threatened to leave him if he fought in such an uncontrolled manner again. 'I got involved in a street fight and I was ashamed of myself,' said Benn at the post-fight press conference. 'I just flipped my lid. I forgot all about what Brian had told me and went out there to blow Logan away.' But other public utterances suggested Benn was inextricably tied to the limitations he had placed on himself. 'I am a fighter, not a boxer,' he said. 'I just love standing there toe-to-toe having a good whack. I know all the manuals say you're not supposed to try to get hit but that's what I relish. I want and need the physical contact, because that's the situation in which I feel superior to anyone else.'

Benn's next victim was Trinidadian David Noel, a 30-fight veteran who had never been knocked out. Noel lasted two minutes and six seconds. Next was Mike Chilambe of Zambia, gone in 67 seconds. Then, in what was supposed to be a tuning fight before his clash with Watson, which had already been set for 21 May 1989, Benn sparked Mbayo Wa Mbayo of Zaire one minute and 24 seconds into the second round. As tuning fights go it was the equivalent of mastering a couple of nursery rhymes before declaring yourself fit for a concert at the Royal Opera House. Complacency was rampant in the Benn camp, with Mendy boasting even before the Mbayo bout that IBF middleweight champion Michael Nunn had offered $3 million to fight his man. 'I think Nigel and Ambrose didn't show Michael Watson the respect they should have,' says Frank Maloney, who promoted a few of Benn's bouts following the fighter's split from Frank Warren. 'They thought they only had to turn up and knock him out.' Mendy described the Watson fight as a 'one-round job'.

There is a saying that the two cheapest things in boxing are talk and imported opponents. Imported opponents summarily dispatched, Benn got down to talking. 'It's war,' declared Benn at the press conference to formally announce the Watson fight. 'I don't think it will go more than six rounds.' Even the normally sober Lynch found himself getting carried away. When Watson referred to himself as 'the quiet man' at the final head-to-head meeting five days before the fight, Lynch couldn't help himself: 'You'll stay quiet. It's going to take a long time to wake you up after Nigel's hit you.' Watson, always scrupulously polite, replied: 'You seem like a very nice man.' 'I'm in the hurt business,' weighed in Benn. 'I'm going to steamroller him over.' Again, Watson rolled with the punches behind his peekaboo guard: 'You are not going to beat me, son.' It was an exchange that said much about the fighters' contrasting personalities at that time. While Watson dealt in logic, Benn was pumped full of platitudes and soundbites. It was the Svengali talking through his puppet. 'I found out that what you said matched what you did,' says Mendy. 'Marketing was my way, Nigel came on board and it was a case of if I've got to do it, you've got to do it.'

As such, Mendy, who owned a large house with a swimming pool in up-market Wanstead and worked out of a modish loft conversion in Tower Bridge, also encouraged Benn to flaunt his new-found wealth. 'Nigel once went on a spending spree in his favourite shop, Jeremiah's in Ilford, shelling out £25,000 in about ten minutes, just on clothes,' says Mendy. 'I said to Nigel, "Whatever you want, you can get". One day we were driving down the King's Road and we stopped in the traffic opposite a Porsche showroom and Nigel was like, "wow", and started giving me the history of the car. He said, "I'd love to get that car" and I said, "You can get it". So we went in there and 15 minutes later he was away down the King's Road in this Porsche. I impressed upon him that if you're prepared to make the sacrifice it will happen.'

While few would have begrudged Benn the fruits of his labour – paying £21,000 in cash for a watch might have seemed extreme to most but in boxing it was pretty much par for the course – and few questioned his commitment to training, some wondered whether Benn's 22 knockouts in as many fights, 19 of them in the first two rounds, had adequately prepared him for a fighter of Watson's class. Veteran American boxing writer Jack Fiske, who had been punching out copy for the *San Francisco Chronicle* since 1947, began his pre-fight preview thus: 'When a fighter has a 22–0 record with 22 KOs it means (a) he is a terrific puncher; (b) he has been stretching strictly stiffs; or (c) he's been so protected that he really can't fight at all. First- and second-round stoppages will get your name in the paper, but it won't teach you anything.'

Others intimate with Benn's career arc pointed out that Logan wasn't the only one to have made the Dark Destroyer see white lights. American Reggie Miller, a last-minute replacement and a natural light-middleweight, had Benn in some discomfort in the Englishman's 12th pro fight before being cut down by a sucker left hook in the seventh round. A few months earlier, Leon Morris, who brought with him from Bogalusa, Louisiana a record of one loss from his only pro fight, stiffened Benn with a left hook before being knocked out himself with the very next punch. 'His stamina was running out against Miller,' noted Warren. 'I don't think he knew what he was going to do and I can tell you his corner was worried.' 'Logan hasn't won since Benn beat him,' said Watson's manager Mickey Duff. 'It wasn't as if Benn was in there with anyone special, just a guy who refused to be intimidated by a reputation.'

In addition, there had been murmurings for some time before the Watson fight that Lynch's unconventional methods would leave his charge dangerously undercooked against a quality fighter. 'Benn has sparred only 12 rounds in training, while Watson will have done nearly 60 when he winds up today,' wrote Colin Hart in the *Sun*. 'Surely no fighter on earth can learn to avoid blows unless he gets right the sparring practice? Lynch may well be right, but I have a feeling the trainers who look after the likes of Joe Louis, Robinson, Ali and Leonard would violently disagree.' Hart picked Watson to stop Benn in the sixth round, and you could have punted on a Watson knockout at what seems a very generous, in hindsight, 7–1. An agitated Lynch responded: 'I don't give a damn what others think. I don't want him leaving all his aggression in the gym on the headguard of some two-bit sparring partner.'

Whether Hart was right and Lynch was wrong is not as easy to decipher as you might imagine. Watson did indeed knock Benn out in six rounds and the champion was made to look like a rank novice who had fought only 40-odd rounds in the professional ranks. Which is exactly what he was. Fighting in spurts behind an exaggeratedly high guard, just as Logan had done, Watson soaked up wave after wave before sensing his rival was spent and pushing him over the edge of the cliff. Fiske reported the decisive punch as 'little more than a jab'. Benn was so exhausted a gust of wind from an errant hook would have done the job. Watson's were the tactics of a man who had fought more than 100 rounds in the professional ranks. Which is exactly what he was. But while victories in boxing have many fathers, defeats are abortions – dumped in a spit bucket and never to be spoken of again. Unless the fathers absolutely have to.

After the fight, Lynch was apoplectic, calling Benn's tactics 'stark raving bonkers'. 'We had the simplest plan but Nigel threw it out of the window. He has got to learn that the best form of attack is defence. I have had a right go at him, but I know he will be back.' Benn, however, laid much of the blame at Lynch's door, claiming he had been overworked, undersparred and lacking in direction. 'In the fifth, I heard my trainer call out, "Go on, Nige, steam him!" said Benn. "Steam him? How do I do that?" I thought. That's not in any of the boxing pamphlets.' The recriminations fly to this day – all that filial respect fostered through days of hard graft in the gym and mornings spent together ploughing through snow in Old Dagenham Park long since forgotten.

'We knocked everyone out, all the way from the ABAs right up to the Watson fight,' says Lynch. 'So no matter what anyone says, I must have been telling him something right, mustn't I? If it wasn't for me he wouldn't have been where he was. You can't teach someone to punch but you can add power to someone. If my way of training him was wrong, why did he only lose one fight? And why did he carry on fighting the same with his next trainers? So let's get it right. He's going to blame someone because he's that type of person. But all that rubbish goes over my head. Nigel was just a raw fighter who wanted to have a row – you'd never make a boxer out of him, not in a thousand years.

'You didn't really have plans with Nigel, he just went in and took the man out as soon as he could. That was it. He had so much confidence in himself he thought he was going to walk through everyone. And he did until he got to Watson. But Watson was a completely different proposition to anyone Nigel had fought before, a good boxer. So we told him to take it easy and use his loaf, but he never listened to no one. And if they're not disciplined enough to listen, well, that's up to them. He had the power to knock anyone out and if he'd have took his time he would have done the same to Watson. But Watson had been around a long time, had lots of experience and he let Nigel wear himself out before taking him out. It worked a treat.'

And while Benn claims he left too much of himself out on the road and in the gym – if not in the sparring ring – Lynch reckons Benn gave too much of himself in the hairdressing salon. 'The day before he fought Watson he was sat in the hairdressers for five hours in boiling heat having his hair plaited,' says Lynch. 'You can't prepare for a fighter of Watson's calibre like he did. He was drained when he got in the ring, went at him at 100 mph and Watson bided his time and done him. All that confidence backfired, he was his own worst enemy. But some can accept it and some can't.' Even Benn conceded his new haircut, as worn by teenage mothers of four from Croydon, contributed to his downfall, stretching his skin so tight it made him more susceptible to swelling: 'I became so slant-eyed that it would only need buck teeth to make me the first black Chinese in the ring,' said Benn.

Legendary American boxing writer Budd Schulberg, after seeing Mike Tyson make a real meal of Evander Holyfield's ears in their 1997 rematch, explained Tyson's actions thus: 'When he did manage to land, Evander had the audacity to hit him back. The look on Tyson's face at the end of that [first] round seemed to say: "No fair, that's not the way Team Tyson tells me it's gonna be: I walk in, I land, they fall down, I go home and count the money."' Benn's attitude was much the same: 'I believe God put Maradona on this earth to score goals, Steve Davis to pot balls and Nigel Benn to kick ass.' It was a cute line that betrayed a corrosive self-belief: convince yourself you are pre-ordained to lay waste to everything in your path and you see no need for self-improvement. But while Tyson had been on the way down for years when he lost to Holyfield second time round, Benn was still a fresh 25 when he lost to Watson. He had time to reflect on his failings, put himself back together as a better fighter and come again.

'The Watson defeat didn't diminish me as a fighter,' says Benn. 'Defeats never diminished me, I was prepared to do everything to make amends. So I packed my bags and went over to the Fifth Street Gym in Miami, where I was getting battered by great fighters, light-heavyweights and cruiser-weights. I went into the lion's den and learnt my trade and learnt it right. And I was always ready to fight anybody: I didn't want to be saying, "I'll fight him but I won't fight him", I wasn't like that. Bring them all on. After Watson beat me I dusted myself down, went to America and came back a world champion. I always had that lion's spirit, it was always alive.'

CHAPTER TWO
Love at first sight

The Friday after Benn's defeat at the hands of Watson, Chris Eubank fought Chicago's Randy Smith at Bethnal Green's fabled York Hall. It was Eubank's first fight for manager and promoter Barry Hearn and Hearn remembers 'doing my absolute bollocks'. 'It was a stinking fight, Eubank won on points and it also clashed with the title decider between Arsenal and Liverpool,' says Hearn. 'I sold 89 tickets and Eubank didn't give a stuff.' And so, in the space of five inauspicious days within a small area of London, the greatest rivalry British boxing has ever seen was born. Hearn could hardly have been blinded by the white heat of invention, but he knew he had a true original on his hands.

'I was at the World Snooker Championship in Sheffield and the referee Len Ganley, old 'Ball Cruncher' Ganley, told me he'd bumped into Eubank and he wanted to have a meeting,' says Hearn. 'I said, "Fine, I'll meet him at the Grosvenor Hotel in Sheffield". He was 12–0 at the time and had just come off a very good win over Anthony Logan [Eubank outpointed Logan over eight rounds, four months after his defeat by Benn], so I knew he could fight. He swanned in, looking sartorially splendid as usual, and his opening line was: "Mr Hearn, before we get started, I am an athlete and I know my value." It was just about the best remark I'd ever heard. Obviously he was pot-less but he had a swagger about him, something special. Sometimes you just get a gut feeling about someone because of the way they carry themselves, their mannerisms, the confidence, the authority in their voice. All that stuff is very important when you're looking to build a sportsman: you need to see something that sets them apart from the norm. And he was also articulate and intelligent. Full of shit as well, but that's OK because that's what you need to sell to the public. I thought, "I can work with this bloke". It was love at first sight.'

But most boxing writers failed to see the appeal of Eubank and thought Hearn had a tricky sell on his hands. 'His prickly arrogance and single-minded, generally unsympathetic nature,' wrote Bob Mee in *Boxing News*, 'make him a difficult man for the public to understand or care about.' Although Mee, one of the most learned historians of the game, added: 'His alternative is to hope that they turn up at the door or switch on their TV sets to see him get beaten, in which case he has to be as arrogant and objectionable as possible.' But Colin Hart also saw what Hearn saw, a fighter with a certain something, a gift from the boxing gods to any self-respecting Fleet Street sports writer. 'I was standing ringside at the Albert Hall, minding my own business,' says Hart, the former boxing correspondent for the *Sun*, 'and a young man came up to me and said, with that wonderful lisp of his: "When are you going to thtart writing about me?" And I looked at him and said: "Who are you?" And he said: "My name'th Chrith Eubank and I've been fighting in America." So I said to him: "When you do something, I'll write about you."' In time, Eubank did plenty for Hart to write about, and much of what Hart wrote was not very complimentary.

Everybody remembers the first time they met Chris Eubank. The itinerant sports writer Jonathan Rendall recalled his first meeting with Eubank at a press conference in Holborn in January 1989, Rendall being the only journalist who turned up. Eubank spoke in an American accent, having lived in New York's South Bronx for much of the previous six years. Explaining away his awkwardness, Eubank said: 'This is difficult, I am not used to seeing white men.' Within a year Eubank was channelling the spirit of P. G. Wodehouse, although his real circumstances were less Wodehouse than Dickens. Short on cash and living in a bedsit, Eubank fell back into a life of petty thieving on returning to England at the beginning of 1988. Indeed, life was not much different than before he left for New York as a 17-year-old in 1982. Except this time he had boxing to help keep him on the straight and narrow.

'It was a Monday night and Chris came into the Jack Pook gym in Brighton and started working out,' says Ronnie Davies. 'I thought, "Wow, this kid looks good, really special". He told me he was looking for a trainer and said he would give me a three-month trial! I read a quote from him recently where he said Chris Eubank taught Ronnie Davies everything he knew. He would, wouldn't he? With Chris, you had to show him a move but make out it was his idea, but that's what made him have this great self-belief: in his mind he didn't need anyone. He used to say: "I want to be a world champion and I know I'll be a world champion." And every time he trained, every time he sparred or boxed, I knew he'd come out on top because everything he did was disciplined. I remember going into his flat when he first came over here from America and everything was in the right position, everything was perfectly laid out, and I knew then he had a very finely tuned mind. I used to say: "Listen mate, when that bell goes, you're on your own, don't go looking for me. I'll help you out in the corner as much as I can, but during those three minutes it's just you and nobody else." To have your own head, your own discipline, your own mind, that's key. He was his own man, so I let him get on with it. It worked for us. I didn't have doubts, I knew from day one he'd be a world champion.'

While Benn, his stock much enhanced by a stellar amateur record and his ability to bang, had solid financial backing at the start of his professional career, Eubank's progress through the paid ranks was a slog from the outset. He juggled training with two jobs at Debenhams and Wimpy before his first manager, a garage owner from Brighton called Keith Miles, started paying him a weekly allowance of £120. 'While all this was going on, Nigel Benn was driving around in a Porsche in his first year as a pro,' says Eubank. 'Frank Warren and Ambrose Mendy were giving Benn Rolex watches and trying to poach him from the other.' So a frustrated Eubank started calling out Commonwealth champion Benn after only his tenth pro fight, a fourth-round stoppage of Wolverhampton's Steve Aquilina at Portsmouth's Guildhall in May 1988. 'Nigel Benn is a coward and a fraud,' Eubank told *Boxing News* in December of that year; 'stand up to the bully and he crumbles. He can bang a bit, but he's so wild and flawed that it's not even funny.' It must have made for amusing reading at the time.

Despite, and often because of, his bristling self-confidence, Eubank's frequent trips to London in search of a big-name promoter had drawn a blank. Mickey Duff, according to Eubank, tried to buy his contract 'for a plate of fish and chips'. Duff later revealed that the meal was partaken in an up-market seafood restaurant and cost £67. Duff won £25,000 damages from the tabloid that reported Eubank's comment. Frank Warren and Ambrose Mendy say they rejected Eubank because of his outlandish financial demands. 'He's always going on about me getting there ten minutes late for the meeting,' says Warren. 'Do me a favour, he's one to talk about showing up on time.'

Frank Maloney, meanwhile, says their negotiations stalled over Eubank's choice of tea and ground to a halt for more prosaic reasons. 'The first time I met Chris Eubank was in Ambrose Mendy's office,' says Maloney. 'He came up from Brighton and we put him on against Anthony Logan on the undercard of Benn-Chilambe at the Royal Albert Hall. I remember he got all upset because Ambrose didn't have any Earl Grey in. But the actual reason we didn't do a deal was because I had so much invested in Lennox Lewis, who had won gold at the 1988 Olympics and who was already pretty well established. I built my career and reputation on Lennox Lewis and I believe that if you've got one great fighter, to conquer Everest you have to put everything into that fighter. I had to be committed to Lennox Lewis 24 hours a day. Eubank wanted every second of your time and he knew he wouldn't be the star of my operation.'

A desperate Eubank took a match against Welshman Simon Collins at six days' notice, eight days before his date with Logan at the Royal Albert Hall. Collins was stopped in four rounds and Logan outpointed over eight. Although Logan had been knocked out by Benn in two rounds, he had also almost knocked Benn out. Therefore Eubank's victory over the Jamaican provided a form guide and got some people thinking: 'Benn-Eubank might be a decent fight after all.' Barry Hearn was one of them. 'Eubank's style wasn't that attractive,' says Hearn, 'but what he did, he did extremely well. And he knew how to win, that was the most important thing. The reason no one else wanted to know about Eubank was because every other promoter at the time was scared of having a fighter with an opinion. A fighter with an opinion would have frightened Frank Warren and certainly frightened Frank Maloney. Eubank knew what he wanted, who he wanted to fight, when he wanted to fight, how he wanted to fight. And he wasn't going to listen to any trainer, any promoter or any financial advisor, which would turn out to be his biggest mistake.'

Maloney, who would guide Lewis to the undisputed world heavyweight crown, disagrees with Hearn's analysis. 'I don't think I could ever be found guilty of being scared of anything,' says Maloney, who locked horns with some of the shadiest characters in boxing during his 12-year association with Lewis, including demonic American promoter Don King. King, who promoted everyone from Muhammad Ali to Mike Tyson in his four decades in boxing, became so vexed at his inability to get his claws into Lewis that he labelled Maloney 'a mental midget' and 'a pugilistic pigmy'. 'To make a statement like that, that I was afraid of Eubank,' adds Maloney, 'Barry Hearn must be going senile.' But it is certainly true that Hearn's way of doing things was at odds with the more established British promoters at the time, who viewed him with scepticism, bordering on contempt. 'He just chucks money around,' said Frank Warren. 'I'm not doubting his honesty but in boxing terms he's a complete prat.' Hearn, meanwhile, was slightly more complimentary about Warren: 'He's the only man I know who knocks down a door before seeing if it's locked.'

Hearn, however, believes he was the only promoter seeing sense in signing the eccentric and untested Eubank. 'I embraced it because I'm not a normal promoter,' says Hearn. 'I'm always looking for something out of the ordinary. As such I appreciate that geniuses in any sport are extraordinary but flawed in some ways because of their genius. So we sat down and worked out a deal. I sent Eubank a letter which he's got framed on his wall: it outlined that his first three fights would be for £2000, £2500 and £3000. In addition to that I paid him something like £3- or £400 a week allowance. And what I liked about him is that he said: "That allowance can stop when I've been beaten once." And I said to him, "No son, sometimes things go wrong, you might get cut or butted or whatever, so it stops when you've been beaten twice". And we did the deal. After the first three fights it became negotiated on a fight-by-fight basis, but in truth we never really had a contract, we had a handshake. And that is something I like very much but which is very unusual in the boxing business.'

Eubank soon put the rather chastening experience of the Randy Smith fight behind him, racking up five stoppages before the end of 1989. This run included a fourth-round knockout of Gloucester's Johnny Melfah, whom Benn had beaten in the ABA middleweight final in 1986, at the Royal Albert Hall. The Eubank-Melfah fight was on the undercard of Jim McDonnell's brutal world title challenge against the great Azumah Nelson, although Eubank was already exhibiting delusions of grandeur. 'In his head he was an all-time great,' says McDonnell, who was knocked out by Nelson, the WBC super-featherweight champion, in the 12th and final round. 'Because I was the main man in our stable at that time he'd talk to me. He used to say he thought I was the only other one who could fight in our gym and he never used to give anyone else the time of day. But even when I was fighting for the world title he'd try to give me advice. At the weigh-in for my Azumah Nelson fight, as I got off the scales I went to shake Chris's hand and wish him good luck. He pulled back, shook his head from side to side and said: "I don't need good luck, Jimthki, you do." I fell about laughing, it was the funniest thing I'd ever heard.

'But with Eubank, what you are seeing is the truth, that's the real Chris Eubank, it ain't an act. I was in New York with him once and we were standing in a hotel room with this martial arts guru called Walter Johnson, whom Chris used to call "The Doctor". And he was doing all that posturing and posing he used to do in the ring. The jumping over the top rope, lifting up the one arm, tapping his gloves together, standing still on the spot and looking into space, he learnt all that from this guy Walter. Eubank said to me: "Jimthki, thith is what you should be doing, thith is the conthept of boxing." I also remember watching Mike McCallum fight Steve Collins in Boston [in February 1990] and Eubank, who was only an eight-round fighter at the time, went up to Bob Arum and told him he could take the pair of them on the same night. He was always different.'

Video of the Melfah fight reveals Eubank was already a villain with British fight fans: at one point in the third round Melfah gets through with a crunching right hand before Eubank circles his opponent contemptuously, almost with his back to him. 'Eubank hamming it up,' says commentator David Brenner, 'what they call showboating in America and the crowd don't like it.' Cue catcalls and boos from the Albert Hall crowd, an angry reaction probably not heard at that grand old venue since the first performance of Stravinsky's *Rite of Spring*. 'I don't know what they made of him in America,' Brenner continues. 'Who's the weird Limey?' But the weird Limey could bang a bit and he sparked Melfah with a crackerjack right hand in the following round.

'Showboating' had long been frowned upon in British boxing rings and is viewed with suspicion to this day. 'I was watching Lee Selby [the British featherweight champion] fight the other day,' says Lloyd Honeyghan, who caused one of the biggest upsets in British boxing history with his defeat of American welterweight king Don Curry in Atlantic City in 1986. 'All of a sudden he started getting all sexy in the ring and the referee stopped the fight. I was shouting at the screen: "Don't do that! That's part of his game!" It's not the referee's job to stop him from doing that, it's his job to stop him from doing something illegal. The referee shouldn't be telling me how to fight. When an American fighter does all this flashy stuff, like Floyd Mayweather or Adrien Broner, everybody goes, "He's brilliant, he's so great", but when a British guy starts doing that stuff in the ring, everybody hates him for it.'

But far from fazing Eubank, the hate that rained down on him from hostile crowds seemed to energise the up-and-coming prospect. 'The problem for my opponent was that I sucked all the venom in,' says Eubank, 'allowed it to well up inside me, transformed it into positive energy, then unleashed it back against him.' And all that venom would make him very rich outside of the ring. 'Before, in the good old days, all you did was make a good match, print your posters and wait for the punters to come and buy their tickets,' said the late Harry Mullan, long-time editor of *Boxing News*. 'Hearn felt that wasn't good enough, you had to go a stage further and go out into the market place and sell it as a product, an entertainment package. He recognised that there has to be a villain, a man you love to hate, and Eubank saw that role wasn't being filled in British boxing and he chose it for himself.'

'Harry was a traditionalist, a great man and a great Corinthian of boxing,' says Hearn, who made the dour Steve Davis into a household name and snooker into one of the most popular television sports of the 1980s. 'But the purists of any sport are small in number. The volume comes from the working men who want to be entertained. When I first started in darts, a lot of people said to me: "What are you doing with all this razz-matazz, it's a game of darts, keep the game respectful and quiet". And I said, "No, that's yesterday". Today is an eight-een- to forty-year-old market place, with more women involved, more alternative forms of entertainment. You're competing for an audience, both on TV and live. For Harry boxing was the Noble Art, but it's not the Noble Art for me. I appreciate the skill involved and the bravery of boxers, but my job is to make that as popular as possible so they get the financial reward, I make a return and my TV companies get a rating. It's not just about the purists in the Blazer Brigade, it's about knowing your target market.'

'Eubank didn't think he was the best fighter on the planet, deep down he knew his limitations,' says the *Guardian*'s Donald McRae, who spent time with Eubank for his classic boxing book *Dark Trade*. 'So I think he felt he had to develop this persona that would make people laugh and piss people off. And like a lot of insecure people he enjoyed the attention. He also understood that boxing at its most pure, its most basic, would alienate a lot of people. And he thought, probably rightly, that boxing then was slowly going into decline and needed to appeal in a different way. So he knew if he could emphasise the music, the lights, the humour and the absurdity, he would open up his fan base and ultimately make more money.' The apparent decline of British boxing was indeed a hot topic of conversation in newspapers and trade magazines of the time, with Mickey Duff's former partner Mike Barrett opining in August 1990, only three months before Eubank's first fight with Benn: 'Where is there a fighter whose appear-ance guarantees a full house? We haven't had a class fighter since Barry McGuigan and nobody with his charisma.'

★ ★ ★

In truth, the 'white hat-black hat' angle had been used to sell fights since bare-knuckle days, and probably beyond. Sonny Liston, one of the most hated heavyweight world champions in history, certainly knew its worth in the early 1960s. 'A boxing match is like a cowboy movie,' said Liston, 'there's got to be the good guys and there's got to be the bad guys. And that's what people pay for – to see the bad guys get beat.' But Hearn, whose first big boxing promotion was the all-British heavyweight contest between Frank Bruno (white hat) and Joe Bugner (black hat) in 1987, milked Eubank's unpopularity for all it was worth. Luckily for Hearn, Eubank loved to be hated. 'He gradually brought all that posing and posturing in,' says Davies. 'I never encouraged it at the start. But once I realised the effect it had on the crowd, I used to say, "Go on mate, give 'em the Full Monty, tell 'em who you are". I think he loved the boos and the hissing. Although he loved it when they cheered him as well.'

In March 1990, Eubank won his first professional title, the lightly regarded WBC International middleweight belt, with an eighth-round stoppage of rugged Argentine Hugo Corti at York Hall. But it was his first title defence against Eduardo Contreras, another Argentine, the following month that announced him to the wider British public. It was Eubank's first fight on ITV – previous bouts had been broadcast on a show called *Seconds Out*, screened only in London, East Anglia and Wales – and viewers were treated to his full repertoire, from the 'Simply The Best'-accompanied ring walk, to the vaulting over the ropes, to the statuesque posturing and funky ring moves. The Blazer Brigade would have been spluttering into their sherries but, more importantly to Eubank, the viewers were learning to love to hate him. En masse. They hated him even more when he labelled the sport they loved 'a mug's game'. 'I turned pro in 1986 and I'm still in this godforsaken business,' added Eubank. 'It's an ordeal. People say it's hypo-critical to hate the dirty business and still take the money. But I can do it very easily. Other people out there are killing for it. Whoring for it, lying, cheating, conning for it. I'm fighting for it. I'm gladiating for it.'

'I wouldn't want to psycho-analyse Eubank, his mind is too complicated to attempt to dissect,' says McRae. 'But he under-stood that boxing, at its core, is about the darkness. He was in enough battles, he suffered enough, and he knew how it felt to get hurt and what he could do to other people. So Eubank's persona was built on a distaste for boxing.' As well as raising the hackles of Fleet Street's dyed-in-the-wool boxing writers, Eubank's avowed distaste for his trade didn't go down too well with some of his fellow pros, whom Eubank claimed to be speaking on behalf of. 'He made it clear that boxing was a mug's game, and he wanted to make as much money as he could by fighting the biggest mugs that he could,' says McDonnell. 'But the mug's game earned him a hell of a lot of money.' 'In any poll for the fighters' fighter,' wrote Alan Hubbard in the *Observer*, 'Eubank would not figure too highly.'

However, Eubank's jaundiced comments about boxing chimed with others within the sport. 'When he said boxing was a mug's game, a lot of black boxers like myself knew where he was coming from,' says Errol Christie, a sparring partner of Eubank who joined the professional ranks in 1982 after a stel-lar amateur career. 'Because we were abused by people in boxing. I was just a street boy from Coventry when I moved to London when I was 17 but I'd never lost a fight for my country and I wasn't treated right. I loved the game but I didn't love a lot of the people in it. The managers, the promot-ers, I hate them. But boxers are now more attuned to what the sport can bring them, and that's a good thing. Both Chris and Nigel saw what I'd done and how I'd been treated and as a result were much more knowledgeable than me.'

'I understood what he was saying and I admired him for saying it,' says Brian Lynch. 'If you're a boxer and you're in there doing all the hard work and there are all these people outside of the gym who are getting all the money, that's not really on. So he put an end to that. He said: "I want X amount, I want to fight this fighter and not this fighter and that's the end of it." Boxers have got a lot shrewder now and some of that is to do with Chris.' 'I don't think he should have made the comment about boxing being a mug's game, I didn't like that,' says Ronnie Davies. 'Because he made a lot of money from the mug's game. But the comment was slightly misunderstood. What he meant was he didn't like seeing fighters being ripped off. A lot of them were, and still are.'

'He had a list of rules for Barry Hearn, especially in the early days,' says McDonnell. 'He wouldn't box anyone who was too tall, he wouldn't box anyone who was a southpaw, he wouldn't box anyone with a zero on their record. He'd say: "Barry, thith ith buthineth." And when Barry would try and make certain fights he'd say: "Barry, thith ith bad buthineth." He wanted the least risk for the most benefit and you can't make him wrong for that. He had it right, he was playing the promoters at their own game. They want you to fight the best boxers out there for the least money you'll accept and he wouldn't have it.'

So while Eubank was dubbed a traitor and a hypocrite and ostracised by his fellow fighters, today he is viewed as something of a pioneer. 'When I started promoting it wasn't uncommon for fighters not to know who they were fighting until the night of the fight and they never bothered asking,' says Hearn. 'Fast forward to today and a novice professional will want to see tapes of his opponents two months before and will walk into your office with his entrance music, which used to be reserved for the very top of the bill, if at all. So a lot of fighters today have followed Eubank's example, some successfully, some not so successfully. In the early days you'd take six options on a fighter and if he was successful you'd make a lot of money because you had him cheap. Today's world doesn't work like that. At Matchroom we work for Carl Froch, the boxer owns the show today. We take a percentage of the show and that's actually very fair, because the fighter gets what he deserves and doesn't get ripped off.'

CHAPTER THREE
Two minds, miles apart?

One of the great absurdities of the Nigel Benn–Chris Eubank rivalry was that the boxer who talked like a toff was actually significantly more street than his rival, who glorified in his black, working-class roots. It was a dynamic that was central to their frayed relationship: Benn despised Eubank for thinking he was a better person than himself – for not being more like he was. Eubank taught himself to speak like a toff via P. G. Wodehouse and the BBC World Service because he wanted to be as different to Benn and his 'wild, uncouth' ilk as it was possible to be. Paradoxically, the deep-seated mutual distrust stemmed from the fact they knew each other intimately.

Eubank was unquestionably the more complicated character, persuading feature writers, from the world of boxing and beyond, to beat a path to his door. Amateur psychoanalysts all of them, they wanted to unpick Eubank's mind and find out what made him tick. Like mechanics working under a car, they tapped and yanked and twisted, determined to work the problem out. Because there must have been a problem. Eubank delighted in confounding them, talking 'philosophically' about everything from Nietzsche to boxing as a metaphor for religion. 'Boxing and Christianity are not much different,' he said. 'You have to treat boxing like Christianity and come away from the world.' He could be genuinely thought-provoking about the trade he practised with such effectiveness but which he professed to find so tedious. 'If it comes down to a fight of will,' Eubank said before his first fight with Benn, 'he can't beat me. Because my will is my skill and his will is primitive.' If Muhammad Ali had said it people would have been proclaiming his poetic genius.

But Eubank's avowed commitment to self-improvement was undermined by a colossal arrogance which meant neither the journalists nor the public who read their words and saw their interviews on television were willing to countenance his overweening ambition. 'The first time I met him I was fasci-nated by him,' says Donald McRae. 'I'd never met a guy like this before. He started out speaking with this booming, lisping intonation and after a while he actually started speaking quite normally, about being a fighter in New York and his early days in the ring in the UK. And I got the feeling that he wasn't that different to Benn and Watson when you got down to the deep core of him. Basically he was a fighting man, too. Even though people laughed at him a lot, I tried not to laugh too much at Eubank. Because I remember he said to me once: "I just want to better myself." He felt by using big words and talking what he called "philosophically" he escaped the limitations of his past. I found that touching.'

Boxing has always been suspicious of fighters who aspire to intellectual and social improvement. Boxing fans prefer their fighters simple and home-spun, like the American heavy-weight Tony Galento, the archetypal ignorant pug. When asked for his views on Shakespeare, Galento, who once floored the great Joe Louis, replied: 'Shakespeare? I ain't never heard of him. I suppose he's one of them foreign heavyweights.'

Gene Tunney, world heavyweight champion in the 1920s, was Galento's opposite. Tunney, 'The Fighting Marine', was from humble Irish-American stock but craved acceptance from the upper echelons of society. His stated aims were 'wealth, education and to marry a prominent woman'. He achieved all three, lecturing on Shakespeare at Yale, wedding a wealthy Connecticut socialite and forming an unlikely friendship with the playwright George Bernard Shaw. Yet he was lampooned for his apparently affected manners by those within the boxing fraternity. Following Tunney's fifth and final fight against his great rival Harry Greb, in which Tunney delivered a fearful beating, Greb was heard to ask: 'There's something I want cleared up – is it true, as the newspapers say, that Gene reads books?' Like Eubank, Tunney was fond of long words and, while he had a greater claim to erudition than Eubank, Tunney wore his learning as heavily. Thus, when Jack Dempsey vowed to 'knock the big bookworm out in eight' before their second fight at Chicago's Soldier Field in 1927, it chimed with the American public. No matter that Tunney was a decorated soldier while Dempsey spent the war years on American soil.

While it was rumoured Tunney read thicker books when reporters were nosing around in his gym, Eubank acquired a reputation for leaving a room mid-interview and returning a few minutes later armed with a barrage of polysyllabic adjectives. 'The journalist Robert Chalmers interviewed him once for the *Observer*,' recalls Kevin Mitchell. 'They were sitting in Chris's hotel room in South Africa, a couple of days before a fight, and Robert asked him a difficult question. Chris got up and left the room, came back five minutes later and shoehorned a handful of extraordinarily long words into his answer. Robert said, "Have you got a dictionary in the next room?" And Chris said, "Yeth, Robert, I have." The first time I remember meeting Chris was when he was giving a talk at the London School of Economics. He was answering questions from students, acting like he was Dr Livingstone. It was packed and I remember he had his most pompous voice on, as if he was a professor of life – which is what he regards himself as. He had them in the palm of his hand, they could hardly believe their eyes. I spoke to him afterwards and the first thing he said to me was: "It is my mission to bring light into people's lives." And I said, "That's very noble Chris, but what about your own life?" And he stopped, deliberated and said: "I'll either be in the gutter looking up at the stars or a rich and famous man for ever more." He got the gutter line from Oscar Wilde.'

'I went to his home quite a few times early in his career for features, so I got to know him quite well,' says Nick Owen, the former ITV sports presenter. 'I found him very humble when I was chatting to him off-camera, underneath it all he was a really nice guy. But boxers put on a persona and the arrogance and the superciliousness were all part of Chris's image. And once the cameras started rolling he always liked to throw in sophisticated words. More than once he asked me the meaning of a word before we went into the studio, just to check it was the right word to use, and I knew I was going to hear that word again in ten minutes' time. He'd usually trot it out in the first part of the interview.'

'Is Chris what it says on the packet?' says Ambrose Mendy. 'No. But he promises to be. He's a doppelganger of himself. Chris doesn't speak like you hear him speaking but have a conversation with him and heaven help you. There's a difference between deliberation and hesitation. When you're deliberate you give a question or subject considera- tion. His delays aren't deliberation, they are hesitation, because he wants to make everything he says structured and therefore make himself sound more intelligent than he actually is.'

Yet Eubank vehemently rejected the suggestion he invented a persona. 'I haven't invented myself,' he said. 'I've become proper. This is what I am. This is not an act. It has not been premeditated.' 'Everything about Chris Eubank was the real thing,' says Ronnie Davies. 'It wasn't an act, it was genuine.' The problem was, despite Eubank's protestations and the claims of Davies, Barry Hearn and others close to him that 'what you see with Chris is what you get', it was difficult to come to any other conclusion. Especially when people remembered him as a rather withdrawn and wary individual with an American accent, which he had been only a few years earlier.

Eubank claims the happiest time of his life was being taken into care by the authorities at the age of 12, which says everything about how rough his life in London must have been. Eubank's mother walked out when he was eight, having grown tired of his father's womanising. His father, a Jamaican immigrant and strict disciplinarian, worked long hours at the Ford plant in Dagenham and had to bring up four unruly children on £90 a week. Dinner most nights was fish and chips, if there was dinner at all. Eubank, the youngest, was bullied by his brothers, leading to a lifelong longing for acceptance. Desperate to be noticed, Eubank acted up, getting into fights, smoking weed, falling into shoplifting. 'I earned very good money, working the streets of the West End,' said Eubank. 'I could make £110 a day.' Eubank flitted from one care home to the next, from Kent to North Wales and back to London. 'It was bliss,' says Eubank. 'There were snooker tables and colour TVs. They had three meals a day, parlours of food, crisps, French fries, fridges, freezers, burgers and sausages. I thought, "This is bloody heaven".' But, having been beaten up by a teacher at a home in Peckham, he slithered out of a bathroom window and spent the next 18 months on the street. Light of finger, fleet of foot and the star turn in a gang of Dickensian-style child thieves, Eubank 'lived like a king'.

Eubank's father eventually tracked him down at the back end of 1982 and packed him off to live with his mother in New York. While the streets of London were paved with gold, the streets of the South Bronx were 'a place of nightmares'. Eubank quit cigarettes, dope, alcohol and thieving, enrolled in high school and, like many lost souls before and since, found sanctuary in a boxing gym, the Jerome Boxing Club on Westchester Avenue. Eubank was unable to pay the $15 a month gym fees, so the co-owner, Adonis Torres, had him sweeping the floors instead. It is a measure of Eubank's enormous mental fortitude that he flourished in such a hostile environment.

'He'd come into the gym with no money, wearing baggy pants and broken shoes,' says Lenny DeJesus, Torres's partner in the Jerome Boxing Club and a man who has worked the corners of some of the greats, including Roberto Duran, Wilfredo Gomez, Hector Camacho and Manny Pacquiao. 'He had a hard life here in New York. His mother was working as a house attendant and he lived with her, but he was more on the street than at home. And when you live that kind of street life in the Bronx, you have to be tough: you have to do your thing to survive, you have to be really wise and you've got to act up. And if you come to the Bronx from another country, you've got to have four eyes and you've got to watch. Because in the Bronx, if you look at someone the wrong way, they'll shoot you. You're dead.'

DeJesus remembers Eubank as an uncertain teenager – 'a nice kid, a gentleman, but with no confidence at all' – who slowly grew in stature as his talent flourished in one of boxing's toughest schools. 'In New York he was more humble, more quiet, a little less forward,' says DeJesus. 'When he went over to England he invented this character to sell himself real good, to become a star. But we wouldn't have tolerated that kind of attitude in our gym. Either you fight or you don't fight, you don't make a mockery of the game or do your own stuff. We teach you and what we put into you, that's what we expect out of you. So Chris came into the gym, he fought, and that was it. But he put in a lot of effort: if you told him to do two hours he put in two hours, if you told him to do three hours he put in three hours. He was a dedicated individual, he liked boxing and he became a decent fighter here in the Bronx.' Eubank spent every day in the gym for the next three and a half years, seeing off 'the fly-by-nights, the triers, the posers, the good-looking guys with no heart'. He watched and listened and learned and began to master his craft, winning 19 of his 26 amateur bouts, the Spanish Golden Gloves light-middleweight title in 1984 and reaching the semi-finals of the even more prestigious New York Golden Gloves.

Eubank turned pro as a 19-year-old, on 3 October 1985. He was still attending Morris High School. He claims he was forced to start punching for money because he racked up a $250 bill on the school phone, talking to a sweetheart back in England. His first fight, against one Tim Brown at the Sands Hotel in Atlantic City, earned him exactly that. Eubank won his next three fights before graduating and signing up for a course in word processing. Eubank began to complement his boxing training with martial arts techniques, taught by an expert called Walter Johnson, the same Walter Johnson Jim McDonnell witnessed imparting his knowledge to Eubank in a New York hotel room a few years later. 'The

Doctor's' impressionable pupil studied the philosophy of martial arts and applied it to boxing. Eubank was suddenly a model student.

'When Chris was with me he was more respectful,' says DeJesus, who shared Eubank's coaching duties with Torres and Maximo Pierret, who would be in Eubank's corner for some of his biggest nights. 'But he was a strong individual and would tend to do a lot of things on his own. The style that he got here was more of a classical American style – we had the "Bronx Bomber", Alex Ramos, who won four New York Golden Gloves, and Wilfredo Gomez, so he picked up a lot of our ways. But he was always trying to invent his own way of doing things. He would do funny things with his leg-work and movement, he learned to be creative. And he had the power – and when you felt his power, that's when he got a little bit arrogant and would want to kick your ass. But even in his early days as a pro, he wasn't overflowing with self-confidence. Every time we would go to a fight he would ask me questions: "Do you know my opponent? Where's he from? What's he like?" And he would get nervous, get butterflies. I'd tell him: "Don't worry, we're gonna win, you're in good condition." And once he threw his first punch, everything came out of him. You learn to walk, then you learn to punch, then you learn confidence.'

There is a sign on the wall of Gleason's, New York's most famous gym, which reads: 'Now whoever has courage, and a strong and collected spirit in his breast, let him come forth, lace up his gloves, and put up his hands.' Eubank's relatively smooth transition from title-winning amateur to promising pro was in large part down to the intensity of sparring in the city. He had the courage, he had the spirit and where others wilted in the heat of battle, he glowed like a rod of iron. 'The sparring was more than real,' remembers Eubank. 'I was seeing tough guys leaving the gym on a stretcher, in an ambulance. Crying.' 'At that time, sparring was like a professional bout, a four-rounder,' says DeJesus. 'We used to bring in fighters from other gyms – even Floyd Patterson used to bring his fighters down from upstate New York – and we used to compete, people would stand back and watch. And people would take particular notice of Chris Eubank, because he was a colourful individual, growing cockier all the time.'

Then, in 1987, Adonis Torres died of a brain clot, depriving Eubank of a second father figure in the space of five years. 'He had a beautiful soul,' says Eubank. 'He had patience. He had time for me. He treated me like a person. He treated me goodly. He taught me things. No one else came close to him for me. I loved him.' Eubank, with five professional victories in the bank but little chance of attracting a top-name American promoter, decided it was time to return home. The South Bronx was where he became a man, where he became a boxer, where he became Chris Eubank. It just never looked that way to the unsuspecting British public he was about to be launched upon. He professed to despise what made him but was never able to escape it. The tragedy being, it didn't make sense to try to escape it. Because boxing was the one thing that made him stand out; the one thing that guaranteed him acceptance.

'He was properly ingrained in that world, even when he was the Eubank the public knows today,' says McDonnell. 'I was in New York with him once and he woke me up at 3 o'clock in the morning and said: "Ring Barry Hearn." He said to Barry: "What do people normally do at 3 o'clock in the morning?" And Barry said: "Are you mad?" And we ended up driving down to the Bronx and hanging about these supermarkets. It was an eerie situation but that's when I knew he was for real. I said to him: "Chris, there's a couple of people in here who look a bit dodgy." But he was cool. When we got in the car he said: "Don't worry, Jimthki, they won't hurt you – they jutht want to fuck your white arth.'"

Eubank once explained the difference between himself and Benn thus: 'It is like two minds which are miles apart, a street brain and a society brain.' Of course, he considered his to be the society brain. But while Eubank thought himself Benn's intellectual and social superior, something that vexed Benn greatly, his real edge came from knowing he was forged in a crucible that was considerably hotter. And perhaps from knowing that Benn knew that, too.

'I've seen pictures of Chris when he was a street boy, I know who Chris is,' says Benn. 'And Chris knows who he is. My upbringing wasn't hard really, my family life was loving. My dad was the guvnor in the house. Not strict, but he just didn't want me to go down the wrong path. He brought me up right, with good morals. When I went out shoplifting in Ilford, my dad would give it to me, because he grafted all his life. I nicked my auntie's purse, I nicked my neighbour's purse, I was a right little tea leaf, but he'd give it to me. He used to have a saying he brought from Barbados: "If you can't hear, you can feel." And many times I felt because I didn't listen. But it was the death of my brother, who was killed by racists, that turned me into an angry person. From a young age I had to deal with that.' Benn's brother Andy, a wild youth who had been in and out of borstal, died when fleeing assailants and falling through a conservatory roof. He was 17, Nigel was eight. 'I wanted to be like my idol,' says Benn. 'A street fighter. The toughest of them all.' So while Benn concedes his darkness became a brand to be marketed, he bridles at the suggestion

46

the darkness wasn't real. 'It wasn't an invention, that was just who I was,' says Benn. 'I was a very angry boy. No one made me, mate, I was the way I was.'

'There was always something about Nigel that was deep,' says Ambrose Mendy. 'At times I got there but Nigel would go into an abyss of the kind I'd never, ever seen before or since. I'm not sure Nigel realised it but I believe he was a manic depressive. And part of that was ugliness and bitterness. He wasn't a bad person but he was never, ever appreciated as a child, not to the extent that he needed to be. And as a result there was this rage. My God, it would surge forward in him. It was unbelievable. And that's why when Nigel went into the ring he genuinely wanted to hurt people.' Benn, despite being the sixth of seven brothers, disputes Mendy's analysis. Indeed, Benn has only kind words for his mother, Mina, and father, Dickson, who was a supervisor at the same Ford plant where Eubank's father worked. Dickson backed his son when he got into trouble at school and even when he was convicted of GBH and threatening behaviour at the age of 15. 'I would have bashed him up as well,' said Dickson. 'Kicking ass was a way of life,' said Benn, who was running amok on the streets of Ilford with lads six or seven years older than himself. 'If you didn't do it, you had it done to you. It was tough but I tell you it was enjoyable.'

It was Benn's mother who, worried by his choice of friends and wayward behaviour, begged him to join his brother John in the army. It was a toss-up as to which were the meaner streets in the early 1980s, those of Belfast or the South Bronx. Although Benn had the advantage of being armed with a gun. But for both Benn and Eubank, the boxing gym provided an escape and was a place they could forge an identity and gain recognition. Benn soon realised being a talented sportsman afforded a soldier special privileges – being signed off menial duties and exercises, better food, lie-ins – while his officers saw the ring as a place where this angry young man could channel his energy while contributing to the greater glory of the battalion.

'He was a fine physical specimen with lots of aggression and it didn't take me too long to work out he wasn't for the army,' says Captain John O'Grady, Benn's battalion boxing chief. 'I remember saying to our physical training head at the time: "This guy is a future world champion." All of his fights were over in 20 or 30 seconds. He would get across the ring so quickly and throw so many punches, his opponents were mesmerised. His brother was a light-heavyweight, a very good technical boxer and a first-class soldier. Not many people went three rounds with John, they normally went to sleep in the second or third. But he didn't have that aggression that Nigel had. Nigel's aggression was magnificent and I always thought: "If this could be harnessed, with the right trainer and the right facilities, he could go far."'

In his first year with the Fusiliers, Benn won the novice, intermediate and open-class titles, a feat that has not been repeated. No opponent was too tall or too wide and in his four years and 256 days in the army he was never defeated. 'He was like a professional boxer even back then,' says Captain O'Grady, 'an absolute joy to watch in training. You have to go back to the times of National Service, when you had all these internationals fighting in the army, to find a boxer of Nigel's calibre. And certainly during his era there was nothing to touch him. I've never seen anything like him since.' Outside of the ring, Captain O'Grady remembers Benn as a good soldier who played by the rules. 'While he was under me, on the boxing team, I never had one ounce of trouble with him,' he says. 'I always congratulated his father and mother on their two sons whenever I saw them, they were a lovely family. It's how you manage these people. They join a disciplined organisation and if they are a little bit wild we can channel that energy into a controlled aggression.'

However, the army did not tame Benn. Alternate bouts of spartan discipline and chaos would become the twin themes of Benn's life and when he wasn't knocking squaddies out in the ring he was knocking them out on the cobbles. Benn, who lost his virginity at the age of 12, was also developing a dangerous addiction to the fairer sex. He juggled girlfriends in England and Germany and narrowly escaped being court-martialled after spending the duration of an escape evasion exercise in Westphalia shacked up with a Fraulein called Anke. And when he wasn't in bed with Anke he was in bed with her best friend Gabby. Another motif of Benn's life that repeatedly exhibited itself in the army was his ambivalent attitude towards authority. Indeed, some of his officers would have recognised Brian Lynch's later criticism of Benn that he 'never listened to no one'. Especially snotty-nosed kids straight out of Sandhurst. 'I can take discipline, but not from little rich kids who wouldn't take the rough stuff with you,' said Benn many years after leaving the army. 'I'd love to meet a few of them in the ring now and give them a good spanking.'

Benn completed two tours of Northern Ireland during the height of The Troubles and lost five of his comrades, three of whom were blown to bits while on a fishing trip in Enniskillen. 'I'm not ashamed to admit that I was scared stiff during most of my time there,' said Benn. 'Northern Ireland put my nerves on the rack and stretched them to the limit.' But Benn also demonstrated a cruel streak during his time in Northern Ireland, abusing his power during a stint as a regimental policeman, 'bashing blokes about if they got in trouble'. Benn would also earn a reputation as a bully during his boxing career. But unlike drunk squaddies, trained fighters hit back. Some of the time.

Despite the numerous hiccups, Benn maintained the army 'made me the man I am today'. 'It was the army that taught me about attitude,' he said. 'I remember finishing second in a race once. The Sergeant Major came up and called me every name under the sun. "Useless! Second is nowhere!" That thinking has driven me ever since.' But in common with many demobbed soldiers he had difficulty adjusting to civilian life. 'After my 18 months in Northern Ireland, it was very hard to adapt to Civvy Street,' says Benn. 'You're checking under your car, looking for booby traps, you're all over the place. You've seen some gruesome things and all of a sudden it's, "Here you go mate, here's your P45".' Armed with a glowing reference, Benn found work as a security guard and store detective but soon grew tired of the long hours and low pay. While Eubank spent almost his entire career decrying the tedium of boxing, Benn wondered if his fists might provide an escape from the humdrum.

CHAPTER FOUR
A monk's life

The morning after Benn's defeat at the hands of Michael Watson the papers were full of talk of a myth having being exploded. To be fair to Fleet Street's boxing writers, many of them had warned it might happen. 'There are people in boxing who are not convinced it is certain to go Benn's way,' wrote the *Independent*'s Ken Jones. 'Instinct suggests the puncher but Watson could be in with a chance if he is still there after six rounds.' John Rodda of the *Guardian* was unequivocal: 'Watson will steer a course to becoming Benn's first conqueror.' Prophesies realised, every man and his dog weighed in with advice for the fallen champion. The consensus was that Benn needed to go back and learn the fundamentals of boxing. Watson's manager Mickey Duff, who had steered his man so skilfully under the radar and into the upper reaches of the middleweight division, told Benn to lose Ambrose Mendy, take six months off from boxing and serve a second apprenticeship under a different trainer. Some, however, wondered if Benn had what it took to come back at all. 'In the end, Benn surrendered,' said *The Times*'s boxing correspondent Srikumar Sen.

Such cutting words from men who had never thrown a punch in anger must have hurt Benn almost as much as some of Watson's blows. Or perhaps he didn't read them. And even if he did, Mendy, who went into full Red Adair mode following the defeat, thought he knew what was best for the Nigel Benn Brand. 'That was the only time a Commonwealth title fight has been shown live coast-to-coast in the United States,' says Mendy, 'and immediately afterwards the NBC anchor shoved a microphone in his face and said: "You were going to do this, going to that, going to be the biggest thing in America since The Beatles – what happened?" Nigel said: "I got my arse kicked. Go and talk to Michael, because he won. But make no fucking mistake, I'll be back." The next day, after the post-fight press conference, I got a call from the ITN newsreader Trevor McDonald, who said: "You guys don't realise, you're creating history." So we were on the *One O'Clock News*, the *Six O'Clock News* and the *Ten O'Clock News*. We had a bigger platform than Michael Watson. Nigel had a big eye and a fat lip but was as honest as the day is long. And he repeated those prophetic words: "Within a year I will be middleweight champion of the world."'

The day after the Watson defeat, Mendy announced that Benn's next fight would take place in the United States in September. Two months later Benn was on a plane to Miami, having resolved to 'live a monk's life'. Some, however, questioned whether Benn possessed the mental fortitude to graduate from such a brutal school. Ireland's former featherweight world champion Barry McGuigan said of his introduction to training in American gyms: 'I boxed a round with a guy, thought that was that, and then saw 11 guys lining up behind him.' Mindful of this, Benn jettisoned Lynch as his trainer and instead hired Vic Andreetti, the former British light-welterweight champion who had long since swapped London's slate-grey East End for the blue skies of Florida.

Benn was soon relishing his role as the only Brit in a gym full of suspicious Yanks: 'In the States I get hurt in the gym,' said Benn. 'One of my first sparring partners smacked me in the mouth and knocked out my gumshield. I couldn't eat for a week and had to drink soup.' 'When we went around the United States I'd say to him: "Nige, just take it easy",' says Mendy. 'But he didn't know how to do it. Sparring? You're joking. He didn't know what friendly sparring was.'

When Benn announced he would be returning to the sort of discipline he had when he was in the army, he was at least being honest. But perhaps only subconsciously so. For while his time with the Royal Regiment of Fusiliers had, as is the way with the army, been marked by periods of subservience and self-restraint, not even the most persuasive sergeant majors managed to drum the naughty boy out of him. And so, one member at a time, Benn's old firm reformed in Miami, soon to be rebranded as 'The Black Pack', embroidered tracksuits and all. Even though half of its members were white. Benn combined his training with wining and carousing, spending his evenings doing his very best impression of a monk gone bad. 'There was a very good club scene in Miami and we took full advantage of it,' says Benn. Occasionally, news of his unruly behaviour would filter back to the UK, as when a Stringfellows 'waitress' told the press Benn had eaten strawberries and cream off 'sensitive parts of her body'. It would take a very hungry monk to do that.

Benn's first fight back was against a journeyman from the Dominican Republic called Jorge Amparo in Atlantic City. It was a stumbling first few steps on the road to redemption. Benn laboured to a 10-round unanimous decision but Mendy was already thinking big, announcing after the fight that his charge could meet the winner of Sugar Ray Leonard–Roberto

Duran III at Old Trafford the following March. It sounded pie in the sky until you discovered the Harvard-educated American promoter Bob Arum was pulling the strings. Arum, the man responsible for several of Muhammad Ali's fights, including Ali-Frazier II, as well as Leonard–Duran I, Hagler–Hearns and Hagler–Leonard, seemed the ideal man to make Mendy's outlandish dreams come true.

There followed a one-round knockout of Puerto Rican Jose Quinones in Las Vegas, before Benn very nearly came unstuck against Sanderline Williams in Atlantic City in January 1990. Williams, who had been the distance with former world champions Frank Tate and Iran Barkley and would secure a draw with future world champion James Toney six months after the Benn fight, was a tough man who would only be stopped once in a 40-fight career. But the regularity with which he was able to penetrate Benn's porous defences had some questioning whether the English exile had learned much in Miami's Fifth Street Gym. It certainly reinforced the impression that he was destined to always struggle against slick, counter-punching boxers. 'He must smooth out,' was Williams's assessment. But, perhaps more importantly in terms of Benn's world title ambitions, the Williams fight went down well on American television and had Arum believing he had a transatlantic star on his hands.

Ambrose Mendy never stopped believing. In anything. Mendy was the fourth of 11 children and grew up in Hackney, East London. Although, if he is to be believed, his lineage is far more exotic. His mother's grandfather, Mendy claims, was a slave who won his freedom working on the Panama Canal. He came to England, became a fairground man and married a Russian Jew called Solomons before settling in Somerset. Mendy's parents were more solid folk – his father was a family welfare officer and his mother a homeworker – so it must have been something of a surprise when their son was jailed for fraud at the age of 22. Mendy attended 21 prisons in four years – 'I had an attitude problem' – but emerged an educated fellow. There followed his ill-fated stint working for Frank Warren, after which Mendy struck out on his own and began to build a rival empire, the grand-sounding World Sports Corporation.

Mendy, who was also the trade development counsellor for Guinea-Bissau and once held the world record for eating three cream crackers in the fastest time (34.78 seconds), soon had a gaggle of top British sports stars on his books, including England footballers Paul Ince, John Barnes and John Fashanu and sprint star Linford Christie. But Benn was his pet. Moreover, the underlying absurdity of boxing allowed Mendy to do things with Benn he never would have attempted with his other charges. 'They spent an awful lot of time together, they were very close,' says Frank Maloney. 'I actually think Ambrose was very good at what he did. He had a great market-ing head on his shoulders and was great at PR, but he never seemed to stay focused on anything. He could have been the most powerful black promoter this country has ever seen, a British version of Don King.'

Frank Warren, unsurprisingly, demurs. 'Do me a favour, that's an insult to Don King,' says Warren, a long-time business partner of the once all-powerful American promoter. 'Don King is a very intelligent and bright man. Lots of people can say things, but saying things and delivering things are two different things. And Mendy's never delivered. The bottom line is, Mendy wasn't capable. Look what he did to Nigel Wenton. Wenton was a good, young fighter and Mendy took him out to America and he got the crap beaten out of him

[Liverpool's Wenton was well beaten by future light-welter-weight world champion Sharmba Mitchell on the undercard of Benn–DeWitt in Atlantic City]. He ruined Nigel Wenton. The reason he was getting the headlines was because of all the stories he was putting about, stuff like Nigel's hands being insured by Lloyd's for 20 million quid. We all knew it was untrue but the press love all that crap. Mendy is what he is, a conman, and that's why he's been jailed on God knows how many occasions.'

'Mendy got up to all kinds of stunts,' says Colin Hart, 'but he could have been the best PR man in British history. The classic of all time was when somebody allegedly made a citizen's arrest on Nigel. Ambrose phoned me in the office and said: "Do you want a world exclusive?"' Mendy takes up the story: 'Nigel appeared in one of those photofit pictures in the London *Evening Standard* and as a result somebody tried to arrest him – in Forest Gate, on the corner of Romford and Nigel roads. I'm glad you're laughing . . .' Scotland Yard admitted it had released a touched-up picture of Benn after the victim of a gunman pointed to a photograph of the fighter in a magazine when trying to describe his attacker. 'One idiot tried to arrest Nigel by jumping on top of him, screaming "he's a wanted man",' said Mendy at the time.

'So Ambrose said he was bringing Nigel to have his hand X-rayed at the London Hospital, because he'd broken it during this citizen's arrest,' continues Hart. 'Knowing Ambrose, I knew there was every possibility it was a load of bollocks. But – and there was always a but with Ambrose – say it was genuine and I refused to turn up and missed a great story? So I got my arse out of the office, into the car, got down to Whitechapel and, sure enough, there were cameras, radio men, newspaper men – he'd told everybody: "Who wants a world exclusive?"

I was bloody livid. To be fair, because they were all news people and the only person he knew was me, he took me into the hospital and straight to Nigel. When I saw him, he had his hand inside his jacket, the one he was supposed to have broken on this assailant's head. And I said to him, "Good to see you, Nige", and put my right hand out. He put his right hand out, I gripped it and realised immediately it was a load of bollocks. Nevertheless, he got the hospital to put the hand in plaster and came out and gave these interviews. He was obviously hoping to sue Scotland Yard and the *Evening Standard* for God knows what.'

'We had this press conference where we had a "magic" box with wires hanging out of it that was going to speed up the healing of Nigel's hand,' continues Mendy. 'It didn't matter that it had changed from his left hand to his right hand overnight. We had this "expert" flown in from France with this box and one journalist was saying "What a load of bollocks, you're telling me that box there is going to cure this, that and the other?" So this guy, who wasn't an expert at all but was actually fresh out of RADA, started elaborating on the functions of this "magic" box. I said, "Never mind all that, if you think it's bollocks, you come and put your hand in this box – switch it on." If this journalist had walked over we would have been totally exposed, but he bottled it by saying there was nothing wrong with his hand. I kept on at him, "Put your hand in it, you'll feel this burning sensation – he's a world champion and he's not too happy about putting his hand in it either" . . .'

'There are so many anecdotes about Ambrose Mendy, you should be writing a book about him,' says Kevin Mitchell. 'I remember his first promotion at York Hall in 1988 and it was the first time there had been this razzle-dazzle, with the ring card girls and the lights and all the stuff you take for granted in British boxing nowadays. Top of the bill was a heavyweight fight between Liverpool's Noel Quarless and an American called John Tate and the combined weight must have been 40 stone. So there was a very real fear that the ring would fall apart. I remember sitting next to Harry Mullan and we weren't watching the fight, we were watching the ring itself, worrying that it was going to collapse on top of us. Only Ambrose could have people flocking to a night like that.'

Mendy glibly referred to such stunts as Benn's citizen's arrest and the 'magic' box as 'glorifying the truth'. Whether it was truth or fiction Mendy was peddling, Benn was happy to go along with it if it got him mentioned in the news bulletins and his picture in the papers, even in the form of a photofit. 'I remember the opening of Trump's Taj Mahal in Atlantic City and there was this whole 1940s Hollywood parody, it was almost like we were Bing Crosby and Bob Hope,' recalls Mendy. 'Then I claimed we'd discovered a McBenn clan and we went up to Scotland and had a photo shoot of us both wearing kilts. My intention was to make him a brand and Nigel knows he was a brand. But I was a lot more aware of what was being created than he was.

'Nigel had not gone much beyond formal education and gone into the army at the first opportunity. But Nigel was as he was and I didn't want to make apologies for his persona. Although he knew he was a brand and was portrayed as the Dark Destroyer and Big Bad Benn, that just allowed Nigel to be himself. I worked on his relationship with ITV, worked on his relationship with the British newspapers, getting everything in synch. And we delivered on their expectations. And it wasn't just the sports writers and the sports editors we were talking to, it was the news editors and particularly the picture desk editors. A lot of research went into what their readerships wanted and we gave them what they wanted. And when we were in Miami or abroad wherever, we'd say to all the boxing writers, "If you don't have the budget, we'll pay for the trip".'

Leonard outpointed a listless Duran over 12 lopsided rounds in December 1989, but Benn ended up fighting neither of them. Leonard, who was defending his WBC super-middle-weight crown against his old rival, was not a realistic target. Duran, who was still the WBC middleweight champion, was a realistic target because Arum had him and Benn under contract. Barry Hearn, meanwhile, had already started plan-ning a multi-million-dollar bout, to take place at a London football stadium in May. However, the WBC stripped Duran of its middleweight belt because he had not defended it within the designated period, meaning Arum and Mendy had to winkle out a new opponent for the coming spring. Enter Doug DeWitt, who was about to sleepwalk into a nightmare from which he still hasn't awoken.

'I'd come off two great wins against Robbie Sims and Matthew Hilton,' says DeWitt, whose victory over Sims, half-brother of the great Marvin Hagler, made him the inaugural WBO middleweight champion. 'People were planning for Hilton to beat me but I gave him a brutal beating, destroyed him. They told me the whole week before the fight that if I beat Hilton I would get a match with Roberto Duran for at least half a million or I would get a rematch with Tommy Hearns. I was very happy about that.' DeWitt had taken Hearns, who would become the first man to win world titles in five weight divisions, the distance in 1986. Hearns was awarded a one-sided decision but DeWitt enhanced his repu-tation as a stand-up contender. However, while DeWitt maintains he could have knocked Hearns out and that he regularly used to outbox Hagler in sparring, his fight record tells a rather different story. The man from Yonkers, New York, was also beaten by former welterweight world champion Milton McCrory in 1986 and knocked out in three rounds by Jose Quinones in 1987, the same Jose Quinones Benn would later spark in one round. He was also knocked cold in seven rounds by Italy's Sumbu Kalambay, the WBA title-holder of the day, in 1988. So while DeWitt saw himself as boxing royalty, to the sport's movers and shakers he was just another pawn.

Still, the tale of how he came to lose his world title to Benn could have been lifted straight from a 1950s film noir boxing movie. Forget 'I coulda been a contender', with DeWitt it was a case of 'Benn shoulda been a man'. 'They conned me into the Benn fight,' says DeWitt. 'I was sitting in a movie theatre when my manager Stan Hoffman came in and asked me down to the Friars Club on 55th Street. Bob Arum was there and he put it to me that I should fight Nigel Benn. I said: "Nigel Benn? I barely know who he is, why am I going backwards?" In England Nigel Benn was a big thing, but over here in the States he was nobody. But I had seen Benn fight Michael Watson, and while Watson defended himself well and ended up stopping him, Benn was still a young, hard, hungry puncher. So why did I need him? I had nothing to gain from fighting him. Why didn't they give me one or two easy fights or give me a huge name, a Leonard or a Hearns, who were past their peak and I had a chance of beating? Not a young, hungry animal like Benn. I wasn't happy about it but they talked me into it and I did say: "I beat Hilton, so I'm sure I'll beat Benn."

'But I also said the only way I'll take this fight is if I get a rider in the contract stating that if Benn beats me, he must give me a rematch. So here's the thing I don't like about Nigel

Benn: Benn agreed to that and he never honoured it. They bullshitted me along and screwed me out of everything, ruined my boxing career. If Benn had given me the rematch, maybe I would have come back and beat him. But he never even thought about me, never even entertained the idea. Benn should have been a man. He should have said: "Doug DeWitt didn't need me after he beat Matthew Hilton, but he gave me a shot. I'll give him a rematch.'"

While DeWitt is of the opinion that he was the victim of a top-to-bottom stitch-up, contemporary reports of the build-up to the Benn fight reveal it was a contest Arum expected, and wanted, the champion to win. And why wouldn't he? As exciting as Benn was, he wasn't American, while the Eubank rivalry was barely a glint in Arum's eye. And it was a fight DeWitt might have won had he not taken Benn so lightly. 'He turned out to be better than I expected,' concedes DeWitt. 'I thought I was going to knock him out for sure because I didn't think he had the greatest chin and I dropped him in the second round with a left hook that didn't even have that much on it. But he was a very hard puncher, a very fast puncher. After only 30 or 40 seconds of the first round he butted me and there was blood running right into my eye, so thick it blinded me. He then hit me with 20 or 30 head shots and I was never in it after that.' And never the same fighter. DeWitt's career trailed off into an extended last gasp following his eight-round defeat at the heavy hands of Benn, which took two years out of his career. 'I took a lot of punishment throughout my career, had a lot of rough fights and the Benn fight was one of the roughest,' says DeWitt. 'When I came back after two years out nothing was there any more.' You might call it boxing's butterfly effect: a fateful tap on the shoulder in a movie theatre that triggers the collapse of your career while setting another man you have never met and will never truly know on the path to glory.

However, Benn was hardly received as an all-conquering hero in his homeland. At the time of Benn's eight-round victory over DeWitt in Atlantic City, the fledgling World Boxing Organization was not recognised by the British Boxing Board of Control, with some justification. In the already splintered world of professional boxing, the formation of the WBO was viewed by many as yet another blow to the credibility of the sport, a further dilution of its purity. It meant there were now four major governing bodies – the others being the World Boxing Council, the World Boxing Association and the International Boxing Federation – and many considered Benn's new title a cardboard crown, with Harry Mullan calling it 'boxing's equivalent of the Zenith Data Systems Cup' and 'bearing no relation to the world middleweight title as won by Randolph Turpin and Alan Minter'. At the time of Benn's victory over DeWitt, the IBF title-holder was unbeaten American Michael Nunn and the WBA title-holder Jamaica's Mike McCallum. Nunn was being groomed as American boxing's next big thing and was cutting a swathe through the 160lb ranks, having claimed the IBF belt from the previously unbeaten Frank Tate and knocked out Sumbu Kalambay in one round; McCallum had only recently administered a thorough beating to Michael Watson, knocking out Benn's conqueror after 11 one-sided rounds. The WBC title was vacant, a fading Roberto Duran, who was still good enough to wrest the belt from Iran Barkley in February 1989, having been stripped.

Benn broke his wrist in two places pounding the hard head of DeWitt and was out of the gym for six weeks. But there was no rest for Arum, who set about manoeuvring Benn into the major leagues, from where DeWitt had fallen. A fight against Tommy Hearns was mooted before the Benn camp plumped for Barkley, a graduate of the same South Bronx streets that had such a galvanising impact on Eubank. Barkley's manager John Reetz described his fighter as having 'an eye that stinks' and 'a body that is deteriorating because he has taken some terrible beatings'. The British Boxing Board of Control agreed, refusing to allow the fight to take place in the UK, largely because Barkley had undergone retinal surgery. The Nevada Athletic Commission had no such compunction and the fight was scheduled to take place at Bally's Hotel and Casino in Las Vegas on 18 August 1990.

While Benn railed against the British authorities for scuppering a glorious homecoming, the British Boxing Board of Control should be applauded for its decision. Barkley, a 30-year-old former gang member, had been in with some of the great middleweights of the day and had the wounds to prove it. In 1988 he sparked Hearns to claim the WBC belt, having been bleeding from cuts over both eyes and on the verge of knockout defeat at the time. Barkley required 70 stitches but was back in the ring eight months later, losing his title to Duran in a bona fide classic. After the Duran defeat, Barkley required plastic surgery to remove scar tissue but was fighting again less than six months later, this time against IBF title-holder Nunn. Once again Barkley was magnificent, losing a decision but convincing one judge he deserved a draw. This trio of marquee fights should have made Barkley a wealthy man, but he was actually out of control, on his uppers and desperate for another big pay-day. 'If he was made to stop boxing now, he would have no future,' said Reetz when asked why Barkley was still fighting. 'He is likely to land up in jail or end up dead with a bullet in him in a South Bronx ghetto.'

In film and literature boxing managers are usually portrayed as unscrupulous operators, with plenty of justification. As Budd Schulberg wrote: 'Boxing is a business where an honest man is automatically down in everybody's book as a suspicious character.' When Schulberg wrote the famous taxi-cab scene in *On The Waterfront*, he had been immersed in the sport for 30-odd years and would have been intimate with the often fractious relationship between a boxer and his connections. Indeed, Schulberg managed a fighter himself, guiding heavy-weight prospect Archie McBride into a fight with future world champion Floyd Patterson in 1955. And so while the words of the embittered Terry Malloy – 'He gets the title shot outdoors in a ball park and whadda I get? A one-way ticket to Palookaville' – have become clichéd, they retain the stamp of authenticity. They could have been spoken by Doug DeWitt himself. But in fairness to Reetz, he was on the horns of a familiar dilemma within the sport. While Barkley claimed Reetz hadn't secured him enough money for his three fights against Hearns, Duran and Nunn, he must have received a considerable sum. And Reetz presumably didn't make Barkley squander the money he did receive on fast cars and jewellery. As it was, Barkley was unable to pay for the funeral of his father, who died of cancer a week before the Benn fight. Reetz covered the $3000 costs. So no matter that Barkley had crashed his car three times since the Nunn fight because the lights of oncoming cars 'looked fuzzy', 'The Blade' had no choice but to lace them up again and do battle with Nigel Benn. If the lights of oncoming cars looked fuzzy, the oncoming fists of Benn would be almost impossible to decipher.

Despite Barkley's well-publicised problems, Benn was only a narrow favourite with the Vegas bookmakers. He made a mockery of the odds. 'Benn's in for a rough night,' predicted

ITV commentator Reg Gutteridge as the protagonists eyed each other from across the ring. In fact, it was all over in two minutes and 57 seconds. Benn came screaming out of his corner on the sound of the opening bell, wobbled Barkley with his first punch thrown, a swingeing right hand, and almost floored him with a left hook 15 seconds later, forcing the referee to deliver a standing eight count. When Barkley had Benn back-pedalling with a left hook of his own barely a minute into the first stanza, it was clear the fight would not last more than a round. Barkley seemingly having weathered the storm, he was sent to the canvas by a clubbing right-left combination with 25 seconds remaining before the fight was stopped on the three knockdown rule, Barkley having touched down again. 'Whatever the long-term judgement on Nigel Benn,' wrote Jack Massarik in the *Guardian*, 'nobody can deny that he possesses a world-class flair for the dramatic.'

While Benn's victory over Barkley had Bob Arum proclaiming his charge 'the best English fighter ever to come to the United States', others weren't as impressed. 'It was a big joke in the boxing world when Benn fought Iran Barkley,' says DeWitt. 'Barkley was way past his prime, went down to flash knockdowns, was hit when he was down and got robbed. Iran in his prime would have knocked Nigel Benn out.' DeWitt's words might be dismissed as the mutterings of a sour man – the assertion that Barkley's visits to the canvas were 'flash' knockdowns is perverse – but there were dissenting voices at the time. For every man who saw the wild Englishman as the most exciting thing to hit the middleweight division since Marvin Hagler, there was another who saw him as an accident waiting to happen and not much better than the fighter who lost to Michael Watson: weather the early storm and you'll get him in the end.

The name on everybody's lips following Benn's latest eye-catching victory was Sugar Ray Leonard, who relinquished his WBC super-middleweight belt shortly after the Englishman's demolition of Barkley. But while Mendy was talking telephone numbers, it is doubtful Leonard ever bothered finding out what Mendy's telephone number was. Leonard, a five-weight world champion who had been beaten once in a stop-start, 37-fight career, had been the blue-eyed boy of American boxing since winning gold at the Montreal Olympics in 1976. But Leonard's slick public persona was greatly at odds with his chaotic private life and he was in the midst of a messy divorce at the time. Tommy Hearns and Roberto Duran were also floated as potential opponents but Benn decided they could wait: there was easier money to be made closer to home. 'It didn't make sense to me,' says Mendy. 'He was a superstar in America, feted by absolutely everybody – Mike Tyson, George Foreman, old-timers like Jersey Joe Walcott, Kid Gavilan and Beau Jack. Everywhere he went, everybody knew who he was. He should never have left the United States, he should have stayed out there, because all of his weaknesses and frailties were here in the UK. And so was Chris Eubank.'

CHAPTER FIVE
A festering volcano

While Eubank's victory over Eduardo Contreras was his first fight screened live on ITV, the 'weird Limey' had been popping up on highlights shows such as Thames's *Midweek Sport Special* as far back as his 15th bout against the Canadian Les Wisniewski. The Wisniewski fight, and the commentary of it, is a crystal-clear snapshot of Eubank's standing in the game at that time. 'It looks as though he's rehearsing for the charleston,' says Reg Gutteridge as Eubank wheels away from his opponent, looking like a man pedalling backwards on a unicycle, 'the Canadian didn't know what to make of that.' Neither did the crowd at the International Centre in Brentwood, where the funereal atmosphere was periodically punctuated by uproarious laughter. 'The Canadian barely landed a punch in the opening round,' continues Gutteridge. 'In fact, the referee's pointed finger at Eubank was causing more damage. He's a quality fighter, Eubank, when he stops the song and dance bit and gets stuck in.'

His fight against Hugo Corti revealed Eubank, his partnership with Barry Hearn now a year old, was pretty much the complete package already. 'This is typical Chris Eubank,' says commentator Jim Rosenthal as Eubank runs through his repertoire. 'And there are certain people that hate the posing, hate the antics and hate the showmanship. Others admire it and say that behind all that there's a very skilful and brilliant fighter. Barry McGuigan: are you an admirer or a hater?' 'I just dislike people being arrogant,' says McGuigan, a man whose main selling point was his humility. As the fight wears on, McGuigan's comments betray a barely disguised disdain for this 'peculiar fella' in his midst. After Eubank's one-sided eight-round victory, it is time for the now obligatory bout of Benn baiting. 'You hear the people, they want Nigel Benn, I want Nigel Benn,' says Eubank, his words not as clipped as they would become. 'I've been wanting him for too long. Let's do it, let's get it on.' Then, prompted by the interviewer, Eubank gives fight fans some of his 'boxing is barbarism' schtick. What they hate him for. What they want. 'Barbaric is right. I would advise that everyone stay away from the ring. This is a dirty business.'

By the spring of 1990, Eubank had cultivated a reputation as a fighter on the verge of world class, a man with most of the shots, a sound defence and a solid punch, particularly on the counter. But he had also become a member of what Mickey Duff liked to call the 'Who Needs Him Club'. Eubank might have become its president if it wasn't for his mouth. '[Eubank] has talked himself into the contest by compiling an unbeaten record against modest opposition and by antagonising Benn,' was *Guardian* boxing correspondent John Rodda's appraisal of Eubank's rise through the ranks. Harry Mullan wrote of Eubank: 'He remains a dedicated non-conformist, whose peculiar posturing and highly personalised ring style repels as many fans as it attracts.' 'Eubank did a lot of martial arts train-ing,' says Kevin Mitchell, 'and you could see it in his movements in the ring. He moved like some Zen artist, like he was going through exercises rather than being involved in a boxing match.' Yet even when the consensus was that Eubank had stunk the place out, he was still able to grab a few headlines with a well-directed barb. When ITV interviewer Gary Newbon suggested Eubank could have put up a better show against Contreras, Eubank replied: 'It shows me immediately that you know nothing about boxing.'

But while Eubank's moves were idiosyncratic – he spent much of the Contreras fight creeping around the ring in an exaggerated crouch, like a cat burglar retreating from a spotlit rooftop – more astute observers knew he had the style to give Benn fits. 'Chris did things that were wrong in the ring but he got away with it,' says Ronnie Davies. 'He was never ortho-dox, he did things completely different from everyone else, but it worked for him. Sometimes he'd only fight for half a minute of a round, the rest of the time he'd be creeping around, messing about. But I used to say to him, "It doesn't matter if you only fight for half a minute, as long as you're not getting hit and you're scoring". And when I saw Chris beat Anthony Logan, I knew then that he had the style to beat Benn, although I respected and rated Benn very, very highly.'

'Nigel Benn was a great, great fighter,' says Barry Hearn. 'But bearing in mind he'd been outboxed by Michael Watson, in trouble against Sanderline Williams and always had trouble against counter-punchers, he should have thought a bit more about it. I've always thought Chris was one of the worst fight-ers going forward but the best counter-puncher I've ever seen. I couldn't believe our luck when they agreed to the fight, especially given that Chris wasn't even the mandatory chal-lenger to Nigel's WBO title at the time.'

Benn is unable to recall when he first became aware of this insufferable upstart saying unspeakable things about him, but

Eubank had been calling Benn out at intervals since returning to England from New York. When Benn was the Commonwealth champion driving a white Porsche and Eubank was a four-round fighter gobbling up journeymen in places like Hove and Copthorne, such flagrant disrespect could be ignored. But when Benn was the WBO middle-weight champion driving a red Bentley and Eubank was knocking out prospects and disrespecting Benn in front of millions on television, the dynamic was altogether different.

'I can't remember the first time I met Chris although I read what he said about me,' says Benn. 'But when he started calling me out I didn't take him seriously. Of course he was going to call me out, I was the blue-eyed boy. When you're world champion you're not thinking about fighters down the rankings running their mouths off, you're thinking about bigger things. Like Leonard and Hearns and Duran. But when he started appearing regularly on TV my hatred for him became all-consuming, the rage was tremendous. He just got my goat, he knew how to get to me, how to poke and prod me. I had this switch and only he could turn it on. All I thought about was him, I just wanted to do a number on him. I really wanted to give it to him big time. I couldn't stand him. I really, really could not stand this guy.'

'This hatred of Eubank, I don't know where it came from or when it started, but I wasn't going to sit back and not capitalise on it once it had taken hold of him,' says Ambrose Mendy. 'Eubank quickly became an obsession and all Nigel would say is, "He's fucking getting on my nerves, I'm gonna do him, I'm gonna do him, I'm gonna do him." We could have made that Sugar Ray Leonard fight happen, or Hearns or Duran, but Nigel wanted to come back to England and shut Eubank's mouth. And when he came back all his mates were saying,

"Nige, you've got to do this Eubank guy." And not just his mates, everybody wanted Nigel to do Eubank. Here was this guy mouthing off, denouncing everything that Nigel had achieved in life, inside and outside of the ring. Eubank got inside him and that fight was a perfect example of how not to go about settling a personal dispute.'

Hatred combined with complacency is a dangerous cocktail but Mendy was only too happy to shake things up once the ingredients had settled in the stomach of his protégé. The exploits of Benn and his 'Pack' in Miami were proof that while the defeat by Watson might have been chastening in the short term, it did not succeed in erasing from Benn an overwhelming sense of self-importance. Benn formed the Billionaire Boys Club, whose stated aims were conspicuous spending and 'living life to the full'. 'When the good times rolled,' says Benn, 'they really rolled.' Chief among the Billionaire Boys Club was Rolex Ray, an Essex boy, like Benn, with a penchant for high-society orgies. 'We did some crazy things,' says Benn. 'Crazy, crazy things. I went to this party when I was about 26 years old, this Roman orgy in a mansion in Surrey, although it might as well have been in Outer Mongolia. I was just this kid from Ilford and there were all these women in ball gowns, others in stockings and suspenders and maids' outfits, all the doors were taken off their hinges, and people were going at it all over the place. There were celebrities there, soap stars, members of the aristocracy, let's just say it was a bit of a shock to the system. I remember I went home in the morning, told my mum and she started laughing. The next week I was at Buckingham Palace, St James's Palace, meeting princes and princesses. It was a rock 'n' roll life.'

Benn remembers those days with fondness but is also acutely aware how self-destructive his behaviour was. 'I couldn't break that addiction to sex, drugs and rock 'n' roll for love nor money,' says Benn. 'I was addicted to that for almost all my career. I had everything, but I lost sight of things. You have an affair and you say, "sorry darlin', here's a new watch; sorry darlin', here's a new mansion". I thought I was the best thing since sliced bread but it was a very shallow life.' However, Benn maintains that his wicked, wicked ways did not diminish him as a fighter and all the evidence suggests that he more than compensated for his louche living when he got down to it in the gym. The realities of an elite boxer's life, whereby they might only fight three or four times a year, mean there are an awful lot of fun days in the diary. This allied with the almost animal magnetism of top-flight boxers – there is a lot of love out there for hard men doing dangerous things in a ring, be it from men or from women – can make for a chaotic, disreputable life.

John L. Sullivan, the first gloved world heavyweight champion, created the template of what a boxer should be, boozing, fighting and fucking his way across the United States in the late 19th Century while managing to hold things together just enough to bust plenty of heads in the ring. Then there was Battling Siki, who celebrated his shock victory over light-heavyweight world champion Georges Carpentier in 1922 with a six-month reign of terror across Paris – dressed in a top hat and tuxedo, with two revolvers on his hips, sometimes accompanied by his pet lion, which he would take for walks down the Champs-Élysées. Alcoholic and penniless, Siki was shot dead in New York in 1925. Cuba's Kid Chocolate was said to have owned 150 suits and was voted New York's best-dressed man in 1931, beating the Prince of Wales into second place. When Chocolate's hotel suite was robbed, he was said to have phoned his manager and opined: 'For God's sake, the bastard has left me with only 20 suits.' His earnings spent on New York's endlessly beguiling night life, Chocolate returned to Cuba and spent the rest of his days living off a state pension in the house he had bought for his mother. The stories of Battling Siki and Kid Chocolate have echoed through the ages, with Mike Tyson making the mightiest roar. Tyson shared Siki's love of furs, jewels and women and had a big cat of his own, in his case a tiger. Actually, three of them. 'I'm in prison and I am loaded,' recalled Tyson. 'This guy on the phone says, "You can be driving your Ferrari with your cub in the front seat". I thought, "Yeah, when I come out, I'm gonna be a cool dude. I'm gonna have a tiger in my car".'

While Tyson was persuaded careering about town with a tiger in his passenger seat – presumably without a seat belt on – was the height of cool, Mendy was able to persuade Benn he had what it took to top the pop charts. 'Simon Cowell was quite well known in the music industry at the time but wasn't earning much money,' says Mendy. 'So he said to me, "Why don't I write a record for Nigel?" And he came up with this song called "Stand and Fight". He got the guy from Snap! involved and invested every penny he had. I was so certain it would go to number one but Simon ended up in court over the ownership of the record.' Benn, meanwhile, has the good grace to sound embarrassed at the memory. '"Stand and Fight", oh my word, what was that all about?' says Benn. 'And it wasn't even me singing, I did a Milli Vanilli.' Not only did Cowell end up in court, it didn't reach number one.

However, many less-heralded fighters than Tyson and Benn have been led down the garden path. Terry Spinks, like Benn an alumni of West Ham Amateur Boxing Club, was a salt-of-the-earth cockney who prepared for his shot at glory at the 1956 Olympics by doing a dustman's round. But having won gold as an 18-year-old in Melbourne, Spinks was seduced by celebrity, which fast corroded him as a fighter. 'When you are a famous personality in the public eye,' said Spinks, 'you've got to look like one. You've got to be seen in smart places with important people.' Benn was simply playing to type.

'On Nigel's stag night,' says Mendy, 'we arranged for a coach to start in Liverpool and pick up John Barnes, Peter Beardsley and loads of the Liverpool lads, head over to Manchester to pick up Paul Ince, Bryan Robson and all the United lads, stop off in the Midlands to pick up Cyrille Regis and then head down to London, where Linford Christie got on. We then went on a tour of a whole series of places, Nigel got merry and we ended up at the Phoenix Apollo, a Caribbean restaurant in East London. Anyway, Sharron turned up – bearing in mind in two days' time we're all heading to Las Vegas to see her marry Nigel in a little white chapel – and wasn't too happy with what she saw. That was it, it was all over, and it cost Nigel a brand new BMW 325 convertible, a brand new wardrobe and loads of humility. Nigel had this magnetism, this allure, and in terms of living the life, he had to do the things that he did because he put the effort in like nobody I've ever come across.' Mendy clearly saw such dissolute behaviour as a necessity: as far as Benn's fixer was concerned, this was merely a warrior blowing off steam between battles, finding an alternate channel for all that pent-up aggression. But others looking in from the outside saw a parallel between Benn's sense of entitlement outside the ring and his sense of security within it. 'I think Nigel was quite complacent before the fight with Eubank,' says Barry Hearn. 'Because he had Ambrose Mendy in his ear, telling him he was the greatest thing since sliced bread. Which he wasn't.'

★ ★ ★

Every bit as dangerous as Mendy's inflated opinion of Benn was his disregard for Eubank. 'We don't consider him a risk,' said Mendy, having announced that his charge would be fighting Tommy Hearns after disposing of Eubank. 'I think he is a fraud. But it's not what I want, it's what Nigel wants, and he wants this fight more than Eubank can possibly imagine.' Mendy's opinion of Eubank was not greatly enhanced by his eight-round defeat of Kid Milo in Brighton in September 1990. It was another performance that had veteran Fleet Street hacks scratching their heads, although it provided further proof that even when winning in second gear, Eubank made for good copy. 'He spends much of each round looking at his opponent as if he is some strange creature washed up on the shore,' said Srikumar Sen of *The Times*. 'The sort that little children turn over with sticks.' 'It is no longer enough to beat your man with skill and determination,' wrote the *Guardian*'s Jack Massarik. 'A star commodity now has to strut, swagger, taunt his opponent and generally act like the bored housewives' favourite baddie on the wrestling circuit.'

But once again Eubank made light of an underwhelming display, spotting Mendy ringside and engaging him in some choice trashtalk. 'I want your boy, he belongs to me, he's mine,' said Eubank. Mendy, king of the non sequitur, fired back with a mashed-up quote from Corinthians, channelled by Nigel Benn, via the Prince of Wales. 'Nigel Benn, if he was here,' said Mendy, 'would say, as Prince Charles once said: "When I was a child I played with childish things, but now I am a man." I was very disappointed with the way Chris fought tonight and we're gonna get you.' 'How could you say such a thing?' replied Eubank, looking genuinely hurt. 'That's ludicrous. You know I can take your boy. You're petrified, I know you are. Your boy's mine, it's done. It's a foregone conclusion.'

Later in Massarik's scathing appraisal he reports, with a degree of schadenfreude, that Eubank returned to his hotel room to discover he had been relieved of £6,500 in cash and jewellery. As if to say: 'That'll learn you.'

On the morning of Friday 21 September, the newspapers reported that a deal had been struck for Benn to defend his WBO middleweight crown on Sunday 18 November at Birmingham's National Exhibition Centre. The negotiations between Hearn and Mendy had been both tortuous and torturous. 'Mendy talks in very big noughts,' said a frayed and frustrated Hearn. Mendy was holding out for a £1m purse for his man but eventually settled for £400,000. As the challenger, Eubank would earn £100,000. But he was already talking like a champion. 'Benn is capable of only knocking out a man, not teaching anybody a lesson,' said Eubank. 'If he is fighting a puncher, he is the man to put your money on. He is the best puncher in the world but he is up against a skillster. He will be exposed. Class will prevail.'

The press conference to announce the fight at London's Café Royal was relatively non-eventful. Relative to what happened when the cameras were off. 'Eubank walked into a room where Nigel and I were sat with Barry Hearn and the head of security for the fight,' says Mendy, 'and Nigel leapt over the table and went at Eubank. Somehow they got somebody between them but Eubank was totally shocked and unnerved. Nigel wanted to iron him out there and then. I was like, "Calm down, Nige, for fuck's sake". I saw it then, and Eubank did too, how much Nigel wanted to kill him. And it was me who had to deal with all this rage, over and over again.' 'I was faced with a monumentally important situation,' says Eubank. 'If Benn had won this little skirmish in that room, in doing so he would have sealed the fight. However, all Benn was trying to do was trick me, but I wasn't going to be intimidated by him and his hostile antics.'

Benn's fuse had been lit the previous evening, when both men signed the contract for the fight live on ITV. 'I remember the enormous tension between the two men, they genuinely did seem to loathe each other,' says Nick Owen, presenter of *Midweek Sport Special*. 'The hatred was almost tangible, which was what made it compulsive viewing. We all know these guys put on an act to a certain extent but if there was ever a genuine antipathy between two fighters, that's as close as you'd get to it. It was a fraught evening, there was a very real fear it might boil over. Chris wouldn't even face Nigel and without question that got under Nigel's skin. The menace in Nigel Benn's eyes was incendiary. It was all calculated and it made for great television. Boxing is about entertainment and television is about entertainment and they both really delivered that day.'

'Nick Owen had to drink gallons of water and God knows what else, he was terrified,' says Mendy. 'Me and Nigel had gone to Hugo Boss earlier that day and picked out green jackets because I'd had some research done and knew that was a colour Eubank professed to dislike. But when Eubank decided to turn away from Nigel, it wasn't that he was frightened of Nigel, it was just a ploy. The man was absolutely off his head. There he was saying: "Nigel Benn hath no clath, the man hath no thtyle." He knew that Nigel didn't have the greatest verbal skills or the greatest confidence. And you've also got to remember that while they were both second-generation immigrants, Nigel's parents came from Barbados and Chris's parents came from Jamaica – and the Bajans and the Jamaicans are about as friendly as the Scots and the English. It was all real, none of it was pretend. After the altercation on *Midweek*

Sport Special, Eubank decided he didn't want to do any more media sessions. But instead of that being a negative we turned that into a positive: "These two guys hate each other so much they can't even be in the same room as each other."'

'It was just so volatile between me and him, it really was,' says Benn. 'The first time I really remember meeting him was when we signed the contract on *Midweek Sport Special*. He was a big, strapping lad, bigger than me, but I knew I could still have him on the cobbles. I would have bitten him and everything. All he had to do was come and get in my face, get in my space and I would have gone "BOOM!" With Chris it could have kicked off at any moment, it was that close. During that interview he had his back towards me, he never faced me, because he knew I would have gone for him. I'm not saying he was scared of me but he had to keep it cool because he knew I was right on the edge and about to jump on him. What annoyed me most was the way he looked down his nose at everybody. He thought he was an eloquent man, but really he needed elocution lessons. He was this black guy who thought he was different class to everybody else. The way he used to carry on was as if he should have been living in Buckingham Palace and the Queen should have been living in Hove. Chris tried to conduct himself as a gentleman, saying stuff like "he's a wild man, I'm different to him, he should be in the jungle". He lit the fuse real good, absolutely he out-psyched me. I just wanted to fight him all the time.'

Eubank steadfastly denies he ever harboured any real hatred towards Benn. And Ronnie Davies contends that his charge's inflammatory rhetoric was merely gamesmanship. 'The hatred was real on Nigel's side but not on Chris's,' says Davies. 'Eubank was a very passionate man but also a very nice person and he didn't have a bad word about anybody.

All that stuff about Benn being uncouth and wild and ungentlemanly, that was just Eubank trying to wind him up.' Others lucky enough to have a ringside seat for the rivalry are not so sure. 'There was actual dislike between the two of them, no question,' says Hearn. 'Eubank would be disdainful, pompous and patronising in his verbal assaults. So poor old Nigel, whilst a very good fighter, got slaughtered at press conferences. Chris claimed he didn't hate Nigel, but if he didn't he was brutal. As far as I could see the hatred was real, it wasn't to sell tickets.'

'He came out with one line at the Café Royal which was horrible. He looked at Nigel and said: "Nigel, we both know, when this is all over, you're going to end up working on the door of a nightclub." This is a bloke who was a great world champion, had gone to America and bashed up Doug DeWitt and Iran Barkley. It was a vicious, vicious line. I compare it to Ali–Frazier: Ali slaughtered Frazier at press conferences and called him all the names under the sun and Frazier never forgave him for the rest of his life. But Nigel's plan was the same as Frazier's: "That's OK, son, say what you like, when we get in the ring I'll fucking kill you." Nigel's found God, he's a really nice human being and the two of them would embrace in the street now. But at the time Nigel had this fire burning inside him and he really, really hated Chris. Nigel was a festering volcano, he wanted to tear Eubank's head off.'

As the fight drew nearer, Eubank's rhetoric took an even more spiteful twist. 'Benn proved to me he was a coward when he lost to Michael Watson,' said the challenger at a press conference five days before the fight. 'But I don't want him to be a coward against me. I want him to come out and face reality. Then we'll see how much of the coward is still there.' 'He is a loudmouth who cannot fight and has made a good living by criticising me,' countered Benn. 'I want to shut Eubank's mouth forever.' 'Who's Fooling Who?' went the promotional tagline. A nation was about to find out. Or so it thought.

CHAPTER SIX
Two shining stars

A nimosity has been used to sell boxing matches since the early days of the sport in any codified form. Pierce Egan, an eyewitness to many of the biggest prize fights in England in the late 18th and early 19th Century and the author of *Boxiana*, which set a standard that every recorder of the sport since has tried to meet, called boxing 'the sweet science of bruising'. It is not known whether Egan was being ironic but there was an awful lot of bruising and very little sweetness in the sport in its pre-Victorian golden age. Fights could last for hours, there were no gloves to soften the blows, bones were regularly broken and claret freely flowed. And if you weren't of Anglo-Saxon stock, the pain was even worse.

Daniel Mendoza was the first Jewish prize fighter to become an English champion and is widely considered to be the father of scientific boxing. The 'Mendoza School' promoted foot-work, the jab and defence rather than toe-to-toe slugging, but while some were taken by this more technical form of pugilism – including the Prince of Wales, who became Mendoza's patron – others professed to be appalled by it. 'The Jew', as Mendoza was often referred to in publications of the time, wasn't, as some claimed, sophisticated but 'cunning'. In 1788, Mendoza had the first of five fights against great rival Richard

Humphreys, 'The Gentleman Fighter'. Taking advantage of the anxiety over the growing Jewish population in England, the fights were promoted along ethnic lines. Having lost the first match after 29 rounds, Mendoza wrote to a newspaper called *The World* to complain about his opponent's cowardly tactics, triggering a war of words between the two men which eventually resulted in a rematch. Of course, the second bout was a sell-out, with many of the crowd there to see the bumptious Jew get knocked out. Mendoza won in 52.

In 1810, a former slave from a plantation in Virginia called Tom Molineaux issued a challenge to Tom Cribb, the celebrated champion of England and a former London porter. Cribb was so tough that he was once crushed by a 500lb crate of oranges and coughed blood for days before making a full recovery. If the idea of a Jew becoming English champion had filled the public with dread, the prospect of a black American prevailing over Cribb had Englishmen of all ranks quaking in taverns across the land. Perhaps only the prospect of an invasion by Napoleon could have engendered such fear. It is likely this fear had as much to do with nationality as race, so intertwined with the idea of supposed English superiority had prize fighting become. 'The national honour was at stake,' wrote Egan.

However, Molineaux was variously described as 'the darkey', 'the nigger' and 'the terrible black' by other writers of the day. William Oxberry, a contemporary of Egan, wrote that the English 'felt somewhat alarmed that a man of colour should dare to look forward to the championship of England, and threaten to decorate his sable brow with the hard-earned laurels of Cribb.' The fear was so real that the English, who prided themselves on their sense of fair play, resorted to cheating to make sure their man won. With Cribb in trouble in the

19th round, a posse of 'Fancy', as boxing spectators were known in Georgian England, stormed the ring and broke one of Molineaux's fingers. In the 28th, Cribb was out on his feet and Molineaux about to be announced the winner when Cribb's second accused Molineaux of fighting with bullets in his fists, the bare-knuckle equivalent of boxing with loaded gloves. Molineaux proved otherwise and the fight went on. Cribb gained the ascendancy and Molineaux, his features barely decipherable, yielded in the 40th round.

Boxing matches were still being promoted on the back of racial tension at the start of the 20th Century and it is likely that no boxer in history was more universally hated than Jack Johnson, the first black heavyweight champion of the world. In many ways Molineaux was the template for Johnson: fast-talking, bombastic, self-destructive and, most pertinently, an unwelcome interloper in a white man's world. The centre of the boxing universe might have shifted from England to the United States in the almost 100 years between Molineaux's failed challenge to Cribb and Johnson winning the greatest prize in sport, but racial attitudes remained much the same on both sides of the Atlantic. But at a time when black people in the United States were oppressed, powerless and almost invisible, Johnson was gloriously conspicuous and a powerful symbol of what a black man could be. Namely, everything a white man could be. And more.

John L. Sullivan, perhaps the most celebrated American of his era, refused to defend his title against black fighters, stating: 'Any fighter who'd get into the ring with a nigger loses my respect.' Jim Jeffries beat the great black boxer Peter Jackson on his way to winning the world title but retired to his alfalfa farm in 1904 rather than defend it against Johnson. Instead, Johnson was forced to chase Jeffries's successor, Tommy Burns, to Australia. 'Citizens who have never prayed before,' said *The Illustrated Sporting and Dramatic News*, 'are supplicating Providence to give the white man a strong right arm with which to belt the coon into oblivion.' It wasn't just newspaper hype, Burns and Johnson genuinely disliked each other. 'The fight with Johnson was the first in which I found myself hating my opponent,' said Burns. Johnson, angered at the disrespect shown him by Burns and his hosts, taunted the champion mercilessly en route to a 14th-round knockout on Boxing Day 1908. The United States was aghast and Jack London was moved to write: 'Jeffries must emerge from his alfalfa farm and remove that smile from Johnson's face. Jeff, it's up to you.' Johnson knocked Jeffries out, too, a 'victory' for black Americans that triggered race riots and lynchings and left as many as 28 people dead. Twenty-two years would pass before another black man, Joe Louis, got a world title shot.

No fight in history has relied more on hatred as a promotional tool than Louis's rematch against reluctant Nazi totem Max Schmeling in 1938. But after the terrible events of World War II, hate was a little out of fashion. In addition, more enlightened attitudes towards race relations meant promoting fights along ethnic lines was far less acceptable, although the mass of white America would have been delighted when Rocky Marciano beat Jersey Joe Walcott in 1952 to become the first white heavyweight world champion for 15 years and appalled when black, illiterate ex-con Sonny Liston ascended to the throne ten years later. That is not to say animosity ceased to exist between boxers, just that it tended to spring up in more spontaneous, organic ways. Such as when Cuba's welterweight world champion Benny Paret taunted challenger Emile Griffith at the weigh-in for their third fight in 1962. As Griffith took to the scales, Paret grabbed Griffith's backside and called him '*maricón*', Spanish slang for faggot. While Griffith would eventually admit he was bisexual, at the time such accusations were potentially fatal to an athlete's career. Later that same day, an enraged Griffith battered Paret to death in front of a television audience of millions.

The principle criticism of Barry Hearn's promotions was that the hatred wasn't organic but fabricated. Or that even if the hatred was organic to begin with it was soon being worked on in press officers' laboratories and twisted into something altogether uglier before being packaged and sold to the public. Three weeks after the announcement of Benn's world title defence against Eubank, a member of the British Boxing Board of Control contacted Hearn and advised him to turn down the animosity. 'It was a concern,' said Hearn, 'it was understood and dealt with.' Eubank, who had told all the women members of his family to stay away from the fight, added: 'You should play down hate if you take the public into consideration. Benn's supporters are not the thinking type of people. If Benn detests me and he makes it clear to them you could have an uprising in there.'

The boxing authorities had reason to be nervous. In common with football, boxing had seen a worrying upsurge in hooliganism in the 1980s. In 1980, a near-riot broke out at Wembley Arena after Marvin Hagler stopped home fighter Alan Minter to claim the world middleweight crown. 'I am not letting any black man take the title from me,' said Minter in the build-up to the fight. There was also trouble at the fights between Colin Jones and Don Curry, Jimmy Cable and Prince Rodney and Pat Cowdell and Azumah Nelson, all in 1985. The common theme? The defeat of a white boxer by a black boxer had sparked the violence, whether in the form of missiles directed towards the ring or direct assault of the victorious black boxer, his team or his fans. It was all proof that while plugging fights along ethnic lines in Britain had become taboo – although it should be noted that as recently as 1979, the British Boxing Board of Control felt the need to state in its regulations that 'promoters shall not advertise a tournament as being a Black v White tournament' – that didn't stop certain fans projecting their unreconstructed attitudes onto a promotion.

In October 1985, the press conference to publicise the British middleweight title eliminator between Mark Kaylor (white) and Errol Christie (black) descended into a brawl after Kaylor attempted to throw Christie into a fountain before attacking his rival in a restaurant. It was alleged that Kaylor's attack was racially motivated – an allegation both boxers denied – and the fight came close to being called off after rumours began circulating that the National Front intended to descend on the fight at Wembley Arena en masse. To put all this into context, the press conference brawl took place only four days after the Broadwater Farm riot, a confrontation between black residents in Tottenham and a largely white police force which left one policeman dead and many injured on both sides. The reaction of promoter Mike Barrett was instructive. On the one hand Barrett banned alcohol from the venue and provided extra stewarding, on the other he issued a poster of the two protagonists eye-balling each other, nose to nose, under the inflammatory tag line: The Battle of Bonfire Night. Hearn was faced with a similar dilemma: needing to be seen to play down the animosity between Benn and Eubank while realising the animosity was the fight's unique selling point. Hate has the capacity to fuel riots, but it also puts plenty of bums on seats that might otherwise be empty.

Harry Mullan became particularly queasy about Hearn's

promotional tactics. 'The boxers themselves may not have liked each other enough to meet socially,' wrote Mullan, 'but that is a long way removed from the extravagant sentiments ascribed to them by the promoter's publicity machine. The "hate" angle has become an ever more frequent feature of major British promotions, in particular those emanating from Barry Hearn's Matchroom organisation.' Hearn is unrepentant. 'There's nothing wrong with animosity,' he says. 'I find it quite unusual that two blokes could go into a ring and beat the living crap out of each other if there is no animosity. Something's got to get me out of bed if I'm going to get punched in the face for 12 rounds. And you have to move with the times: what is going to make 20–30,000 people buy tickets for a fight at White Hart Lane in September? It's got to be better than someone saying: "This is going to be a good fight." When Gary Stretch fought Eubank [in 1991] he said: "I'd rather die than lose." Gary didn't really want to die, he just didn't want to lose. But that remark probably sold 2,000 tickets.'

'That could have come out of my mouth, although I don't honestly recall,' says Stretch, a former British light-middle-weight champion and male model who has carved out a career for himself as an actor and director in Hollywood. 'I'm older now, so I certainly wouldn't rather die than be beaten, but as a young man I was very different: I used to get caught up in the moment, there might have been a little bit of needle and I didn't like getting beat. So while I wasn't afraid of getting hurt, I was afraid of losing. But for the most part, I think most of the boys took all that promotional stuff with a pinch of salt. Most of the boys don't know each other, we're just selling the fight. When I fought Eubank I didn't know him, so how could I hate him? It's just the business. The promoters do what they do but if the fighters are being honest, all they're thinking about is going home safely at the end of the night with their record intact, hopefully having won the fight.'

Unsurprisingly, as long as there were no serious injuries in the ring and nobody actually died, television executives and those tasked with commentating on fights were happy to broadcast live pictures of two men knocking lumps out of each other into millions of living rooms across the land. 'I'd love to say I was uneasy about it but I don't think I was,' recalls Jim Rosenthal, the main anchor for ITV's boxing output in its 1980s and '90s pomp. 'I just viewed all that pre-fight chat as part and parcel of the build-up. The word hate was bandied around a lot around the time of the first Benn–Eubank fight but I didn't buy into that at all, I think it was largely for promotional purposes. Neither of them was stupid, they knew which buttons to push, how to create a fight, they were good salesmen. There is a certain amount of hoopla before any fight but I got the feeling that deep down neither Benn nor Eubank believed there was genuine hatred. Because they knew how much their opponent was doing for them in terms of keeping boxing on the front pages and raising their own profile.'

Whether the hatred was real or not, and however inflammatory some thought Hearn's promotional methods to be, many were simply pleased to see two black fighters get this kind of blanket coverage. When Jamaican-born Bunny Sterling became the first immigrant to win a British title by wresting the middleweight crown from Mark Rowe in 1970, his trainer and manager George Francis received 'lots of nasty letters calling me "nigger lover".' Francis's involvement with black fighters in the 1960s and '70s wasn't necessarily frowned upon by promoters because of any inherent racial prejudice on their part but on more pragmatic grounds. 'In the 1960s it was virtually unheard of,' said Francis, who would later guide Frank Bruno to a world heavyweight crown. 'Black boxers had no fan following. They could not get fights.'

As a result, some black fighters in Britain adopted flamboyant alter egos in an attempt to get noticed. Achille Mitchell was a welterweight from Coventry via the Dominican Republic who lost an eliminator for the British title against fellow Caribbean immigrant Kirkland Laing in 1978. But Mitchell's talent alone wasn't enough to make him stand out from the crowd, so he took to wearing a scarlet-trimmed black fedora and gave himself the nickname 'Speedy'. 'My manager told me in strong terms before I turned pro,' said Mitchell, '"Look, you're black, you've got to be different."' However, in an era when Britain's white population was largely suspicious of 'uppity' black men, such attempts at self-promotion weren't necessarily the most productive course of action.

'The race issue was very prevalent when I was fighting,' says Errol Christie. 'In Coventry, where I came from, I had to fight the National Front and the views of many members of the general public. When people saw a black man in a shop in those days, straightaway they thought "this guy's a thief". I'd have women clutching their purses to their chests in case I was going to nick it, you were being pre-judged all the time. And in my era, black fighters weren't treated the same as white fighters, we had a lot of racist attitudes spat at us. We had to be more subdued, we had to watch what we said. So it was my generation, the generation that came before Nigel Benn and Chris Eubank, we were the ones who really suffered racially.'

White athletes had been used to sell everything from newspapers to cigarettes to hair pomade since before World War II.

Jack Dempsey, a man famed for his untameable virility and animal ferocity in the ring rather than his looks, said as far back as 1921: 'It's no longer enough to have speed and a good right arm to be the favourite. You have to be good looking, too, now that ladies go to the fights.' And as the American sports writer and broadcaster John R. Tunis noted eight years later: 'The modern pugilist is last of all a fighter. A lecturer, and endorser of belts, underwear, shaving cream and storage batteries he must be. An apt speaker on the radio . . . knowing in the art of publicity – these are the gifts that must be culti-vated by the pugilists of today.'

But it would be many years before the CEOs of blue-chip companies and the editors of 'respectable' lifestyle magazines started turning to black athletes to help sell their products. And it didn't matter how well you spoke or how good looking you were, as Sugar Ray Leonard found out after winning Olympic gold in 1976. 'Bruce Jenner, the decathlon winner from the Montreal Games, was raking in the real dough,' said Leonard, 'pitching every product on the planet. I had no problem with Bruce doing well. He earned it. But there was no doubt in my mind that if I were white, I would have done a lot better.' Instead of appearing on the front of cereal boxes and getting paid tens of thousands of dollars for the privilege, Leonard eked out a few bucks appearing at local businesses and signing autographs at car shows before belatedly deciding to turn pro. Leonard would become a darling of Madison Avenue, advertising everything from fried chicken to 7UP, but he was at the tip of the vanguard.

In Britain, the way was paved by a select few athletes, nota-bly double Olympic champion Daley Thompson, the face of Lucozade in the 1980s, and Frank Bruno, whose crossover appeal was as much down to his double-act with BBC commentator Harry Carpenter as any feats in the ring. 'We were getting Nigel on sofas, which was all new, it hadn't been done by any boxer, white or black, since Freddie Mills in the 1950s,' says Mendy, presumably forgetting about Bruno. 'The *Mail on Sunday* did a piece where Nigel was done up as d'Artagnan and it was the first time a black sports star had been on the front cover of their colour supplement. And this was when Linford Christie was in his element, Daley Thompson was still around.' It is certainly true that Mendy ran a slicker operation than those behind Thompson and Bruno.

Indeed, in Thompson's case, there appeared to be no one running the show at all. When cricket legend Sir Garfield Sobers presented Thompson with the Sports Personality of the Year trophy in 1982, the tracksuited athlete declared: 'I feel like shit.' It would have caused a minor stir today but for some in Middle England in the early 1980s it would have elicited a similar feeling to that of discovering their daughter's black boyfriend relieving himself over the family china. It was as if Thompson was on a mission to undermine his commercial potential. After winning gold at the 1984 Olympics in Los Angeles, Thompson raised the hackles of patriots by grinning and whistling the national anthem as the Union flag was hoisted. He then rocked up to the winner's press conference wearing a T-shirt bearing the legend 'Is the world's 2nd greatest athlete gay?', a clear reference to US track and field star Carl Lewis. Asked by an American reporter what defending his decathlon title meant to him, Thompson replied: 'I haven't been this happy since my granny caught her tit in a mangle.' When the next day's newspapers should have been praising him to the heavens, they were instead taking him to task for his lack of decency.

Bruno was a very different type of black man. Possessing a

fraction of Thompson's talent for his chosen sport, Bruno managed to manoeuvre himself into the mainstream through a mixture of a bomb of a right hand, some affable patter and a willingness to make fun of himself. Asked what Bruno's appeal was, the marketing director of HP Foods, the sauce people, said: 'He's everything that we are, and that we wish to be known for. Homely, unpretentious, well loved. And of course, very British.' But while journalists were falling over themselves to anoint Bruno the most popular black man in British history, which he may well have been, others were distinctly uncomfortable with what they suspected was an affectedly humble persona and his unceasing malleability. 'Bruno wasn't a pioneer, he wasn't one of us,' says Lloyd Honeyghan. 'You never saw me in Hyde Park, on my hands and knees, with some white guy dressed as a jockey riding me. If you want to promote yourself like that, go for it. But what the fuck is that all about? I don't judge, but I'm just saying.'

Promoter Mickey Duff openly admitted he thought Bruno was an easier sell than other black British fighters because he could be packaged as a white man. Whether he was dressed in a frock in pantomime, playing Man Friday in an HP Sauce ad or engaging in easy chat-show bonhomie, Bruno was seen as easily influenced and unthreatening. But Bruno walked a thin line between gaining acceptance among the wider British public, in other words the white British public, and losing acceptance in the black one. It was the sort of behaviour that led his fellow black British heavyweight Lennox Lewis to label him an Uncle Tom before they fought in 1993, a perception that haunted Bruno throughout his career. After beating Oliver McCall to finally claim a world heavyweight title in 1995, Bruno's first words into the microphone were: 'I love my brother, I'm not an Uncle Tom.'

England cricket legend Ian Botham, that other great British sporting exponent of pantomime, was not said to have let down white folk when he appeared in *Jack and the Beanstalk* at the Bradford Alhambra. Then again, he was playing the King. 'When I came into boxing,' said Bruno, 'I brought it to the next level with adverts and doing pantomime and people just got jealous of me doing that. And they started calling me all sorts of different names. But if they'd had the opportunity to do it, they would have. You know Chris Eubank told me he would have loved to have got into pantomime?' In public, Eubank claimed pantomime would be beneath him. 'I would not do pantomime,' he said, 'or be ridiculed for money.' It was a statement dripping in a lack of self-awareness: Eubank – courtesy of his English gentleman schtick, haughty demeanour and host of gaudy props – was a walking, talking pantomime character and would be roundly ridiculed as such throughout his career.

In contrast to Bruno, Honeyghan was everything Middle England didn't want the country's black men to be. Confident, assertive and a wildly flamboyant dresser, years before Eubank came on the scene, Honeyghan didn't seem to care what anybody thought about him. At the time of his victory over Curry, Honeyghan had four children by three different women and had just walked out on Terry Lawless, the avuncular manager who led Bruno into the hearts of a nation. 'I was the original pioneer, not Bruno,' says Honeyghan, who had two stints as world champion between 1986 and 1990. 'But I had nothing easy, it was tough having all these racist cockroaches looking after my career. When British fighters express them-selves in the way I did and Chris Eubank did, they all have a go at us. But we were just being ourselves. When an American tries to be himself, everything is hunky-dory. It's all about the jealousy. The way I dress or Chris Eubank dresses, the way we talk, what's it got to do with you? Why should it upset you?'

But the confident and assertive pair of Eubank and Benn did upset people, on either side of the fence. 'In some ways, Chris was what so many Afro-Caribbean immigrants wanted their children to be,' says Ambrose Mendy. 'You come to England and you become affluent and respectable, you make something of yourself. But by talking like he did and dressing like he did, especially when he went from wearing Hugo Boss to being totally immersed in Jermyn Street – the suit maker, the shirt maker, the boot maker – he was flirting with a stereotype that many black children of immigrants found objectionable.' It was an issue complicated by the fact that Eubank's flamboyancy echoed the sartorial spirit of the first wave of black immigrants from the Caribbean in the 1940s and '50s, as photographs and television footage of elegantly dressed Jamaican men disembarking the *Empire Windrush* in 1948 clearly demonstrate.

Benn, whose spending sprees were legendary, was almost as fastidious about his appearance as Eubank, at least in the early days of their rivalry, before Eubank moved into his monocle and jodhpurs phase. But Benn alternated sharp suits with a 'street' image that was more in tune with the youth of the day. However, whether dressed in pristine riding boots and twirling a cane (Eubank) or decked out in bling and a satin-finish Joe Bloggs tracksuit (Benn), neither man could please everybody. While Eubank was accused by some of aping the white man with his quintessentially English dress and speech patterns, Benn's apparent crime was communicating his success in more base and vulgar terms. Wrote the *Guardian*'s Dave Hill after Benn's win over Iran Barkley: 'Pridefully coiffured and sumptuously groomed, the boxer Nigel Benn and his manager

Ambrose Mendy returned to London for their victory press conference, Mendy talking power politics from behind the ultimate prop: a fat wad of freshly minted US dollar bills. Even in triumph, black success is reduced to a cartoon, a process in which its victims approach complicity.'

The mainstream media had no time for such beard stroking: here were two blokes who looked different, sounded different, thought different, fought different and apparently hated each other. Who cares if they're black? Stick them on the box and in the paper and watch the figures rise. 'In those days there were more television regions, so you could build up fighters around the country,' says Jim Rosenthal. 'We followed Nigel to all sorts of venues – Windsor, Wisbech, Stafford – and built him up as a character. As a result, by the time they met each other in the ring, the public knew almost everything about them. And if you had to create a boxing double-act to get people interested, you'd DNA those two and say, "Those two profiles will do us absolutely fine." In one corner, you had this vaguely eccentric, posing, superior enigma wearing very strange clothes, driving very strange vehicles and giving massive, long answers to questions that nobody really understood; in the other corner you had an ex-squaddie who just wanted to rip his head off.'

For Errol Christie, who witnessed the National Front descend on Coventry in 1981, '*sieg heil*-ing' their way through his home city, Benn and Eubank's entrance into the mainstream – however they articulated themselves and whatever they chose to wear – could only be a good thing. 'Attitudes had certainly eased off quite a bit by the time Nigel and Chris came along,' says Christie. 'They got there at the right time, I was too soon. When Frank Bruno came on the scene, people started being more accustomed to seeing black guys being flamboyant on TV. And after Bruno, Nigel and Chris came through and it was brilliant to see black sportsmen coming into their own. They were seen as people like anybody else, whereas in the past we were just seen as black guys. Nigel and Chris were like two shining stars in the sky: people followed them whether they were black, white or whatever, everyone joined in.'

CHAPTER SEVEN
Ghosts at the feast

Only in the warped world of boxing do you have competitors who are too good for their own good, what Budd Schulberg called 'a tough club of guys-ya-want-no-part-of'. Of Archie Moore, who finally got a shot at the world light-heavyweight title at the age of 39, after 14 years hard slog as a professional, Schulberg wrote: 'If it had been tennis, his ranking would have top-seeded him into a shot at the champions. But this was boxing, a bitter and slippery business, where the challenger your manager picked for you was the one who guaranteed the high money – and who didn't figure to be as tough as Archie Moore.' Moore was one of the luckier ones. Charley Burley beat three different world champions in three different weight classes, including Moore, and was ranked in the top ten at welterweight and middleweight throughout the 1940s, yet he never got a shot at a world title. Hall of fame fighters who avoided Burley included world champions Rocky Graziano, Tony Zale, Marcel Cerdan, Jake LaMotta and Billy Conn. But it wasn't necessarily a black thing. Sugar Ray Robinson, the greatest fighter ever to lace up gloves but also as shrewd as they came, was reported to have said: 'I'm too pretty to fight Charley Burley.'

Burley, whom Joe Frazier's trainer Eddie Futch called 'the

finest all-round fighter I ever saw', was only one of a gaggle of great fighters who should have been contenders during the years either side of World War II. Schulberg dubbed this exclusively unlucky group 'The Black Murderers' Row', fighters nobody wanted any part of, except each other. That so many top-class operators were able to be frozen out of the world title picture was in large part down to the particularly sordid nature of American boxing at that time, when the sport was infested with mobsters who secretly owned shares in certain boxers and controlled managers, matchmakers, officials and promoters. Chief among these mobsters were Frankie Carbo and Frank 'Blinky' Palermo, who orchestrated the fixed fight between LaMotta and Billy Fox in 1947 (which LaMotta 'lost') and had many of Madison Square Garden's movers and shakers in their expansive pockets. The law eventually caught up with Carbo and Palermo and the mobsters' grip on the sport was loosened, with Sonny Liston the last world heavyweight champion to have proven Mafia connections. But the dawning of the age of Muhammad Ali did not bring with it the 100 per cent transparency many in the game had hoped for.

Indeed, the beautiful and charismatic Ali merely reinforced that old boxing adage that the fight game was actually 'show business with blood', with as much in common with Broadway and Hollywood as other athletic pursuits. Mike Jacobs may have been the most powerful man in boxing from the mid-1930s until his effective retirement shortly after the war but he cornered his first market in Grand Opera. Schulberg wrote of Jacobs, whom he called 'Machiavelli on Eighth Avenue': 'Opera stars, famous beauties, Mansfields and Barrymores, six-day bike racers, or a boy with two heads were all grist to Mike's opportunistic mill.' When British suffragette leader Emmeline Pankhurst arrived for an American tour, Jacobs briefly enlisted in the cause of women's emancipation. 'It'll be a shot in the arm for the matinee business,' said Jacobs of his new-found political calling.

So while practitioners of other sports have always been able to rise to the top on the back of athletic prowess alone, boxing has always taken account of aesthetic considerations. Because, as the American sports writer Pat Putnam memorably put it, 'most fight fans would not spend a dime to watch Van Gogh paint sunflowers, but they would fill Yankee Stadium to see him cut his ear off'. Of course, how 'good' something is is a matter of personal opinion, but the history of boxing is littered with fighters who had the purists drawling into their programmes and the 'rip-his-fucking-head-off' merchants streaming towards the exits. Unfortunately for the purists, the 'rip-his-fucking-head-off' merchants shout loudest and make more financial sense. Take Pernell Whitaker, once ranked by *Ring* magazine as the tenth best boxer of the last 100 years but whose slippery, elusive style many fight fans considered dull. 'Who the hell wants to see Whitaker fight again?' said Bob Arum after seeing his fighter Oscar de la Hoya wrest the WBC welterweight crown from Whitaker in controversial fashion in 1997. 'He clowned around.' Whitaker, who also got the raw end of a shocking decision against all-action Mexican Julio Cesar Chavez in 1993, never got the rematch he craved and that the purists felt was owed to him.

The rules are no different in Britain. Billy Walker, a solid domestic heavyweight who was well beaten by Henry Cooper in 1967 when challenging for the British title, earned the nickname 'Golden Boy' on account of his dashing good looks rather than his boxing ability. Walker never won a professional title but was able to retire at the age of 30, the loyal support of impressionable London fight fans having made him a wealthy celebrity. Far better fighters than Walker never made anything like the money he made, while there are many more examples of fighters who earned more than they might have courtesy of a winning personality or some headline-grabbing trashtalk. Frank Bruno is the most obvious, while Manchester's two-weight world champion Ricky Hatton managed to become the most popular British fighter of the last 20 years despite never fighting on terrestrial television.

Hatton was more than the brawler his detractors made him out to be, especially during his brief peak years, before the Guinness and curry diminished him. But the millions he made were hardly commensurate with his talent in the ring. Anything between 5000 and 10,000 British fans followed their relentlessly down-to-earth hero to Las Vegas in 2007, only to see him get knocked out by the great Floyd Mayweather. And many of them returned two years later to see him get knocked out by the great Manny Pacquiao. There was no shame in either defeat, it was just that Hatton had found his level. A couple of months before Hatton's blockbuster clash with Mayweather at the MGM Grand, Sheffield's Junior Witter defended his WBC light-welterweight title against Guyana's Vivian Harris at the Doncaster Dome. Many thought the awkward Witter had the style to give his more straight-forward rival fits, and Hatton probably agreed. Luckily for Hatton, Witter also had the style to put punters to sleep. 'I'd close the curtains if Junior Witter was fighting in my back garden,' was Hatton's well-worn and entirely justifiable excuse for the fight never happening.

Witter was a product of Brendan Ingle's fabled gym in Wincobank, Sheffield, which also sprung world champions Naseem Hamed and Johnny Nelson onto an unsuspecting and suspicious public. But the progenitor of what would become known as the Ingle 'way' was Herol Graham, a gentle soul with a childlike sense of humour and some of the funkiest moves ever seen in a British ring. Indeed, if Britain can be said to have had its own version of Whitaker it was Graham, who was variously described as a ballerina, a limbo dancer and a pacifist. 'I hate the sight of blood,' said Graham. 'When I see it on an opponent's face I can't go on hitting him. I glance at the referee to encourage him to do something about it. If he won't, I'll go to the body or I'll throw a little flurry of punches to make the referee stop it.'

Graham began developing his own inimitable technique when he was a boy in his home town of Nottingham, boxing for Radford Boys, and further refined it under the tutelage of Ingle, a former professional fighter from Ireland who had an altogether more prosaic style in the ring. 'He had all the boxing techniques wrong yet managed to do everything right,' was how Ingle described his quietly spoken young charge. Ingle took Graham on exhibition tours around the smoky working men's clubs of Yorkshire, where miners drunk on pints of mild sparred with 'The Bomber' in makeshift rings. Ingle would offer £10 to any man who could knock Graham down, knowing full well no one could lay a glove on him. It was much the same in Ingle's gym, where seasoned pros were only made to look like drunken miners. Ingle was far too quick on the draw with 'The Bomber', he should have nicknamed his protégé 'Houdini'.

But while Graham's trickery went down a storm with the pissed-up patrons of Batley and Wakefield, the boxing world beyond the pit communities of Yorkshire was slower to recognise his genius. 'Graham's style,' wrote Harry Mullan, 'is seen by some as a mockery, a travesty of fighting and an insult to more orthodox practitioners. Yet there is another school of thought – to which I subscribe – which sees it as a refinement of the art of self-defence to its purest degree.' Putting aside his personal taste, Mullan was well aware which was the most commonly held view: 'Celebrations of non-violence do not tend to attract huge purses – punters want action, not artistry.'

Graham won the British light-middleweight title in only his 17th fight and the British middleweight title four years later, in 1985, with a first-round knockout of Jimmy Price. Nevertheless, Ingle and Graham knew they would need more clout to break through to the mainstream. Enter Barney Eastwood, the Irish bookmaker who had guided Barry McGuigan to a world featherweight title. The ambitious Eastwood wasted no time calling out Marvin Hagler, who some suspected was over the hill. However, talk of challenging the undisputed world middleweight champion was wildly optimistic when even Graham's domestic rivals didn't want to know about him. First, Mark Kaylor pulled out of a challenge for Graham's British title at the tail end of 1985, before Tony Sibson pulled out of a challenge for Graham's recently won European title. When Kaylor was finally tempted into a challenge for Graham's European strap in 1986, Graham demonstrated to every other middleweight on the planet exactly why it would be unwise to fight him. 'I have never had such a frustrating night of boxing,' said Kaylor, who was withdrawn by trainer Terry Lawless in the eighth round. 'I never enjoyed it one minute.'

'That's why no one wanted to know,' says Graham. 'These fighters weren't above me in the rankings, they were around me, but they just sidestepped me all the time. They avoided me like the plague because I am the plague! My hands were all over the place, they hated my movement – "Excuse me, wait a minute, he's supposed to be here, he's supposed to be there . . . no he's not, he's here, where is he now? He's over there!" They couldn't cope with that, they just couldn't cope with that at all. They say boxing is unfair and it is. I wanted to prove I was the best but not everybody wanted to box me. Because they couldn't stand the idea of me tipping and tapping and them trying to throw the big, heavy shots at me and missing. My opponents and the fans just wanted a tear-up but I wanted more than that. I was in a fight every now and again, but I was more tactical in my approach. I was like water dripping on a stone, it slowly wears the stone down and eventually the stone breaks. After round after round of being worn down, my opponents would look for the canvas, take a dive. I was torment for them. They'd start cursing, as if to say: "This is too much for me, I don't care where you punch me, let the ref count me out!"'

Following the Kaylor fight, more talk of fighting Hagler or Tommy Hearns quickly melted away, before Eastwood's attentions turned to Iran Barkley, who was himself on the verge of a world title shot. Instead, Graham had to make do with Charles Boston, who had knocked out Errol Christie only a month earlier. Graham stopped his American opponent after seven one-sided rounds. Hagler, unsurprisingly, opted to fight Sugar Ray Leonard instead of Graham, while a fight against Barkley, mooted for the autumn of 1987, again fell through. Graham, briefly estranged from his long-time mentor Ingle, was persuaded by Eastwood to put his world title ambitions on hold and concentrate on defending his European title instead. With Ingle out of the picture, Eastwood brought in two trainers from the United States to assist Barry McGuigan's long-time cornerman Eddie Shaw. 'Graham has turned defensive boxing into a poetic art,' said Shaw. 'The trouble is, nobody ever knocked anybody out with a poem.' Therefore, Shaw and co. attempted to transform the poet into a rock-breaker, with disastrous results. Confused by the conflict between his natural instincts and the new techniques that had been foisted upon him, and without the soothing presence of Ingle in his corner, Graham put in a dismal performance and lost his title to Italy's Sumbu Kalambay at a half-empty Wembley Arena, as well as his world ranking. 'They have tried to turn him into a fighter,' lamented Ingle, as if he was talking about some broken balladeer.

Graham reunited with Ingle after the Kalambay debacle, while simultaneously trying to rid himself of Eastwood. 'He promised me the world but all he gave me was peanuts,' said Graham of Eastwood, who refused to budge. Despite his woes beyond the ropes, Graham soon regained the British title with a fifth-round stoppage of London's James Cook. His first defence was another fifth-round stoppage, this time of Gloucester's Johnny Melfah, in November 1988, and it provided plenty of evidence that Graham remained best avoided. However, Graham was soon to receive the news he had been hoping for since turning professional ten years earlier, namely that he had been nominated for a world title shot. Graham's opponent at the Royal Albert Hall on 10 May 1989 would be Jamaica's Mike McCallum, a former light-middleweight world champion who, like Graham, had one defeat on his record, also against Kalambay. As a light-middleweight, McCallum had knockout wins over top-drawer fighters Julian Jackson, Donald Curry and Milton McCrory on his record and brought with him to England an iron chin and a fearsome reputation for body punching. A cocky young fighter from Brighton was chosen to replicate the teak-tough McCallum in Graham's gym, a certain Chris Eubank.

'I came to bust him up,' said Eubank. 'I was so determined to get him. But he's not there. Mr Eastwood told me to go forward, to press him. I told him he should stick to managing. When you go in close with Graham, you just get hurt.' 'I didn't know who he was,' says Graham, 'he was just this brash boy who came into Brendan's gym for a spar. But even then he was the Chris Eubank we now know. He was my sparring partner, but he'd make up his own rules, tell me he'd have to be away at weekends. Even then he thought he was the best. The first day he put me on my arse but I got up so quick I didn't know it had happened and he never, ever touched me after that. He was there for a week and he got so frustrated he said to me: "Herol, we will never, ever box if I win a championship." And he stayed true to his word.' 'Herol Graham was such an inspiration,' says Eubank, 'a magnificent fighter. I hit him once in two weeks – and it was a great shot – but I got punched to pieces every day. I said publicly after I beat Nigel Benn for the world championship: "I will never fight Herol Graham – why would you fight a man you can't hit?"'

Graham's fight against McCallum, for the vacant WBA middleweight belt, was considered by most in the game to be a 50–50 affair, with shrewd judges such as Mickey Duff picking the Englishman to win it. But Graham's preparations were hardly ideal, with Ingle and Eastwood still at each others' throats and the contractual dispute with Eastwood rumbling on. On fight night, Graham was bombarded with conflicting advice from manager and trainer. McCallum also managed to do what none of Graham's previous 42 opponents had done, namely pin him down for long enough to land with hurtful punches on the inside. 'I can send Mike out to do any job and he'll do it,' said McCallum's venerable trainer Eddie Futch. 'He is like a mechanic.' Graham was level on the scorecards midway through the fight but deducted a point for wrestling in the eighth round and eventually defeated on a split decision. 'Your Herol's a classy boxer,' said Futch, 'but he doesn't want to fight.' Terry Lawless, the promoter of the bout, called Graham's performance 'bewildering'. It is telling that even in one of Graham's finest hours, old heads such as Futch and

Lawless should damn him. In truth, Graham's performance wasn't bewildering at all, it was very much par for the course: mastery of technique, hitting and not being hit, the elevation of self-defence over attacking instinct, boxing at its purest. But still some people didn't get it.

'Benn and Eubank were getting all the adulation, but for what?' says Graham. 'For fighting, not for boxing. What was Nigel Benn's plan? "I'm going to go out there and bang him out in the first round?" I used to think: "No, I'm better than that. I'm going to go out there and move around and when he comes to me I'm going to jab, move to my left, move to my right. And if he leans forward to throw a jab, I'm going to sit back and counter with the backhand and follow that with a hook, catch them off-balance." My opponents hated it, they'd be mesmerised by me. But boxing is as much about show business as it is about sport. Look at Naz [Naseem Hamed] and the show business side of him – the flash, the entrances, the posing and posturing. The people loved it. They'd go for the razzmatazz and then they'd get to see the fighting side of him, demolishing the guy, banging him out. The build-up would lure people in and then they'd get the boxing. And what a brilliant night they'd have.'

Eleven days after Graham's defeat at the hands of McCallum, Michael Watson knocked out Nigel Benn. While some intimate with the fight game had suggested it might happen – Colin Hart of the *Sun* predicted a sixth-round knockout for Watson – to an awful lot of experts, and especially the general sports fan, it came as something of a shock. British middleweight greats Alan Minter, Tony Sibson, Terry Downes and Herol Graham all picked Benn to win. Benn, after all, was the 'Dark Destroyer', 'Rambo', 'The Mean Machine', 'The

People's Champion', 'Mr Punch' – born to kick ass. Watson, on the other hand, was just a boxer. 'My boxing said it all,' says Watson. 'My entertainment was my boxing and my boxing alone. I was the gentleman, that was my role.'

Watson started boxing at The Crown and Manor club in Hoxton, East London, before moving down the road to Colvestone Boxing Club at the age of 17. 'I went to the gym but I was a timid, church-going boy,' says Watson. 'I wasn't street-wise, I was brought up very gently, so a lot of people couldn't believe I became a fighter. But life is full of surprises.' Despite his initial timidity, Watson, a keen all-round sports-man, soon began to blossom in the Colvestone gym, which was established by a London cabbie and former ABA finalist called Harry Griver, inevitably known as 'Griver the Driver'. Griver was responsible for refining the crude natural talent of future light-heavyweight world champion Dennis Andries, while the lavishly gifted but fatally self-destructive Kirkland Laing was also a Watson sparring partner for a time. Watson was talent spotted at Colvestone by another cabbie and former amateur boxer called Eric Seccombe. Excited by Watson's potential, Seccombe took an ABA coaching course and got down to polishing his rough diamond. In 1984, Watson won a London ABA title but his Olympic hopes went up in smoke when he was outpointed by Scotland's Russell Barker in the semi-finals of the nationals. 'I boxed his head off,' says Watson. 'I won the fight but he got the decision. I couldn't believe it. It was the same as my first fight with Eubank.'

Watson turned pro in October 1984 and won his first seven fights in the paid ranks, stopping his first six opponents. However, in his eighth fight he was outpointed over eight rounds by former Southern Area champion James Cook. 'That defeat made me realise that I cannot rely solely on my natural ability,' said Watson. 'There and then I decided to stop messing around. I suppose you could say I became a man overnight.' Watson, who also had a wife and daughter to consider, bounced back with a first-round knockout of Welsh journeyman Simon Collins but his breakthrough fight was against 'Dangerous' Don Lee, a top-rated middleweight from Milwaukee with a reputation for turning deadly when wounded. Lee had a win over Tony Sibson, whom he floored four times, and a draw with Doug DeWitt on his record but was no match for Watson, who stopped him in five. 'Watson showed talent and determination beyond anything revealed in his previous fights,' commented *Boxing News*. 'He proved himself a middleweight to be reckoned with.'

There followed a string of wins over journeymen Americans, which prompted Watson to quit his job as a mini-cab driver to concentrate on boxing full time. In May 1988, Watson stopped Ricky Stackhouse in five, a victory that provided a form guide: Herol Graham took eight rounds to see off Stackhouse, IBF title-holder Frank Tate six and Roberto Duran was taken the distance. A month earlier, Nigel Benn claimed the Commonwealth crown and Watson's impressive victory over Stackhouse made a meeting between the rival Londoners a tantalising possibility. Watson and his connections, however, were willing to bide their time. Indeed, while Watson would later claim he was mismanaged by Mickey Duff, many in boxing thought he was being far more sensibly handled than Benn. 'While Benn opted for the high-profile showbiz route to the top,' said the *Sunday Times*, 'Watson and his trainer Eric Seccombe stuck to the formula which Duff has perfected over the years. While Benn was knocking over a weary line-up of "Mexican roadsweepers", Watson was honing his skills on good pros.' Perhaps the best example of Duff's ability to move a fighter into the world rankings virtually unnoticed was with Lloyd Honeyghan, who came from nowhere to upset the supposedly unbeatable Don Curry for the world welterweight title in 1986.

However, while Watson was content taking the quiet route – his local paper in Islington once called him the 'Smooth Mover with a Hoover', a reference to his willingness to help out his mum with the housework – he crackled with self-assurance when asked to assess his abilities and those of his rivals. 'I think my record compares more than favourably [to Nigel Benn's],' said Watson, when the Benn fight was still some way off. 'I've nothing against Nigel, but in my opinion he has met several blown-up middleweights. My opponents have been of a much better class. In my humble opinion, I'm the number one. No one has yet seen what I can really do.' They soon would. After a routine three-round win over another American trial horse, Franklin Owens, in March 1989, Duff and Ambrose Mendy hammered out a deal. Watson would challenge Benn for his Commonwealth middleweight title on 21 May 1989, in a tent in Finsbury Park, spitting distance from the house Watson grew up in.

'When I fought Nigel it was the highlight of my entire life,' says Watson, who claims even Duff and Seccombe feared he would lose. 'Nigel was one of the most devastating hitters of all time and was red hot when I fought him, with 22 explosive knockouts in a row. He was like an English Mike Tyson, regarded as invincible. But I never trained so hard. People say he was complacent before that fight, but he was ringside when I beat Don Lee, and I made Don Lee look like nothing. And at the final press conference, Nigel tried to intimidate me. But I just looked at him, right into his eyes, and said: "Nigel, when I beat you, I just hope we can be good friends." He knew then that he couldn't intimidate me, that I wouldn't be bullied. So he knew he was in for a fight. So I fought Nigel at his best and I beat him at his best. He would have knocked out anybody else at that time but that was the best fight I ever fought. I ruined his reputation in that tent in Finsbury Park, but I launched my own.'

But it didn't exactly pan out like that. The day after his greatest achievement, Watson watched in shock from his living room as Benn and Mendy appeared on news bulletin after news bulletin, concocting excuses for the defeat and outlining future plans. 'He was going to America, he was going to win a world title and then he would come back and fight me,' says Watson. 'It was a joke. I was angry because he had stolen my thunder and that hurt me more than any of his insults before the fight.' Watson splashed out on an Escort XR3i and toyed with the idea of starting his own furniture removal business before receiving the news he had been hoping for: he had been made number one contender for Mike McCallum's WBA middleweight belt. For the second fight in a row Duff was outbid, this time by Barry Hearn, who had only recently hooked up with Chris Eubank. The fight against McCallum was set for November 1989 at Alexandra Palace in North London. Watson was so confident of victory he had white tracksuits made up for himself and Seccombe, bearing the legend: 'Michael Watson, WBA Middleweight Champion of the World 1989'. If it was out of character, it was also an admission that he had something of an image problem: bombast had never done Nigel Benn any harm.

Having got himself into the shape of his life, disaster struck in Watson's final sparring session, a broken nose causing the fight to be postponed until the following April. McCallum stayed sharp, taking a voluntary defence against a tough young

Boston-based Irishman called Steve Collins. McCallum won on points after 12 rugged rounds. Watson, meanwhile, was going stale in his gym. By the time the bout came round, Watson hadn't fought for 11 months and he was hacked into submission by 'The Body Snatcher' after 11 brutal rounds. 'I was totally out of shape for that McCallum fight and still gave him one of the hardest fights of his life,' says Watson. 'If I had been at my best I would have stopped Mike McCallum.' Two weeks after Watson's defeat by McCallum, Benn won the WBO middleweight title from Doug DeWitt. Watson was down and out while the man he'd beaten less than a year earlier was cock of the roost.

'It's not what you know in boxing, it's who you know and having the right connections,' says Watson, who set a legal precedent by breaking his British Boxing Board of Control contract with Duff in the wake of the McCallum defeat. 'Mickey Duff wasn't the right man. If I had had the right people around me at the time, I would have gone on to be one of the greatest fighters of all time. But all they were inter-ested in was making money, they didn't care about me. I didn't even have a trainer, my trainer knew nothing. If I'd had a better trainer I would have gone sky high. They should have directed me down the right path, picked the right fighters, looked after me a bit better. How much more would I have received if I was well looked after? It broke my heart that I didn't get what I was due for being a great fighter.'

'Michael was a modest man but, like any fighter, he also had a huge ego,' says the *Guardian*'s Donald McRae, who conducted a chillingly prophetic interview with Watson for his book *Dark Trade*. 'He didn't like the fact he was better than both of them and he was third in the pecking order, even though he had totally outclassed Benn. But Michael was never going to be box office, he would never put bums on seats in the way Benn or Eubank could do. I always felt Michael Watson was much more comfortable just being himself, he didn't need any artifice, and that's why he was less popular, because he didn't have a persona. Most boxers, whether it's Muhammad Ali, Mike Tyson, Floyd Mayweather, Eubank or Benn, they have personas and we get sucked in and seduced as much by the persona as the person and what they can do in a ring.' 'Michael was like me,' says Errol Christie, 'and neither of us understood how powerful we were. We were just down-to-earth guys – all we were bothered about was shaking hands before the fight, having the fight, shaking hands after the fight and then having a cup of tea and a chat. Nigel and Chris were more aware of their own publicity and how to make money. They were sharper than we were. They certainly had more brains than me.'

Having cast off Duff, Watson swallowed his pride and sought advice from Ambrose Mendy, whose charge was preparing for his WBO title defence against Iran Barkley in Las Vegas. 'I've never met a manager who was so creative, so imaginative,' says Watson. 'Before the fight against Nigel, I was watching *EastEnders* and all of a sudden Nigel was on the telly in the Queen Vic, shouting: "Watson, I'm gonna get you, you better run for your life!" Ambrose was so unique, I sometimes wish he had been in charge of my career, he would have taken me a lot further and made me a lot more well known. He's a good character and a true gentleman, I take my hat off to him.

'I was just flourishing when I beat Nigel and if I had been managed in the right way I would have gone on to great things in my life. Nigel went on to beat Iran Barkley and Gerald McClellan, and that was after I'd burst his bubble. I would have beaten all the great fighters around at that time, including the Americans. Even Marvin Hagler said he hadn't seen a fighter like me, with my body strength and my versatility. I could have adjusted my style to beat any fighter.' After much soul-searching Watson, who claims he was grossly underpaid for his efforts against Benn and McCallum, placed his destiny in the hands of Barry Hearn, who put him on the undercard of Benn–Eubank I in Birmingham. 'It seemed like a bad joke,' says Watson. 'But what could I do?' While Benn and Eubank would trouser six-figure purses for their efforts, Watson would earn £15,000 for his three-round blowout of Errol Christie.

'That says it all about what makes sport tick today,' says Hearn, 'it is character-led. Michael was a very, very good fighter but the old-style promotional activities of the incumbent promoters – Mickey Duff, Jarvis Astaire, Terry Lawless, Mike Barrett – didn't take into account the characterisation of sportsmen, they only took into account their technical ability. Unfortunately, technical ability doesn't necessarily sell tickets. Even the great ticket sellers of the 1960s, Henry Cooper and Billy Walker, weren't necessarily the greatest fighters but had something about them that the public responded to. You can shape personalities, which I've done with most of the sports I've been involved in, but you need the basic ingredients to work with: you can't install something in someone that's not basically in them. Michael Watson couldn't have been a nicer person and his technical ability, as he showed in beating Nigel Benn, was at a very high level. But he wasn't a ticket seller. Being good at what you do is only half the battle, you need something to sell. And whether they boo you or cheer you, it really doesn't make any difference.'

The absurd nature of Watson's predicament was not lost on the boxing press or his fellow pros, some of whom were of the opinion that the contest between Benn and Eubank was a mockery of a world title fight. 'I don't want to pour water on it but let's have some semblance of reality,' says Jim McDonnell, 'it was a British title fight, despite the fact the WBO belt was on the line. The best fighters in and around that weight at the time were Mike McCallum, Michael Nunn and James Toney. These were all guys Eubank in particular avoided like the plague. It was great TV, great entertainment and the media got caught up in the hype. But I called the WBO the 'World Barry Organisation' because it was how Barry Hearn got his fighters world title shots at the time. Barry could sell sand to the Arabs and he did a great job with Eubank, drummed up that fight massively, sold it as the middleweight championship of the world. The truth was they weren't even the two best middleweights in Britain. The best middleweight in Britain was Herol Graham, and not by a short margin either, he was leagues ahead of the pair of them. And Watson was better than both of them, as well. Graham and Watson were like ghosts at the feast.'

The *Guardian*'s John Rodda summed up the mood of the press pack: 'Nigel Benn and Chris Eubank come together in an intriguing domestic middleweight contest tomorrow night at the NEC in Birmingham. It is, indeed, little more than that, despite the promotional ghetto-blasting which has generated the hype of a world championship contest . . . the WBO is not regarded seriously by anyone other than the fighters, managers, promoters and TV executives.' Wrote Harry Mullan in *Boxing News*: 'WBO champions are still, undeniably, the poor relations of the boxing world.' Even Barry Hearn, in an unguarded moment of honesty, declared: 'It's a paper crown. This is nothing to do with titles, this is about two men who are both proud athletes who want to find out who's the better man on the night.' Said Graham's trainer Brendan Ingle: 'Herol would stand the pair of them on their heads.'

CHAPTER EIGHT
Who's Fooling Who?

It is the early hours of 18 November 1990 and Nigel Benn should be sprawled out in bed in his Birmingham hotel. Relaxing the body, tuning the mind. Mulling over the rhythm, the feel and the timing. Instead he is trussed up in a sweat suit, pounding away on a treadmill in an otherwise deserted gym. 'On the Friday night before the fight I attended a show as promised but Nigel wanted to stay in his room,' says Ambrose Mendy. 'And it was discovered that there was a bird in there with him. I wasn't really worried about that because I figured it was pretty emotionless, but between them they'd drunk a bottle of champagne. Nigel was adamant he hadn't drunk any of it but when we had the recce meeting at 6 o'clock on the Sunday morning of the fight, we were all sat round a table planning the TV show and Nigel's trainer Vic Andreetti turned up at the door and asked me to come outside. Vic said: "Ambrose, you're never going to believe this, but he's six and a quarter pounds overweight." He had drunk the champagne and the alcohol had caused the weight retention.' 'Nigel got complacent and the complacency did the worst thing to him, it messed up his weight,' contends Barry Hearn. 'Because Nigel thought: "This upstart, all he can do is talk, when I hit him he'll go down – I don't need to take him seriously."'

'There was no time to start going nuts,' says Mendy. 'I told Nigel we could postpone the fight but he said, "No, no, no, I want to fucking do him". So I said, "Right, let's get this weight off". I explained to Gary Newbon, head of boxing at ITV, what had happened and it turned out he had a friend who owned a fitness centre in the middle of Birmingham. Gary said, "You go there, I promise you it will be in confidence". So Nigel put a sweat suit on and ran three miles, shadow boxed and did pad work in the steam room, then went on the bike before resting. Eventually he lost six and a half pounds and weighed in a quarter of a pound under the 11st 6lb middleweight limit. The weigh-in was about 11 o'clock and once he'd done that he could go and have a solid six-hour sleep.'

Benn, however, claims there were no women in his bed and that he was tucked up with a Hollywood legend and a bunch of grapes rather than a bottle of champagne. 'I remember sitting in my room watching *On The Waterfront* with Marlon Brando,' says Benn, 'eating grapes, no problem at all. I wasn't struggling at the weight, because I wasn't as big as Chris and the other lot, they were virtually natural light-heavyweights. But when I got on the scales after getting out of bed I was almost 12st. I couldn't believe it, the morning of the fight and I'm six pounds over the limit. I was eating all healthy but I was locked in my room and not training it off, which meant I put on six pounds in three days. I couldn't go to the gym because there would be people down there. That's the only thing that Ambrose did wrong, putting me in a high-rise hotel with other punters in the middle of town. So on the morning of the fight I had to do five three and a half minutes in the steam room, between sessions on the treadmill, and I managed to get it all off. But there's a picture of me on the scales for the actual weigh-in where my eye's going wonky. Please understand, I'm not making excuses, but I wasn't right for that first Eubank fight.'

Benn's struggles with weight on the morning of the fight are well documented. What is less well-known is Eubank's cavalier approach to weight loss, which on one occasion moved trainer Ronnie Davies to report his fighter to the boxing authorities. 'He was murder in terms of his weight,' says Davies, 'I used to have terrible rows with him over it. I reported him to the Board of Control once. It was before a fight in South Africa, he just wouldn't get on the scales until a week before the fight. I don't know why he put us through all that worry. Sometimes he cut it too fine and had to get a load of weight off at the last minute. But that was the only flaw he had, everything else he did right.' 'He used to worry me because he would lose a stone in seven days,' says Jim Rosenthal, who got to know Eubank well during his years covering his fights for ITV. 'He would basically fast. I once saw him at a weigh-in in Cardiff, had a close look at him and he was so dry. I said: "Chris, I've got to say this, you look awful." And he said to me: "Jim, my eyeballs feel dry." Of course he made the weight but he broke every boxing rule and it worried me about him.'

Jim McDonnell, who was intimately acquainted with his gym-mate's training methods, disagrees with Davies that Eubank 'did everything else right'. 'I don't even think he trained that hard,' says McDonnell. 'He used to spar hard, he used to have wars in the gym, and he used to do straightforward roadwork, that's how he used to prepare for fights. Against Michael Watson he was 15lb over the limit about 36 hours before the first fight. And Eubank was massively overweight before the first Benn fight. I was in camp with him and he took off about 17lb between Thursday and the weigh-in.

After the fight, a journalist said to Eubank at the press conference: "Has this taken away from your achievement, Nigel having to lose 6lb on the morning of the fight?" And Eubank said: "What do I think? I think this is totally unprofessional." I wanted to fall off my chair. He was famous for this in our gym, this is how he used to operate. That's why Chris never used to fight three minutes of every round, he used to box in spasms. He got away with it to a degree but would he have got away with it against James Toney or Michael Nunn or Mike McCallum? No.'

At the same time as Benn was dripping off the pounds in a Birmingham gym, Barry Hearn was putting the final touches to the promotion, waiting for a visit that never came. 'The complacency in the Benn camp extended to one of the best promoters in the world, and certainly one of the most professional, Bob Arum,' says Hearn. 'I made Benn a decent offer – £400,000 to Eubank's £100,000 – so it was a fairly risky fight. It made a little bit of money, although not very much. And throughout the whole of the build-up I was waiting for somebody to ask me for options on Eubank if Benn won. I thought what was going to happen was that I'd get to the weigh-in and someone would put a gun to my head and say: "If you don't sign this, the fight's off." But nobody ever did, which is amazing, especially since I was dealing with someone normally as savvy as Arum.'

That Arum did not insist on options in the fight contract, which would have granted him control over Eubank's future career and earnings, was the most startling indication of the supreme confidence swirling around the Benn camp and of how little Arum thought of Eubank and his potential earning power. But some pretty good judges were suggesting Eubank had it in him to win it. 'If the fight goes over six rounds

Eubank will win inside the distance,' said Barry McGuigan. Herol Graham, who was set to fight Julian Jackson for the WBC middleweight title the following week, said: 'Eubank can punch and he can do what he threatens. I'd put my money on him to win, if not in the first then maybe after seven or eight. I'm not convinced Benn is all that durable.' That Michael Watson came down so forcefully on the side of Benn might have been more the result of wishful thinking rather than any deep consideration. 'Benn will win inside the distance and Eubank will be quickly forgotten,' said Watson.

Graham, a former sparring partner, knew Eubank better than most. And it is instructive that many who knew Eubank in a personal capacity, however tenuous, found it difficult to countenance him losing, such was the enormity of his belief. 'When the fight was first announced I thought Nigel Benn was going to kill Chris Eubank,' says Lloyd Honeyghan, 'mainly because I didn't know much about Eubank, I just thought he chatted a lot. But I was down in Brighton one weekend, staying in this sexy hotel. I was in the pool one morning, swimming with some bird, and I heard someone shouting: "Honeyghan! Honeyghan!" I thought, "Fuck me, no one knows I'm here". So I looked round and saw this black geezer at the other end of the pool. He swam over and said: "I'm Chrith Eubank, I'm fighting Nigel Benn." And in my head I'm thinking, "Nigel Benn's gonna kick the shit out of you". But we talked and talked and by the time I got out of the pool I thought, "This guy's going to kick the shit out of Benn". I'd never met a boxer with so much confidence, it was like I was talking to myself.'

It should be noted that Eubank did have his supporters among the British public. 'Concerning all the boxing writers and fans who are constantly insulting Chris Eubank,' wrote

Jenny Andrews of Thetford, in a letter to *Boxing News*. 'I think that Chris is OK! Chris is an intelligent and amusing man, and I find his strutting and "boasting" very entertaining and appealing.' Most fight fans, however, were unable or unwilling to look beyond Eubank's posturing and preening. This was in no small part down to the tabloid press, in particular Colin Hart of the hugely influential *Sun*, who wrote a scathing appraisal of Eubank and his chances against Benn the day before the fight, under the headline: 'BENN WILL CLOCK EU IN 3 ROUNDS'. Hart's article is worth quoting at length: 'Nigel Benn will do Britain's close boxing family a big favour if he can crush Chris Eubank and wipe the silly smile off his face. There is no doubt the strutting, egotistical Eubank is loathed by the vast majority of his fellow professionals. Fighters, trainers, managers and promoters find his brand of high-handed haughtiness detestable. For the first time we are going to find out if Eubank is an expensive original or simply a useless fake. Once Eubank feels those hooks crushing into his ribs, his hands will come down and he will be rendered helpless by the third round.' Say what you really think, Colin.

The champion, meanwhile, was everything a boxer was meant to be: an all-action knockout artist, seemingly bent on entertaining the fans, with little or no thought for his own safety. One of Benn's biggest fans was a nine-year-old kid from South London called David Haye, who would be inspired to take up boxing by this vicious, unbridled spirit burning through his television screen. 'Nigel Benn was my first boxing idol,' says Haye, who would take up boxing at ten and become a cruiserweight and heavyweight world champion. 'When I first started boxing I used to wear solid black shorts, black boots with no socks, just like Benn, and I moulded my aggressive style on Nigel. I wasn't the most skilled fighter, I used to just get in there and bowl people over recklessly, like Nigel at the time. If you see footage of my early amateur fights it's just me swinging and trying to knock my opponent out, and nine times out of ten, I did. I wasn't big on jabbing or looking stylish, it was just all-out, I'm going to knock you out. I was a very aggressive kid myself and it was Nigel's raw aggressiveness I loved. He would seek and destroy, blast people out. Occasionally he'd get tagged and wobbled, but when he got hurt was when he was at his most dangerous.'

'Proper boxing people knew it was going to be a close fight but most punters expected Nigel to win,' says Kevin Mitchell. 'Nigel was on a roll, he was the hot property in British boxing. Nigel was always vulnerable but people wanted him to succeed because they wanted excitement: Nigel would throw punches from everywhere, get knocked down, pick himself up off the canvas and knock you halfway across the ring. Chris was very mannered and a lot stiffer than Nigel's free-swinging style. Chris would move around a bit, jab properly and lunge in with his right hand, stiff-backed, slightly wooden. The public didn't need Chris Eubank, while Nigel was the very image of what the British public wanted from a fighter.' 'A lot of people dismissed Eubank in that first fight as this pussy, this big mouth, this buffoon,' says Donald McRae, 'while they thought hardcore Nigel Benn was going to show him up. But I knew enough by then that Eubank was not going to go under easily, because he had this indomitable will and this iron chin.'

Eubank arrived at his dressing room at 6.30 p.m. and set about making sure everything was in its correct place. Which was more difficult than it might have been. 'Ambrose Mendy and his team pulled all sorts of strokes,' says Hearn. 'They knew Eubank liked nice, white towels and they gave us shitty, horrible towels; we liked to warm up properly but they gave us the smallest dressing room we'd ever seen.' As Eubank went about his business, seemingly oblivious to Mendy's King-like machinations, Ronnie Davies soothed him by singing Irish rebel songs. At some point, referee Richard Steele came into the dressing room and gave Eubank his pre-fight instructions. The appearance of Steele, America's most high-profile and respected official, had a galvanising effect on the challenger. 'You're fighting for the championship of the world,' said Steele. 'This can make or break you but it will not be a dirty fight. I am the man in this ring, you do as you are told. You are not going to win this fight by cheating and I am telling Nigel Benn the same things.' Said Eubank: 'I was proud to be spoken to like that.'

Meanwhile, down the corridor in Benn's dressing room, Mendy was wrestling with his charge's demonic fury. The seconds marching by, enormous. 'First it was a case of trying to knock the nervousness out of him,' says Mendy. 'Then we went through the opening sequence, stressing that the first 30 seconds were really important, reminding him Eubank had promised to knock him out. Right before a fight I'd always get everybody out of the room and we'd usually have a hug and say some really personal things – about his well-being, about what would happen if he was hurt, because you can get killed in the ring. And he'd morph from someone who was uncertain into a frightening, frightening character. It was incredible to witness, this brooding intensity. But this time the intensity is so great that Nigel is not listening to anything I'm saying. He's in the zone, he's elsewhere. Nigel is already in the fight. So there were no words this time, just a glare. It was almost as if there was him on the inside and a different Nigel Benn on the outside: I looked into his eyes and I could almost see inside him. When he looked at you it was almost as if he paralysed you, you couldn't move.'

Mendy wasn't in Benn's corner for the fight, which allowed him to concentrate his efforts elsewhere, namely in attempting to cause as much unrest in the Eubank camp as possible. 'I knew that I had to unhinge Eubank, somehow, some way,' says Mendy. 'Because of the issue with Nigel's weight loss I couldn't be there when Eubank weighed in but I knew I had one more chance to get to him, and that was the witnessing of his hands being wrapped. Ronnie Davies came into our changing room and it was all orderly. But five minutes later I went into Eubank's changing room and he went absolutely nuts and attacked me. It was chaos. He's trying to choke me up against a wall and I'm trying to knee him in the bollocks and right hook him. If I'd got close enough I would have bitten him, make no mistake about that whatsoever. The guy from the WBO jumped in, Barry Hearn was involved, and Chris is screaming: "Get him out of my fucking changing room, I don't want him involved." Meanwhile, Barry's trying to reason with him, saying: "Calm down, Chris, he has to be in here, he's got to witness your hands being wrapped and sign your gloves." In hindsight, I should have left it at that, walked out and said no one from our camp is going in there, until we got him at the point where he was demoralised. Instead, he calmed down immediately – as if someone had flicked a switch – smiled at me and said: "Thmart move. Thmart move. OK, fine." I picked up the pen and calmly wrote on his gloves: "Dopey cunt", and walked out of the changing room.'

However, Mendy had one last trick up his sleeve. 'Chris is strolling out to "Simply The Best" and when he gets ten yards inside the arena my mate, who was the DJ for the night, ripped the music off,' says Mendy. 'And Eubank stretches out his arms and says: "Barry – what the fuck?!"'

'That was Ambrose who cut off Chris's entrance music,' says Benn. 'I wouldn't have done it and it wasn't my idea. Ambrose was into all that psychological warfare, but I didn't have time for any of that.'

'I said to Eubank, "Right, back to the dressing room",' says Hearn, 'and I went upstairs and had a row with the geezer in the DJ booth.'

'Barry's gone upstairs, but I've had two gorillas stationed outside the DJ booth,' says Mendy. 'And they said to Barry, "Not tonight, go away". So Barry had to go back down and say: "Chris, we ain't got no music."'

'I came back down after this steaming row, with foam coming out of my mouth,' says Hearn. 'And I've got ITV saying to me: "We're live!" And I went, "Chris, dressing room, now!" But Eubank just looked at me and said: "Bazza – they gave me shitty towels, they gave me a shitty dressing room, they've fucked up my music. Just keep calm and let me punish this man." And suddenly I felt like a little child standing next to him. Before that I wanted to chin everyone. Now I was like, "OK, Chris, I trust you, off you go . . ."'

'I was nervous in the dressing room,' admits Ronnie Davies. 'Ambrose Mendy was a very clever man and it was very intimidating. But Chris wasn't fazed at all. Barry was saying: "Let's go back and walk out." But Chris just said: "No, we won't, we'll go ahead without the music." Nothing got to him, I've never seen anything like it, he had this tremendous inner strength.'

More than two minutes after his entrance had been sabotaged, Eubank reappeared. The cacophony of boos and catcalls no longer masked by Tina Turner's incongruous moans and groans, the lack of music lending the occasion a stark, old-school air. Eubank, wearing a simple white, towelling tabard, climbed the ringside steps and stopped for a moment on the apron, looking halfway over his shoulder, a tacit acknowledgement of the hatred of the crowd. From men who smelt of cigarettes and pubs, men who thought they were hard but had never laced up gloves, calling Eubank a bastard and a cunt. Eubank negotiated the ring post, tested the tension of the top rope and vaulted into the ring, before turning on his heels and back-pedalling across the canvas. There were cheers, so he did have supporters – indeed, Eubank recalled he had a crowd of 'about 40 or so up from Brighton' – but mostly it was boos and catcalls. 'I stood in the ring and sucked in the hate from the Benn supporters,' said Eubank. 'I redirected it towards Nigel Benn. I was like a prism.'

'Once we'd done the walk and got into the ring I thought I was all right, which surprised me,' says Davies. 'But Ambrose Mendy had arranged for all these soldiers to play Nigel into the ring, with the drums and everything else, and that was bloody intimidating again.' 'They can't all be on the pay roll, surely,' quipped David Brenner, commentating on the fight for early satellite outfit Screensport, as the Royal Regiment of Fusiliers band led in what looked like the whole of Benn's old battalion. And then it was time for some Phil Collins and his seminal 'In the Air Tonight'. 'They were fantastic fights but the music was the antithesis of what, ultimately, those battles became,' says Donald McRae. 'Phil Collins and Tina Turner?! Fucking hell . . .' Mercifully, Phil Collins eventually gave way to what Eubank liked to call 'Ragamuffin music' and Benn finally appeared from the bowels of the arena, leading out a hefty rearguard, all decked out in black and gold satin tracksuits.

As Benn bounded towards the ring, his black, sequined gown shimmering under the lights, Eubank remained rooted to the spot. 'Chris Eubank, we can see, is totally dispassionate,' said Brenner. 'He has not moved a muscle since getting in.' 'Very few fighters can get in the ring and stand absolutely static,' said Brenner's co-commentator and Eubank's stable-mate, Jim McDonnell. 'It's all part of his temperament, his self-control, and it looks magnificent.' 'He'll need it tonight, I'm telling you,' said fellow co-commentator Barry McGuigan, 'he'll need it tonight . . .' When Benn finally made it into the ring, McDonnell thought he resembled 'a wild tiger'. But to many, he looked like a man on the verge of a nervous break-down. 'Ambrose Mendy calming him down a little bit,' said Brenner, 'he is one very, very hyped-up guy.'

'He put everything on the line that night,' says Mendy. 'When he got into that ring he was ready to kill Eubank. No fighter was more aptly named: he was dark and his sole inten-tion was to destroy. After everyone had been cleared out of the ring, Eubank had his head slanted to one side and his gloves held together; Nigel was snarling, his hands down by his side. I remember the intensity of his stare across the ring: it was like Superman's X-ray vision, you could almost see the rays coming out of his eyes.' Eubank had vowed not to meet Benn's gaze until they came face to face in the ring. And he had carried out meticulous mental planning for when the moment came. 'In the lead-up to the fight myself and my fiancée Karron always referred to him as 'Benjamin',' said Eubank. 'To think of actually fighting Nigel Benn would have been too awesome. In the ring I looked at him and saw a relentless savage. But I also saw a man with a slight doubt on his mind. When he looked into my eyes he needed reassurance. I thought: "It's too late for that, mate. You're mine."'

'My lords, ladies and gentlemen,' begins MC Alan Hughes, somewhat disingenuously, as Eubank stands stone still in his corner. Chin tucked in, nostrils flared, right glove across his chest. Then, like a statue coming to life, Eubank launches into a couple of extravagant lunges. A photographer peers up at him through the ropes, eyebrows raised with wonder, when he should be taking pictures. 'Ladies and gentlemen,' continues Hughes, 'presenting, and introducing to you, in the blue corner, with the white and the red shorts, with 24 wins from 24 contests, 14 inside the distance, the challenger for the title, from Brighton in Sussex, Chris Euuuuubank . . .' Cue a torrent of whistles and jeers as Eubank, gloves touching in front of him, swaggers towards the middle of the ring, comes to a halt and nods three times. Referee Steele shoots him a wry look that seems to say: 'Not in all my years have I seen anything like this . . .' Eubank bows and retreats, as if someone has pressed rewind. Cue more whistles and jeers. From men who smell of cigarettes and pubs, men who think they are hard but have never laced up gloves, calling Eubank a bastard and a cunt.

'That hatred was real, I could feel it,' says Steele, who refereed 167 world title fights in all, including Hagler–Hearns in 1985, three of the most brutal rounds, nine of the most brutal minutes, in boxing history. 'You could say that British fight fans are more savage than fight fans in the States and you could feel the hatred in the air in Birmingham that night. But Chris Eubank was so arrogant in the way he carried himself, he really shoved that hatred down their throats.' From his ringside trench, Brenner suddenly cuts through the whistles and the jeers to point out a butterfly, 'fluttering around in the ring, one of these daft little things that you notice at a world title fight'. Like a soldier, knee deep in squalor, trying to ignore the bullets screaming overhead, the grenades exploding all around him, clinging to any sign of God's beauty.

'. . . And ladies and gentlemen, his opponent, in the red corner, with the black shorts, with 27 wins from 28 contests, 25 inside the distance, defending the title, from West Ham in London, the WBO middleweight champion of the world, Nigel Beeeeenn . . .' Benn makes his way to the middle of the ring, raises his arms and drinks in the adulation. Looking out at the frothing mass of expectant faces. People who want Benn to do Eubank like Benn wants to do Eubank. People who want Benn to fuck Eubank up, rip his head off, spit down his neck. The bastard. The cunt. 'The atmosphere inside the arena was astonishing,' recalls Benn. 'There were about 12,000 people in there and you could just feel it coming off of every one of them, like electricity. So I was already psyched up before I got to the ring because I knew I was going to beat him. I knew I was going to beat him.' And now Richard Steele waves them in . . .

As Steele delivers his instructions, Eubank leans back exaggeratedly, so that it looks like Ronnie Davies is holding him upright with his hand on his neck. In Eubank's mind he is Charles Bronson, the mysterious harmonica-playing gunman in *Once Upon a Time in the West*. No, really. 'Benn entered the ring like an uncaged tiger,' said Eubank. 'I just stood there, cool. It reminds me of those movies, I am following Bronson's lead. Like him, this was the moment I had been waiting for for many years.' Benn, meanwhile, is salivating, so that it looks as if his head might disconnect from his shoulders: eyes bulging, neck straining, jaw jutting, a rabid dog tethered in front of a prime piece of beef. 'Benn giving Eubank the sort of look that sometimes comes with a tax demand,' says Brenner. 'Not friendly.' Steele's sermon complete, Benn brings his right fist downwards so that Eubank's arm goes spinning, before both fighters turn on their heels and head towards their respective bunkers. 'That was a mistake,' said Eubank. 'When he hit my glove I knew. I could feel the power. I didn't need to test one of his punches like I usually do. I thought: "You've educated me and that goes against you, too."'

One by one the canvas clears until it is only Benn, Eubank and Steele left in the ring. A particularly lonely place to be when, in addition to the thousands of eyes pointed your way in the arena, there are millions gathered around radios and watching on TV. In living rooms across Britain, in gentlemen's clubs, working men's clubs, wine bars and spit and sawdust pubs, people gather up their drinks, gird their loins and prepare themselves mentally for the brutality they have been promised. Nothing less will do. 'Boxing on terrestrial television in the late '80s and early '90s used to stop the country,' says Jim Rosenthal, presenter of ITV's coverage that night. 'And it was people right across the social spectrum tuning in, from people piling into pubs and clubs to the upper strata, if you like, breaking up dinner parties and saying, "We've got to watch this fight". The status that boxing had at that time was absolutely enormous and when Benn and Eubank fought each other, that was the absolute pinnacle.'

Ringside, Barry Hearn is seated next to Bob Arum and Ambrose Mendy. Hearn just can't help himself. 'I was thinking, "I'm certain I'm going to win this fight, I've gambled everything on this fight". I'd invested a huge amount of money into Eubank, about a quarter of a million pounds, because he didn't sell tickets when he started out. And this was the night we were going to find out if we'd been wasting two or three years of our time. I remember my chief executive saying to me on the night: "Do you know how much money we stand to lose here?" And I kept saying: "Don't worry, we're gonna win – styles make fights, Eubank has the perfect style to beat Nigel Benn, he's a counter-puncher, Benn's aggressive." If I was kidding myself I was doing a pretty good job because I 100 per cent believed it. So I just couldn't resist it. When the bell went for round one, I turned round to Bob Arum and said: "You know you're fucked, don't you?" And he said: "Why's that?" And I said: "Because you haven't got any options." And he went: "We don't need options, do we Ambrose?" And Ambrose said: "Nah, nah, this is a straightforward fight." And I went: "Trust me, son, you're fucked." It was a beautiful moment.'

'It will be interesting to see whether Benn has learned from his experience against Watson,' says McGuigan, seconds before the action begins. 'Will he go in and use the jab or will he get stuck straight in? There's been so many bad things said about one another they'll not be able to refuse a slam-up in the first round, I don't think.' When the first bell finally tolls, both men tip-toe towards each other, as if 'ooh-aahing' across hot sand. Chins slightly raised, gloves pawing the air, for a moment they look like marionettes on strings. As Eubank draws close he tilts his body, so that when he finally reaches Benn he has his back to him, as if his strings have become twisted up in the arena rafters. Eubank suddenly swivels and launches a screech-ing right cross that misses. 'No fancy boxing,' says McGuigan, answering his own question, 'it's just slam-bang.' 'I came out and threw the right hand,' said Eubank, who had placed a £1000 bet on himself at 40-1 to knock Benn out in the first round. 'If he'd come out bombing like I thought he would, it probably would have hit him. It missed by an inch.' Benn, head twitching wildly, predatory animal that he is, stalks Eubank remorselessly to all corners of the ring. Eubank wheels backwards towards the ropes, before landing with a juddering right hand. Benn, momentarily stiffened on pipe-cleaner legs, breaks into a smile. Eubank sends home another juddering right hand. 'Nigel's gotta keep those hands up,' screams McGuigan, as Benn goes wading into the mayhem again.

'Man, when that first bell went, those punches were fast and they were hard,' says Benn. 'He was a strong man with an incredible physique and I felt that power. Some punches I took, I could see little birds flying around my head. He could bang, he really could.' When the bell sounds to end the first round, Eubank turns his back on the champion, like a matador waving through a bull. Benn, wounded and frustrated, staggers past him towards his stool. As the champion is being washed and brushed up in his corner, Eubank is strutting around the ring. Sucking in more hate, ready to spew it out on Benn.

Early in the second, the champion finds the target with a huge right hand. Eubank, despite pulling away from the punch, takes it well. Entering the final minute of the round, Eubank loads up with an uppercut and Benn lands with another right hand. It is a shot that would have fallen most trees. Eubank sways backwards, like a tall pine being tugged by a breeze, before returning to his full height and scuttling out of range. 'Eubank has taken that, Reg,' says Reg Gutteridge's co-commentator Jim Watt, over on ITV, 'so he can take a shot. That was the one.' And it's Eubank who finishes the round the strongest, taking Benn's legs away from him with a snappy left hook. The champion staggers backwards onto the ropes, momentarily extricates himself courtesy of some wild flails, before finding himself pinned in the corner again. At the sound of the bell, referee Steele flings himself between the combatants, who glare at each other between outstretched arms, which must resemble the bars of a jail in the circum-stances. Eubank turns his shoulder towards Benn, flairs his nostrils and strikes that familiar pose; thinks about going for a stroll, thinks better of it, finds sanctuary in his stool. The crowd sounds subdued, confused even. Benn is not going to give this bastard, this cunt, the hiding they demanded. Actually, he might, it's just that he's going to get one as well.

Two rounds gone and still barely a jab. At the start of the third, Benn goes head-hunting again and finds his mark with a swingeing cross. Eubank, in full retreat, talks to his assail-ant, waving him on. Benn obliges, only for Eubank to stop him in his tracks with a thunderous uppercut. For a split second Benn is motionless, like a man with lumbago stuck halfway out of his chair, before suddenly recovering his composure and landing with a strafing right hand. 'This man is lethal when he's hurt,' says Brenner, 'he's like a wounded tiger.' Eubank ships a paralysing left hook and an uppercut for luck. The crowd feed on the hate and the frenzy multi-plies with every connection. 'For a fellow who openly says he doesn't like the game,' notes Gutteridge, 'he's a brave guy.' 'The pace was hot,' said Eubank, 'his power surprised me. He was on me, in an 18-foot ring, nowhere to go. On your back foot, right hands coming, right hands coming . . .' 'He was just so tough,' says Benn. 'All I wanted to do was work his body and he was in a bit of bother early on. But he was covering up real good.' Three rounds gone and already McDonnell is talking about who wants it most, a topic usually held back for the championship rounds. 'Tremendous,' says McDonnell, 'a lot of hatred being expended . . .'

Watt, meanwhile, is questioning Eubank's tactics, implor-ing him to stop swaying back from the waist, get his hands up and his chin down. 'We didn't go in with a game-plan and never did,' says Ronnie Davies. 'It might sound stupid to a lot of people but I'm an old-school trainer who doesn't believe in watching videos of other fighters. You can watch a fighter on video but that doesn't mean to say he'll box that same way again against you. Any fighter, if he trains properly, should have enough in his artillery to know what to do, learn to fight all ways. If you learn to fight all ways, you can produce on the night.'

Early in the fourth, Eubank lands with a booming cross. 'Jesus!' says McDonnell, all sense of decorum or professionalism suspended, 'look at that right hand!' Benn staggers backwards on spaghetti legs and covers up on the ropes, bobbing from side to side like a boat marooned on some rocks. Benn rides out the storm but his left eye is purple and swollen. 'I can't remember much about the early rounds and I don't know what my plan was,' says Benn. 'But I do remember that by midway through the fourth round my eye was up and couldn't see anything. Every time he hit me it was like I had a migraine, someone was pricking me with a needle and the pain was going up to my brain. OOOH! It really hurt, it was horrible. And all the time I'm thinking, "I don't want to lose to this man, I'm going to do everything in my power not to lose to this man".' 'I was sticking to one-twos,' said Eubank, 'keeping my form. I was jabbing, throwing right-hand leads. His left eye was closing. He couldn't see my right hands.' Eubank, meanwhile, is bleeding from the mouth. 'You can't have bombs like this flying about without signs of damage,' says Brenner.

'We were in a clinch and I had dropped my head onto his shoulder,' says Eubank. 'My jaw relaxed and my tongue slipped in between my bottom teeth and my gumshield. At that exact second, Benn nudged me off his shoulder with a jolt and

BOOM! He hit me with a mammoth right uppercut. The seismic impact guillotined my tongue with my own teeth.' 'He didn't tell me, I could just see blood coming out of his mouth,' says Davies. 'I thought it was just a cut lip and he said afterwards he didn't tell me in case I pulled him out, because he was swallowing a load of blood. And I would have done, I had to look after his interests. But there was so much on the line he'd have never forgiven me. He would sooner have died.' Benn finishes the fourth looking the far more likely, dismantling Eubank's defences and even breaking into a smile at one stage while waving his exhausted rival in. 'Nigel Benn was without doubt the most menacing British fighter I ever saw,' says Davies. 'I never witnessed power like it. They were both hitting each other with terrific shots but talking right the way through the fight: "Is that all you've got? You hit like a woman." I've never seen such a vicious fight and to witness it at such close quarters, well . . .'At the sound of the bell both fighters head in the wrong direction and Benn has to be shown to his stool by referee Steele.

Round five is a breather round but referee Steele remains virtually invisible, the ghost at a shambolic feast of pounded flesh and shattered bones. Benn and Eubank eschew the traditional recuperative tactics of throw and hold – this pair hate each other so much they're not about to snuggle – instead staying at range and warding each other off with sniping jabs. But the slower pace favours Eubank, who slips into a groove, setting traps, making Benn miss and landing on the counter. 'He wasn't the hardest man I fought, not by far,' says Benn. 'But Chris was the most solid. And I couldn't get Chris on his chin: he'd crouch down, lean to the side and offer you this funny-shaped head, like a mallet. Then, just as you had him lined up, he'd skip back out of this funny stance.' If round five was an armistice of sorts, it was a short-lived one. A minute into the sixth and Steele, a particularly ghoulish spirit, on this night at least, is clapping his hands and asking for action. Eubank obliges with a chopping right-hand lead, before Benn replies with a left to the Eubank crown jewels. The crowd assail the bent-over Eubank with a chorus of boos, as if to say: 'Stop fucking about, Eubank, this is our fight, not yours.'

'I have almost no recollection whatsoever of rounds four to six,' says Eubank. 'I assume I was just dealing with the dire situation – watching the video confirms that.' Eubank sucks up the low blow and rejoins the battle but Benn, reminded that Eubank's body is the route to victory – and that his head has eyes – hammers away at the challenger's kidneys, like a man tamping down concrete with a length of four-by-two. Eubank spends the last 30 seconds of the round crabbing round the ring in an exaggerated crouch, gloves drawn towards his chin, forearms acting as a shield for his body, looking like a man protecting his modesty with a towel. 'What I remember most is the intensity, the ferocity,' says Jim Rosenthal. 'These guys really were giving absolutely everything because there was just so much at stake. It was the climax of a lot of pre-match chat but that fight surpassed the hype. It was two really proud guys who didn't want to give an inch. Everyone goes on about Hagler–Hearns and the ferocity of those three rounds, but this one lasted more than double that. It was raw.'

In the seventh, Benn looks to have found a second wind, bouncing on his toes and managing to crowd most of Eubank's work. But with a minute to go in the round Eubank pushes him off with his left hand, creating some distance, and locates Benn's chin with a pinging left–right combination. Benn, who was about to release some grenades of his own, is left flailing wildly at mid-air. The champion shakes his head, flashes his gumshield and beckons Eubank back in, a study in defiance. Eubank needs no second invitation, shifting into fifth gear, ramming down the accelerator and running Benn over again, landing with a beast of a right cross on the bell. By the end of the round, Benn is effectively a one-eyed fighter – but still sensing victory. 'Never once did I feel like I was going to lose that fight,' he says. 'You never think that. But he was a strong man with an incredible physique and I really felt that power.'

'When you have a fight like that you've got to go in with the mentality of "this is gonna hurt and I'm going to have to take a lot of punishment if I want to win it",' says Hearn. 'If you believe in yourself you will have your moment. And you could see the pendulum swing, from the quick start from Benn to Eubank taking control in the middle rounds. You could hit Eubank in the body all day, he was like a rock. And you could hit him on the chin all night, he wasn't going to go anywhere. I can't think of too many fighters who have had the same ability to take punishment. We had his jaw X-rayed once and the bloke who X-rayed it said he'd never seen a jaw that thick. So it was God-given ability and a certain amount of luck in the way he was designed as a human being. Unless you closed his eyes or cut him or nutted him, he would not have a problem because, as well as his physical attributes, his mental belief was so strong: he knew he had to go through that barrier because Benn had the prize.'

Benn's corner works furiously on his swollen eye between rounds but to no avail – if he is going to hang onto his title he will have to complete the task half-blind. The champion tags Eubank with a left hook, hunts down his wounded prey and lets fly with a looping right hand that clips the top of Eubank's head and sends him to the canvas. The commentators struggle to make themselves heard over the din as Eubank shakes his head and pleads with referee Steele not to award the knock-down. 'When he went down I remember him saying: "It was a thlip! It was a thlip! It was a thlip!"' says Benn. 'Yeh mate, you slipped over a right hand.' Steele rejects Eubank's claims and delivers a compulsory eight count. Benn's corner roars its man forwards into the minefield as Eubank continues to send out distress signals, grimacing and complaining about border-line low blows and a whack to the back of the head. The bell sounds and Benn has secured what could be a crucial 10–8 round. Eubank breaks into his muscle-man pose and Benn impersonates him, a moment of jet-black humour amid the carnage. Eubank wastes ten seconds of his minute's break swaggering around the ring, drinking in the boos and the jeers. 'I don't know why Eubank doesn't go straight back to his corner,' says Brenner, 'it seems a daft thing to me.' We know now it was Eubank taking in one last hit of hatred: 'One last hit, just one last hit, that's all I need to get the job done . . .'

At the start of the ninth Watt has it even, McGuigan has Benn marginally ahead, although it is agreed that the three American judges sat ringside are likely to favour Benn's greater aggression should it go to the cards. Which sounds like some kind of sick joke. Benn digs in a ferocious right to the kidney, causing Eubank to grimace and stiffen and twist himself side-ways, as if he is being assailed by flames. Eubank motions Benn in, overreaches with a right hand and Benn sends him to the canvas again with a left hook to the backside. But this time it is ruled a slip. Eubank clambers to his feet and circles the champion, as if measuring him for a suit. 'Keep those hands up, Nigel,' someone shouts from the crowd. Eubank steps in, plants his feet and lands with a sickening right hand to the side of Benn's jaw. 'His leg went, he went back and I knew there was no power left,' says Eubank.

Benn is momentarily mummified, legs straightened, arms out in front of him, until his survival instincts kick in again and he takes refuge on the ropes. 'This is it! This is the end of it!' screams McGuigan. Only it isn't, not quite yet. Benn fights his way out of the corner and back into the middle of the ring, a wounded animal in a jungle clearing. Eight seconds left in the round. Eubank measures his stricken quarry from a safe distance before moving in. Seven seconds left in the round. Eubank cocks his right hand and delivers the killer blow. 'I'd broken his spirit,' says Eubank. 'No more resilience left. Right hand, straight left, right upper-cut, left hook, the referee steps in.' Steele takes Benn in his arms and cradles his head on his left shoulder. Suddenly, so tender. 'The referee did the right thing but only when Richard Steele stepped in and stopped the fight did I think I was going to lose,' says Benn. 'And that was it. Over. It was one of those fights I wanted to win. I would have rather lost to anyone else but him.' Eubank, ever the aesthete, falls to his knees in the centre of the ring and is immediately engulfed by hatred. The bastard. The cunt. Has only gone and won. 'I closed my eyes and roared,' says Eubank. 'Then the pain came, in my mouth and my chest. I was broken, but I wasn't beaten. I'd brought Benn to his knees, but when I watched the videotape of the fight and saw him sobbing into Steele's shoulder I felt sorry for Benn because he's still a man, he has a mother.'

Who had been fooling who? Unusually in boxing, nobody had been fooling anyone. But one man who remembered what it had actually all been about was Barry Hearn, wading through the gore in his tuxedo and reminding his charge what he had perhaps forgotten. What he had perhaps forgotten as his brain slopped against the hard, inner surface of his skull. What he had perhaps forgotten as his kidneys became first tenderised and then pulped. What he had perhaps forgotten as he swallowed pint after pint of his own blood. That this was still show business, after all. 'Eubank had split his tongue right down the middle – he looked like a snake,' says Hearn. 'So at the end of his post-fight interview with Gary Newbon, he said to me: "Could we finish now, please, I think I need to go to hospital." I said to him: "You can get married now, propose, let's have it live, we might as well milk the moment." And there he was: "Karron, will you marry me?" It was one of the greatest fights ever seen in a British ring, between two great fighters. But that was the showbiz part.'

'It ranks in the top ten of all the fights I refereed,' says referee Steele. 'It was two guys that hated each other and it was brutal. It was the same intensity as the Hagler–Hearns fight and it affected me a whole lot. The referee's job is a very dangerous, very crucial job. You've got two kids' lives in your hands but you've got to make sure you give them every opportunity to display their talents. I had to give Benn a chance to redeem himself, despite the closed eye, and he was still fighting and willing and still able to do damage, up to a point. But sometimes the fighters have to be saved from themselves. There's no point asking the boxers because they're going to carry on regardless of their injuries. They fight with their hearts, not with their minds.' Says Benn: 'Is it any consolation that Richard Steele thought that was one of the most ferocious fights he'd refereed? No, not really.'

Boxing writers who had been eager to point out that neither Benn nor Eubank had proved themselves the best middle-weights in the Southern Area, never mind the world, were suddenly falling over themselves to heap praise on the two brave warriors. 'The championship belt was, in the end, an irrelevance,' said Harry Mullan. 'They were struggling for victory, pure and simple, and I don't think I have ever seen two men with a more intense will to win. Who could complain about any aspect of this truly unforgettable encounter?' 'It was one of the great British contests,' wrote Srikumar Sen in *The Times*. 'I have not seen two men trade punches with such venom in recent times.' The *Guardian*'s John Rodda said 'the fight had all the mayhem and drama that the protagonists had forecast'. Ken Jones, who regularly used his columns in the *Independent* to prophesise the end of boxing as we knew it, wrote: 'It was a thrilling contest, fluctuating dramatically, not of the highest class but nevertheless intense and demanding much of both men.' Before adding a proviso: 'We are left with irony, the knowledge that Eubank, who believes boxing to be unworthy of his intellect, defeated the one British fighter guaranteed to draw a crowd.'

One journalist whom Eubank had proved spectacularly wrong was Colin Hart of the *Sun*. Two days after the fight, a smug-looking Eubank and an embarrassed-looking Hart were pictured together under the headline: 'I FORGIVE EU, COLIN'. 'I picked Benn to beat Eubank the first time because he was a far heavier puncher and at that stage we were wondering whether Mr Eubank was more a poser than anything else,' says Hart. 'But Eubank proved in that fight he had all the balls in the world and if you wanted to draw him into a fight he would certainly accommodate you. I was led astray. I knew the boy could box but I was beginning to think that when push came to shove, he would be the one who would bend the knee. He proved me completely wrong on that particular night. From that moment on I realised Eubank was a bit special, and the most special thing about him was the size of his heart.'

'I can honestly say that was the best moment of my life,' says Ronnie Davies. 'I was a good-class professional boxer myself, a Southern Area champion, but to have my career all over again at a higher level was a fantastic feeling. I went straight out and got really drunk. But the day after the fight I came downstairs from my hotel room and all the press were there and Nigel Benn was bent over like an old man, with this overcoat draped over him. I went back upstairs and said to Chris, "The press want to see you downstairs", but he couldn't get out of bed. I had to help him up and help him shower, because he was so badly bruised up. He passed blood for a week after that fight, from the punches to the kidneys. When he eventually came downstairs they both put their arms round each other and everyone clapped. It was quite an emotional thing. Benn was a lovely man deep down, a great fighter and a very nice person.'

However, the traditional post-fight garlanding of mutual admiration and respect masked deeper emotional truths. For Hearn, there was an overriding sense of relief. A sense of relief that his project, which he had pumped so much time and so much money into – and which so many people had told him he was wasting his time on – had borne such bountiful fruit. 'I'd rolled the dice,' says Hearn, 'and I'm not sure if Eubank had got beaten by Nigel that he would have been anywhere near the fighter he turned out to be.' Eubank claimed the material gains outweighed the psychological benefits. 'One day someone will bring me to my knees,' said Eubank. 'When that happens, my pride will be hurt. But is my pride more important than my wife's security, or my child's education, my child's standard of living? No. That is why I box.' However, victory for Eubank also translated into acceptance. If not acceptance of him as a person but at least of his skills, his will and his monumental courage.

For Benn, who had been stripped mentally, physically and materially, there was more desolation. 'He was somebody who was in a dark place, struggling to find some normality in his life and he exorcised lots of demons in his life by confronting them,' says Ambrose Mendy. 'Chris's bravery was second to none. Second to none. And the fans got more than they wanted, I had never witnessed such violence in a boxing ring. But Chris had decried him, denounced him. So that defeat was as raw and as real as anything could be.'

'I handled defeat graciously,' says Benn. 'Chris won and I wasn't going to run him down and make excuses – he prepared like the champion, and I said that. But Michael Watson was a gentleman. And while Chris was gracious in victory in the ring, I knew that I was going to get it from him in time. And when the dust settled, he carried on his bravado. I was beneath him, those were his words. It was really hard to deal with that. There was a lot to take in, a lot going on. I'm not the world champion any more, my world has crumbled. I'd lost what I'd worked for all my life. I was a 400 grand fighter and now I'd dropped a nought. So I was thinking: "Mortgage, kids, all these other things I've got." I found it difficult to think straight. But I had to start putting things in perspective, pick myself up, dust myself down and get back out there. It was in my head – "What if I lose next time?" – but I never seriously thought about quitting. Like my dad used to say, "The dog that runs away lives to fight another day".'

Benn might have detected a chink of light at the end of the tunnel but many in the press were busy bricking the tunnel up. 'His credibility as a world-class performer is now in shreds after inside the distance defeats by Watson and Eubank,' wrote Harry Mullan. 'The boastful world of Nigel Benn will never be the same again,' wrote Srikumar Sen of *The Times*. 'The hot air that fills it was let out last night.' Benn's defeat did indeed see him tumble out of the world title picture. Worse, he was considered by many to be only the fourth best middle-weight in Britain, with Eubank, Michael Watson and Herol Graham all above him in the pecking order. Given the thrilling nature of his fight against Eubank and the public clamour that came in its wake, Benn thought a rematch was a natural. But a natural rematch is one that makes most money and Eubank and Hearn were more than happy to wait.

'Don't start getting hung up on the semantics of the noble art, that's all bollocks,' says Hearn. 'The boxing business is all about money.' As such, Hearn, who apparently believed Benn would come again, decided to build the suspense. 'No one was going to forget that first fight, there was no rush,' says Hearn. 'So whenever the rematch did happen it was going to be a huge, huge fight.' Eubank, as Benn had suspected he would be, was insufferably smug in victory. 'Be prepared for the worst and hope for the best,' Eubank said in a television interview shortly after the fight. 'I'm the man now and if I decide to give you the opportunity to fight me again you should think yourself privileged. But as for now I think I'll make you wait in the queue for a little while.'

CHAPTER NINE
Seeing dogs fight

A week after Eubank's victory over Benn, Herol Graham challenged for a world title for a second time. 'You've heard this one before, and recently,' wrote Harry Mullan in his *Boxing News* preview. 'An eccentric, oddball British middleweight, hated by as many fans as love him, takes on a thunderous-hitting opponent for a version of the world title and punches him to a standstill.' Only this time it didn't turn out like that. Graham was on the verge of stopping Julian Jackson in the fourth round when he switched off momentarily and left his chin exposed. It was a silly thing to do against any top-class boxer, but against Jackson it was suicidal. Virgin Islander Jackson, who was knocked out himself by Mike McCallum in 1986, had already earned himself a reputation as one of the most explosive punchers in boxing history and none of his previous 33 fights had gone the distance. Jackson drilled a crackerjack right hand into Graham's jaw, rendering the Englishman unconscious before he hit the boards.

'I was smashing him,' says Graham, who won the first three rounds at a canter, making Jackson miss by embarrassing margins. 'He had a dodgy eye, dodgy nose, dodgy mouth and the referee came over after the third round and said, "If nothing happens in this round, I'm stopping the fight". That stirred him up big style. And instead of thinking, "All I have to do is run away, do my normal stuff", I wanted to play the big shot, take him out. I'll have to take a look at what happened . . . oh, that's right, he knocked me clean out! Six minutes, was it? Or was I out for a bit longer than that? Jeez, it haunts me to this day. If I had that fight again I would have run and run, I would have been Usain Bolt.'

While an estimated ten million British viewers witnessed Eubank and Benn's caveman savagery in Birmingham, the latest defeat of British boxing's pugilist-poet went comparatively unnoticed. The British Boxing Board of Control had refused to host the bout for the vacant WBC belt because of Jackson's two retina operations, one on each eye, and so Graham's world title hopes ended up in a crumpled heap on the floor of an obscure hotel on Spain's Costa del Sol. There was a hint of romance about it but mainly it was cruel. 'I was royally fucked,' says Graham. 'Two world title losses in a year, in my 30s, still rowing with my manager and with a pretty dim view of the world. Was this how it was meant to be?' Graham's defeat saw him tumble out of the world title picture. None of the world's top-ranked middleweights had ever wanted to fight him anyway, now they had a cast-iron excuse: 'What does Herol bring to the table apart from some fancy footwork and a bit of limbo dancing?'

One of the world's top-ranked middleweights who had never wanted to fight Graham was Chris Eubank. But in the aftermath of Eubank's victory over Benn, it seemed like Eubank didn't really want to fight anyone. A rematch with Benn having been immediately ruled out – 'no way am I getting back in the ring with him' – Eubank also pooh-poohed the idea of a unification match against IBF title-holder Michael

Nunn. 'Nunn is 6ft 2in and a southpaw,' said Eubank. 'He is therefore a liability.' 'Chris is his own man and will have a good look at who's around,' said Barry Hearn. 'Why should Chris want to go back in with such a threatening opponent?' Hearn's statement also seemed to rule out Julian Jackson, and indeed WBA champion Mike McCallum, who had beaten both Graham and Michael Watson. Rated Irishman Steve Collins, who had also been beaten by McCallum, and American Dennis Milton, who had wins over Gerald McClellan and former world title challenger Robbie Sims on his record, were also mooted. But in the end Eubank plumped for an unknown Canadian called Dan Sherry. Eubank, as was his way, ranked Sherry a seven out of ten as a fighter. Few outside of Sherry's home town of Burlington, Ontario had ever heard of him. Nevertheless, after the brutality of his fight against Benn, Eubank could be forgiven for setting out on the path of less resistance.

That Sherry came so close to relieving Eubank of his WBO title persuaded some observers that his heroics against Benn had been a flash in the pan, albeit an almighty one that almost took your hair off. Eubank was leading on two of the judges' scorecards and behind on one when he deliberately butted the challenger in the 10th round. The referee deducted two points from the champion, Sherry was stretchered from the ring and Eubank won on a split technical decision. Many thought Eubank should have been disqualified (under British or European rules he would have been), while plenty of others thought he was behind when the premature end came. Either way, it was a very close shave. 'He should have been disqualified,' says Jim McDonnell. 'But he was good TV, filling up halls. The other fella didn't mean jack. Wasn't he from Kansas or something? They weren't going to give him the title.'

Following the Sherry fight, the press pack roundly criticised Eubank's performance and behaviour and he was fined
£10,000 by the British Boxing Board of Control. The fight
also left some questioning Eubank's talent as a matchmaker,
because while Eubank accused Sherry of running all night,
most sitting ringside thought the challenger outboxed him. As
his next opponent Eubank chose Gary Stretch, who had
fought only once as a middleweight, 11 months earlier. With
11,000 seats to fill at the Kensington Olympia, the build-up
wasn't pretty. As well as Stretch apparently saying he would
'rather die than lose' the fight, which was inevitably dubbed
'Beauty v The Best', Eubank said he would like 10 per cent of
the plastic surgeon's fees after he had made a mess of Stretch's
face. Eubank needed an eye-catching win to placate the
boxing writers, who were already beginning to weary of his
arrogance and studied eccentricity and whom Eubank accused
of giving him a bad name. 'I am a misunderstood champion,'
said Eubank. 'It is you, the press, who are giving a wrong
impression of me, with what you say. I am not a bad man or a
villain. I can understand people thinking I am rather strange.
Anything that is not the norm is intriguing.' Eubank bludg-
eoned Stretch to defeat in the sixth round. Yet still there were
question marks over his performance, because the elegant
Stretch was ahead on all three scorecards when the end came.

While Eubank was capitalising on his victory over Benn,
Michael Watson was hammering his way back into world title
contention. Having smashed Errol Christie in three rounds on
the undercard of Eubank–Benn, Watson defended his
Commonwealth crown with a sixth-round stoppage of
Australian Craig Trotter. Shortly after Eubank's defeat of Stretch,
the WBO champion, having decided ageing Brit-basher Mike

McCallum could wait, signed to fight Watson instead. 'What can McCallum bring?' said Barry Hearn, '£5000 from Jamaican television?' The press, needing an angle, quickly installed Watson as the 'People's Champion', as Benn had been for his fight against Eubank. Such was Eubank's standing with the public, Satan would have been dubbed the 'People's Champion' in a fight against a man one newspaper called 'Britain's most disliked world champion ever'. 'Eubank refuses to show respect for me or anyone else,' said Watson. 'He is trying to portray himself as something he is not. He carries on as if he belongs to royalty. Well, he has not intimidated me. He might as well surrender now because he has lost this battle. And when this is over he has the public to face.'

Others had a more charitable view of Eubank, as a clever man simply chiselling out a niche in a crowded market. 'To some, he is a fraud who compensates for lack of talent with an arrogance which borders on dementia,' wrote Harry Mullan. 'My own view is that he is an inspired self-publicist who, virtually alone among British fighters, has grasped the truth of what Muhammad Ali was about in his Cassius Clay incarnation: that it does not matter whether people come to see you win or in the hope of seeing you trounced, so long as they come and the cheques do not bounce.' Lenny DeJesus, one of Eubank's former trainers from his New York days, couldn't believe his eyes when he saw how his old charge had turned out. 'It was a big surprise to be honest with you,' says DeJesus. 'But that's what made him over there in England: he sold, and he sold real good. He had become a Jack Johnson character, making people angry with his arrogance, his expensive clothes, by driving around in fast cars. But it was just a show to get people into the stadium. He let loose over there – we had instilled the basics in him and it was only when he went to

England that he broke the rules and created his own style. But I don't think he would have made it in the United States in that manner. The competition here was tougher, we had real fighters. Chris was intelligent enough to find a good promoter in England who knew how to push him and knew how to sell him. That's why he made it.'

Stretch, meanwhile, was at least one fellow professional who appreciated Eubank's rare gift for self-promotion. 'I first met him in Frank Warren's office,' says Stretch. 'I remember Frank saying: "You're going to meet someone who's very different." He'd just come over from New York and he was a little distant. Then we fought and I still didn't know who he was, he was just another fight, albeit a big one. But as the years went by I had many sit-downs with Chris and it became clear he didn't mind being the one they loved to hate, he played that role to perfection. Boxing is very similar to acting in many ways: to be a good actor you've got to really know who you are and what makes you tick, and to be a good boxer it's the same. I think he liked the fact that no one really got behind the facade and it worked for him. He said to me once: "You know, Gary, I don't mind if they don't like me, at least they turn up to see me get beat. This is a business for me, I'm not in it to please them all and they don't really know me anyway. I've created a persona and as long as I sell tickets, I'll take that." Boxing isn't show business but there is an element of show business in boxing. The fighters that put arses on seats are the entertainers. Eubank put a little bit of theatre into it, brought something different to the game, which is not easy. There are a million fighters out there but there is only one Chris Eubank.'

It was only when he became a professional boxer himself that David Haye, who was a rabid Benn supporter as a kid, worked out he had also been a huge Eubank fan all along. 'My mum loved Chris, but I didn't get it,' says Haye. 'I didn't understand it was just a show, I couldn't relate to it. I was a fan, though, I just didn't realise it. I'd read about him in the paper, watch the TV any time he was on. I'd have to know about everything the man did because everything he did was so captivating. But it wasn't until I appreciated the art and business of boxing that I started looking beyond the voice and the posturing and thought: "This guy's actually a classy dude, inside and outside the ring." He wasn't following fashion, he was a trend-setter. If you look at Naseem Hamed's ring entrances, they were almost carbon copies of Chris Eubank's: vaulting the top rope, standing on the ring apron, tapping his gloves together. And like Eubank, Naz would get booed a lot of the time – but at least people were there, at least people felt passionately about him. Chris told everyone that came after him, including me, that it's OK to put on a show and whip that crowd into a frenzy, it's OK to say controversial things that people might not like. Now I really do appreciate what Chris Eubank brought to the table.'

Whatever Eubank's motives, and whether the persona he portrayed had much to do with the real Eubank or not, Watson's dislike of him was entirely understandable. 'The reason I earn the most money is that I have a little bit of everything,' said Eubank, in an attempt to explain why he was box office and Watson was not. 'I can box, I can fight, I can dance, I can strut, I can show off, I can behave arrogantly, I can charm, I can communicate with people who have PhDs in philosophy and make them feel intimidated. Michael Watson can only box so he has none of my presence or my money. It's that simple.'

'Watson genuinely didn't like him,' says Donald McRae. 'Michael was similar to Nigel Benn, a real fighting man, and I interviewed him at an archetypal boxing gym behind King's Cross station, a dingy, dark place. In contrast, I had to meet Eubank at the Grand Hotel in Brighton. Michael was much more secure in his own self, he didn't need any artifice. But maybe Eubank understood boxing better than Michael. Eubank knew that, in the end, it was about fucking knocking someone down, causing them damage. But he also understood you needed artifice and humour to bring more people in. Eubank liked to talk about having a silver spoon in his mouth and how well-educated he was and Watson just thought that was a load of bollocks. Even now when I speak to Michael the bitterness is there. He always felt that he didn't get the money he deserved and that the money went to Eubank based on him doing outlandish things – strutting about in his jodhpurs and monocle, riding in on motor bikes. Michael thought it was all bullshit.'

'People thought it was all part of the business, the hype, about putting flavour into the system,' says Watson. 'But you know what? I did hate him. It wasn't an act, it was serious, because Chris had an attitude problem. He was scum. He was ignorant, had no respect, thought he was above everybody else. And still does. Nothing he said or did made sense. He called boxing a mug's game, so why was he boxing? Of course he loved boxing, it's boxing that made him who he was. He thinks he's too regal to mix with scumbags like us, but he was a typical ghetto boy, from the streets. Somewhere along the way he lost his identity. He doesn't know who he is, whether he's white or black. He's confused, totally mixed up. He's ashamed of himself. Wouldn't you be?'

Unlike against Benn, few were picking Watson to beat Eubank. Citing the fact he was managing himself and suggesting that his sparring had been inadequate, Hugh McIlvanney, the doyen of British boxing journalism, didn't give Watson much hope. Added McIlvanney: 'In the three wins Watson has scored since suffering his cruellest night [Watson's defeat by Mike McCallum] there has been little to indicate that he is the one to give the fantasist a bitter dose of reality.' Watson's former manager Mickey Duff seemed to relish putting the boot in. 'Mentally, Eubank will destroy Watson,' said Duff, who also revealed that Watson 'lived off crumbs' for the last three days before a fight in order to make weight. 'I don't expect Eubank to lose a round.' Hell hath no fury like a boxing manager scorned. Herol Graham, however, gave Watson a chance. 'I think Eubank may have to do it inside the distance to keep his title,' said Graham. 'If it goes to the final bell, Watson could be the new champion.'

It wasn't only Watson who was living off crumbs. Eubank, as was his wont, was more than a stone overweight the Tuesday before the fight and ended up losing 19lb in four days. The evening before the day of the fight, Eubank claims he blacked out after trying and failing to pick up a carrier bag. Given the eyewitness accounts of those who knew him well, it seems entirely believable. It is one of the diabolical truths of professional boxing that the two men bearing their souls for the fans' delectation are sometimes little more than dried-out husks and not the sweetly tuned athletes some believe them to be. 'Watson's appearance,' wrote McIlvanney, 'gave the impression it would be difficult to lose any appreciable weight without the assistance of a carpenter's plane.'

What transpired at Earls Court on the evening of 22 June 1991 left pretty much everyone watching feeling angry as hell and sick to their stomachs. 'Most of the 11,500 watchers in the hall were convinced that Watson's performance represented a triumph for honest orthodoxy over imaginative bombast,' wrote McIlvanney, although it should be noted that most of the 11,500 watchers were Watson fans. Unfortunately for Watson, the three judges that mattered disagreed, with one making Eubank the winner by an astonishing three rounds, another by two and the third making it a draw. Even more remarkably, two of the judges hailed from the United States and one from Puerto Rico, both nations with a tradition of favouring come-forward fighters. While Watson's perform-ance in an underwhelming, awkward fight had been less than eye-catching – 'it was a good fight for the third division,' said Herol Graham – it was he who had shown the most initiative, especially in the second half of the fight as Eubank tired. Past and present champions ringside who had Watson winning included Graham, McCallum, Alan Minter and Jim Watt, who was co-commentating on the fight for ITV.

'Waiting for the verdict, I thought it would be unanimous in my favour,' says Watson. 'The journalists and photographers were already saying to me, "When you get the belt, come straight over here". So I could have died when I heard the result, it felt as if my heart had left my body. I gave Chris such a pasting, I was in total control and enjoying myself so much. Everywhere I wanted him to be, he was there, and I was hitting him from pillar to post.' Eubank, unsurprisingly, thought he had done enough to hang on to his belt, although the haunted look on Hearn's face as he waited for the score-cards to be announced told a different story. The atmosphere in the arena having turned medieval in its malignity, Eubank was harangued all the way to the exit by an angry mob. Coins, phlegm, the rudest gestures and the basest epithets were slung the champion's way – presumably their pitchforks had been confiscated at the gates. 'I was regarded as the villain of the villains,' says Eubank.

Backed by the British Boxing Board of Control, Watson lodged a formal protest to the WBO. Meanwhile, Hearn performed a sudden about-face, declaring that while he had Eubank three rounds ahead on the night, having watched the fight again on video, he now thought it had been a draw. Funny, that. The shadowy officials based at WBO HQ in San Juan, Puerto Rico soon passed down their decree and a rematch was arranged to take place at White Hart Lane on 21 September. This time the fight would be in the super-middleweight division, Eubank having seen sense and given up his WBO middleweight belt. In addition, it would be for the WBO super-middleweight belt made vacant by Tommy Hearns, with the governing body's previous numbers one and two contenders (Juan Carlos Gimenez of Paraguay and Michele Mastrodonato of Italy) vanishing from the top ten. Rather than condemn this shambolic state of affairs, the British Boxing Board of Control suddenly decided to give the WBO formal recognition.

While the 168lb division had a short and undistinguished history – veteran American boxing writer George Kimball referred to it as 'yet another bastard weight class' – it would become a happy hunting ground for British-based fighters over the next two decades, with Eubank, Benn, Steve Collins, Richie Woodhall, Robin Reid, Joe Calzaghe and Carl Froch all holding versions of the world title. But for Watson any belt was of little real importance and interviews Watson gave before the second Eubank fight reveal a brooding, bitter man bent on revenge. 'I want Chris Eubank,' Watson told Donald McRae. 'On my mind it's just Eubank, Eubank, Eubank . . . this is a fight at the crossroads – one fork leads to the light, the other into darkness.'

The build-up to the fight was even more vitriolic than first time round, with Watson's sense of righteousness stoked by a mischievous media and a public high on a sense of vicarious victimhood. At the press conference to formally announce the fight, a clearly rattled Eubank stated: 'You make me sick, you're pitiful. You lost the fight and you're still whingeing like a child. If I was to get up and walk out of this room now, you'd be left starving.' Eubank promptly got up and walked out, before returning a few minutes later, jangling his car keys, as if he'd just popped out to top up the parking meter. Later, Watson stated: 'The sport has to be resurrected, he has pushed boxing down into the gutter, he has torn boxing apart.' 'I have a lot of contempt for this man, for his frame of mind,' said Eubank. 'His point of view is weak.'

Watson dismissed his long-serving trainer Eric Seccombe and upgraded Jimmy Tibbs, a former top-class amateur who had trained former flyweight world champion Charlie Magri and Barry McGuigan among many others, to chief second. Watson believed Tibbs leant his camp more professionalism but boxing insiders were concerned by what they saw as more upheaval in Watson's life. Seccombe, after all, had known Watson since he was a budding amateur and had been in his corner for all 29 of his professional fights. And while the bookmakers had the rematch even, many in the game thought the extra weight would work to Eubank's advantage. 'The result [of the first fight] has woken Eubank up,' said Jim Watt. 'He can do so much better. I don't think Watson can do better, so I think Eubank has the edge.' But Watson thought he knew what he had to do. 'I needed to destroy, to knock him out,' says Watson. 'I had to do a complete job on him, I couldn't risk it going to a decision.'

Everyone agreed the second fight between Chris Eubank and Michael Watson was a great fight – one of the greatest fights seen in a British ring in recent history. Always 'in recent history' write the reporters, as if to make quite clear that however hard these modern fighters are, the old-timers were so much harder. While in the first bout a weight-drained Watson had been forced to fight sporadically, in fits and starts, in the return he poured it on from the start, backing a startled Eubank up from the sound of the first bell and forcing him to fight at a pace he was unaccustomed with. Says Eubank: 'I came back to my corner after the first round and Ronnie Davies said: "Don't worry kid, if he keeps up this pace you'll stop him in five to six rounds."' Watson's attacks left openings and Eubank obliged, landing with jolting uppercuts and looping rights. Eubank was cut in the fourth, a round Watson clearly won, before the fight juddered into a groove and careered into the distance, like a runaway train with no driver. While millions watched and did nothing. 'I knew from round six that the man was too strong for me,' said Eubank. 'But I knew I could go the distance. I didn't think he could survive at the pace.' 'That fight showed you the bravery of Eubank, because he was beaten that night,' says the *Sun*'s Colin Hart. 'I used to have arguments with a lot of my colleagues and one of them, who will remain nameless, kept telling me Eubank was a fraud and that when push came to shove he would be exposed. But I was right and he was wrong.'

At the end of the eighth Eubank appeared to turn his back towards Watson while punches were still flying, the first real suggestion that his will might be sagging. And Eubank continued to ship fearful punishment in the ninth, including a number of howitzer rights over the top. 'I remember thinking of Watson as a flame,' says Eubank. 'I remember thinking, "If you so much as flicker, I will do my best to finish you".' 'I suppose I was enjoying beating him,' says Watson, while rejecting Eubank's suggestion that he was consciously humiliating him. 'I would have preferred to have stopped him and put an end to the night.' Before the start of the 10th, Watson was so keen to get to Eubank that referee Roy Francis had to place his hand on his chest to stop him jumping the bell. Once again, it was Watson's round. Before the start of the 11th – what Watson calls 'the greatest round', with no apparent irony – Davies implored his fighter to summon one last effort.

Eubank looked to have worked up a second wind at the start of the 11th but quickly found himself on the retreat. But he got through with a ramrod right about halfway through the round, forcing Watson to tie him up on the back foot. Eubank, sensing blood, kept coming forward, windmilling punches like a pub drunk at kicking-out time. Watson managed to step to the side, leaving Eubank lolling over the slackened ropes, as if the exertion had been too much and he was depositing beer and kebab over the ringside patrons. 'You can't fault Eubank's desire but he seems to have used up an awful lot in that round,' said ITV co-commentator Jim Watt. Right on cue, Eubank was sent tottering round the ring by a sustained assault by Watson. 'There it is,' said Reg Gutteridge, 'can he have him over?' Seconds later, a rat-a-tat left-right combination from Watson turned Eubank to stone and another right cross had him down.

'When I put Chris down,' says Watson, 'I thought, "I am the champ at last".' Says Eubank: 'My nervous system shorted. But when my knee hit the canvas, it was almost as though I was earthed. I was completely recovered.' Eubank was down on his hands and knees for barely two seconds and almost back on his feet before Watson had reached a neutral corner. Eubank gobbed on the canvas before herding his scattered thoughts. With ten seconds left in the round, Eubank took three steps forward, listed almost imperceptibly to his right and drilled a right uppercut between Watson's guard. This time it was Watson who was turned to stone, before a left from Eubank sent him sprawling, Watson's neck pinging off the second-bottom rope on his way down. Watson clambered to his feet before the bell for the end of the round intervened.

'Despite what he said,' says Davies, 'Chris loved boxing, deep down. You can't have that much will to win just for money. He had this deep desire to overcome things. In the second Watson fight, he could have said: "I'm getting paid well, I'll stay down here – what do I need to risk my life for?" But he didn't. He had tremendous pride and he loved boxing in his own way.' Watson heaved in air between rounds as his seconds attempted to rejuvenate him. 'I got up for the last with one thing in my mind,' says Watson. 'Keep your hands up. Survive one more round and you're the champion.' But Watson was on spaghetti legs at the start of the final round. Eubank, looking vital again, extended his left arm to touch gloves but Watson, apparently through absent-mindedness rather than a lack of respect, had to be dragged into the centre of the ring by referee Francis. Eubank, sensing Watson was already gone, went in for the kill, like a spider scuttling across his web. And then began his grim work. For 20 or so seconds, Eubank flailed away at his prey before referee Francis had seen enough and stepped between them. 'I wanted to keep going,' says Watson. 'I was so angry when it was stopped. But then everything went dark.'

'The ring's invaded,' said Gutteridge as Eubank's arm was raised. 'It's a jamboree in there now.' Beyond the ropes, scuffles had broken out between rival sets of fans. And so the runaway train with no driver clattered ever onwards. Meanwhile, in his corner, Watson was slipping into a deep sleep. Nobody really knows how the damage was done – whether the clots that were forming on Watson's brain were the result of the upper-cut that took him off his feet or the snapping of his head on the rope as he landed. All anyone knows was that Watson was dying. Back in the middle of the ring, Eubank was being interviewed by ITV's Gary Newbon. 'I want him tested,' said Eubank, 'to see if he had anything in his blood. Because no one is that strong.' Watson would later sue Eubank for libel and slander and Eubank was forced to settle out of court.

The ringside scuffles were eventually quelled, at least for as long as it took for Watson's still body to be lowered from the ring on a stretcher. The men carrying the stretcher nearly dropped him on the BBC radio commentary team. Watson was initially taken to nearby North Middlesex Hospital but stopped breathing before he got there. Medical staff managed to keep him alive but the hospital lacked the facilities to operate on him. By the time Watson arrived at St Bartholomew's more than 90 minutes had passed. Watson had two procedures in the early hours of Sunday morning, to remove blood clots from the brain. Consultant neurosurgeon Peter Hamlyn had stared more dying boxers in the face than anyone, having performed life-saving operations on Robert Darko in 1990 and Rod Douglas in 1989, after his loss to Herol Graham. But Hamlyn told Watson's mother, Joan, to prepare for the worst. 'Michael was closer to death than anybody that I had ever operated on,' said Hamlyn. Everyone agreed the second fight between Chris Eubank and Michael Watson was a great fight – one of the greatest fights seen in a British ring in recent history. There was only one problem: Michael Watson almost died.

★ ★ ★

The events of the evening of Saturday 21 September left many in the boxing fraternity examining their moral compasses. Men who earned a living writing about other men punching each other for show now had to explain to an equally confused public exactly why Chris Eubank had been allowed to almost kill Michael Watson in front of a paying audience of 20,000 and millions watching on television. Wrote Hugh McIlvanney, who had been covering fights for more than 30 years, in the *Observer*: 'How much mileage is left in ambivalence, you may ask, as Michael Watson clings precariously to life in a London hospital? The answer, rendered no more adequate by being honest, is that I don't know.' Donald McRae would later write: 'I knew that eleventh-round punch from Eubank had been what I always wanted to see most in a ring. The kind of last-gasp blow which turns defeat into stunning victory. When else as an adult, if not in sex or sleep, had I been so far beyond the mundane?' Most writers came to the conclusion that, fighting and the love of watching it being such an integral part of human nature, the only logical way forward for the sport of boxing was to minimise the risks involved.

'I've always thought it's a bit daft to cover boxing over a long period of time and decide one or two fights are too brutal for your tastes but the others aren't,' says the *Guardian*'s Kevin Mitchell. 'Howard Cosell [the American sportscaster] suddenly decided, after seeing Randall "Tex' Cobb" get cut to pieces by Larry Holmes in 1982, that boxing was an inhuman sport. That he didn't think that beforehand was a bit ridiculous because he'd covered the twilight years of Muhammad Ali's career. It's difficult to be ambivalent about the violence of boxing and still cover the sport – boxing and ambivalence don't go. You either deal with your doubts about whether it's legitimate as a sport or walk away. Whatever happens in a fight, it's not something you didn't know before, or at least should have done. It's the only sport where it's legal to kill someone. It's a frightening concept but that's the way it is. So you can't suddenly decide, having had a good innings being associated with it, that maybe it's too much.'

That boxing's central aim was to commit violence against another person left it dangerously exposed in times of tragedy. Defenders of the sport were quick to point out that there had been more injuries and fatalities in other sports, in terms of the ratio of injuries and fatalities to competitors involved, but this argument suddenly seemed wilfully naive to anyone who had witnessed the almost primeval savagery at White Hart Lane. Racing drivers were maimed or killed by speed, not by the fists of another human being. A more convincing argument involved freedom of choice, the fact that both Watson and Eubank knew the risks involved and the difficult-to-escape – even for the abolitionists – truth that boxing had given a voice to generations of mostly working-class boys and young men who otherwise might have led lives of humdrum desperation. There would always be boxers and boxing, the argument went, as long as there was social deprivation.

But such arguments cut no ice with many medical practitioners, politicians and social commentators. James Callaghan, Labour MP for Heywood and Middleton, said: 'It is a throwback to the days of gladiatorial contests. There is only one winner in professional boxing: I have never known a promoter suffering from punch-drunkenness or brain damage.' Said Menzies Campbell, the Liberal Democrat spokesman on sport: 'In modern-day Britain, boxing jars the conscience of all who love sport. We must not allow the enthusiasm of young men to cause them to put their lives at risk.' Journalists were particularly damning of the pre-fight hype, with Eubank coming in for some fearful stick. 'Those of us who defend a man's right to explore his limits,' wrote Michael Calvin in the *Daily Telegraph*, 'be it up a mountain, on the high seas or in the claustrophobic confines of a boxing ring, are undermined by the contrivance of a man's character for commercial reasons.'

But the most valuable words, certainly as far as the sport of boxing was concerned, were spoken by Peter Hamlyn, the man charged with saving Watson's life. 'Boxing is not a safe activity,' said Hamlyn. 'As long as it goes on people will be damaged and die.' Crucially, however, Hamlyn did not call for boxing to be abolished. Nevertheless, on the front and back pages of newspapers, in leader articles, on television news bulletins, on magazine shows, on radio phone-ins, in pubs and offices across Britain, everybody seemed to be asking: what is to be done with boxing? Fewer rounds? Shorter rounds? Longer breaks? Headguards? Heavier gloves? Ban the whole bloody spectacle? Or would that only serve to drive boxing underground? While the arguments raged and Michael Watson lay stricken on a hospital bed, the band played on.

Two days after the tragic events at White Hart Lane, Lennox Lewis made a £2 million offer to Frank Bruno; a day later Frank Warren held a press conference to publicise a promotion at the Royal Albert Hall at the end of October; and a day later a Barry Hearn-promoted event went ahead in Basildon. 'I thought of calling the show off but the fighters were under contract,' said Hearn. 'We are a business and the fighters have to earn money.' And so 600 boxing fans crammed into the Festival Hall to watch Sheffield's Slugger O'Toole, aka Fidel Castro Smith, beat local boy Ian Strudwick to claim the vacant British super-middleweight crown. Apparently subdued but not unduly worried by the blood that streamed from a weal above Strudwick's right eye and caused the referee to step in. 'It's what people love to see,' says Watson, explaining the enduring attraction of the sport 22 years after his fateful clash with Eubank. 'It's human nature. No different to seeing dogs fight.'

CHAPTER TEN
So beneath me

S ome wicked ironies emerged from Eubank–Watson II. First, that a man who professed to hate boxing had almost killed a man who professed to love it. Second, that a fight that should have been the making of Chris Eubank seemed to threaten the future of the sport he professed to hate. And third, that a fight that should have finally gained Eubank acceptance made him only more hated by many. 'By producing a move of such quality in his moment of supreme crisis,' wrote Harry Mullan of the punch that put Watson in a coma, 'Eubank made the transition from strutting showman to a champion of genuine worth.' While Eubank agreed with Mullan that it was 'by far the most special' fight of his career, there were less charitable souls who thought it should have been Eubank in a coma and not Watson. On one occasion, Eubank was removing his bike from his Range Rover on Brighton seafront when an elderly woman wound down her car window and told him so.

Having been admitted to hospital for treatment himself, Eubank arrived at his stricken rival's bedside in the early hours of Sunday morning. 'My very soul shuddered,' says Eubank. But as the days turned into weeks and Watson still hadn't emerged from his coma, some sections of the media decided

Eubank didn't seem sorry enough. 'For years afterwards, people would look at me in the street and I'd know what they were thinking,' said Eubank. 'But should I feel responsible? No. I don't think so. I was doing a job.' At least now Eubank felt able to round on those who had condemned him for condemning boxing. As far as Eubank was concerned, Watson's plight was all the proof he needed that he had been right all along. 'For anyone who says that this is not a mug's game,' said Eubank, 'and that I am not a mug to take this risk, I'd say: "Tell that to Michael Watson."'

At the end of October Watson started showing the first glimmers of life and in early November he opened his eyes and began to communicate through blinking. But mostly he stared at the ceiling of his ward, asking God to deliver him from this terrible predicament. In January 1992 Watson was moved to Homerton Hospital's special rehabilitation unit and four months later a broken-down Muhammad Ali paid a visit, photographers in tow, so that the world could be reminded what this barbaric sport could do to even its greatest practitioners. But for Watson, for whom Ali was a childhood hero, it was a breakthrough moment. As Ali shuffled into the room, Watson's eyes widened and he smiled for the first time since that September night. Ali moved close to Watson's ear and whispered: 'Boy, you're pretty. But I'm prettier than you.'

Meanwhile, Eubank wrestled with his demons. 'I never thought I could inflict such damage on an opponent,' he said. 'I still haven't come to terms with it. It makes me think whether I can go on with a sport like this.' Many assumed Eubank would indeed hang up his gloves. But a little over two months after sending Watson into a coma, Eubank announced his intention to carry on. 'My view of boxing

Master and pupil, Ambrose Mendy and Nigel Benn. 'Whatever you want, you can get.'

British boxing's next big thing, Frank Warren. 'I lived and breathed boxing – and still do.'

The Odd Couple, Chris Eubank and Barry Hearn. 'Love at first sight.'

A myth exploded, Benn–Watson. 'The worst defeat ever. Complete devastation.'

Press Association

Who's Fooling Who? Benn–Eubank I. 'My hatred for him was all-consuming.'

Victorious and vindicated. 'I closed my eyes and roared. Then the pain came.'

Blessed are the deal-makers? Frank Warren, Don King and Barry Hearn. 'The hardest men in boxing.'

Action Images

Judgement Day, Benn–Eubank II. 'The ego has landed.'

Forget the controversy, feel the hatred. 'I detest him as a man and always will.'

At the crossroads, Eubank–Watson II. 'No different to seeing dogs fight.'

The greatest fight? Benn–McClellan. 'You got what you wanted to see.'

Sucking in the hate, Eubank–Wharton. 'I'm abnormal in many ways.'

Losing like a gentleman, Eubank–Thompson I. 'The higher one soars the less people care.'

How quickly they forget, Benn–Collins II. 'I knew I was kind of gone.'

Simply The Best, no longer. 'I can't seem to win these days.'

The fuse is lit? 'That's fucking it.'

Bygones let be? 'Chris is ashamed of himself. Wouldn't you be?'

Third time unlucky, Herol Graham–Charles Brewer.
'I was too scary for Eubank and Benn.'

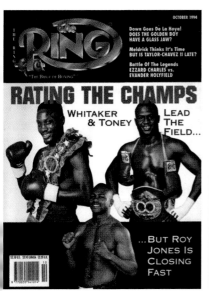

Avoidable truth, James Toney and Roy
Jones Jr. 'Like the plague.'

Beautiful monstrosity, Eubank and his
rig. 'People still stare at me.'

Action Images

Still in the game, Frank Warren. 'I don't care what anyone else does.'

Meet the new boss, Eddie and Barry Hearn. 'You've got to have someone to compete with.'

Best of enemies, Eubank and Benn. 'Only you can do this to me . . .'

has not changed,' he said. 'I asked myself the question: "What are you going to do to earn money?" When I can stand on my own two feet, I'll get out of boxing before you can say one-two.' Such were the tragic circumstances of Chris Eubank: that this thing he professed to hate, this thing that liberated him and afforded him some semblance of recognition, also entrapped him. Watson, however, had little sympathy for his rival's plight. 'No, I didn't feel sorry for him,' says Watson. 'I was amazed that he decided to carry on. Having called boxing a mug's game and after doing that kind of damage to someone, I would have retired immediately. I thought maybe what happened in that fight would wake him up from the foolish way he had been carrying on, make him pull himself together. But has he changed? No. It just goes to show what sort of person he is: a liar.'

In February 1992, five months after his fight against Watson, Eubank ploughed into a labourer when his Range Rover spun out of control on the A23 and was subsequently found guilty of driving without due care and attention. It only increased his sense of isolation. In the space of 15 months, Eubank had beaten two 'people's champions', sent one of them into a coma and killed a man. Yet those who thought this succession of events might make him any less bombastic and any more humble were to be gravely disappointed. In April 1992, Eubank gave an interview to Karen Pierce of the *Independent* that was breathtaking in its arrogance, jaw-droppingly insensitive and baffling in its lack of self-awareness. 'The topics that average people talk about are so small and so beneath me that I can't handle it,' said Eubank, explaining why he didn't socialise. Asked whether the recent car crash weighed heavily on his conscience, Eubank, in full noble victim mode, replied: 'Don't judge me as in accordance with the way you would feel because you are average in comparison to me.' Eubank went on to tell Pierce how proud he was of his Range Rover, revealing he washed it at least once a day. To top it all off, Eubank said of his wife: 'I have often told her: "You are common in comparison to people like me."'

While Eubank complained bitterly about his treatment in the media – 'they've transformed me into some kind of cartoon character' – he provided so much grist for their mills that they struggled to store it all. Eubank had always been a natty dresser – 'that's one thing I've got to give him credit for,' says Nigel Benn, 'he was the sharpest dresser around' – but in the months following his victory over Watson he began to morph into a full-blown grotesque. The genesis of what Eubank likes to call his 'English gentleman look' was a shoot for *Esquire* magazine in May 1992, when he was photographed wearing whipcord jodhpurs and riding boots for the first time. It wasn't long before he was twirling a gold-topped cane and sporting a monocle. Many wondered how a man who complained of having been turned into a cartoon character could carry on in such a manner. Even Eubank sounded confused. 'The media sees me as a commodity for filling their back pages,' he said. 'One who's not real, who's outrageous, a showman. Which I am. But that's only part of me.' During an interview with Jonathan Rendall, Eubank admitted that his public persona was an act. 'What did you think it was?' said Eubank. When Rendall pointed out that Eubank had claimed, on many occasions, that he wasn't playing a character, Eubank replied: 'It is me, but I am a character. OK?'

Some saw Eubank's sartorial outrageousness as another manifestation of his innate courage. But most saw it as more evidence that this man was a total buffoon. Many of his public utterances did little to dispel this view. The *Sunday Times* voted Eubank 'mouth of the year' for 1992, including in its round-up the following quote: 'I'm trying to get into Cambridge University. I want to study psychology. I think I am naturally a master of psychology.' He developed a habit of stalking hotel rooms with his interrogator's dictaphone in his hands, turning it on and off as he pleased, disregarding questions that didn't interest him, making up others that did. He spoke of his desire to be a musician or an artist and quoted Kipling and Nietzsche. In a typically bonkers interview with Robert Chalmers for the *Observer*, Eubank was quoted as saying: '*Thus Spake Zarathustra* is a book I've read . . . bits of.' Chalmers quipped: 'This is almost certainly true; it is the last title that a man with Eubank's pronounced lisp would bring up unless it was absolutely unavoidable. You do not have to listen to Eubank for long to realise that, beyond the hype, he is genuinely – some might say worryingly – unusual.'

'So many of the things he did were so comical, you couldn't take him seriously,' says Kevin Mitchell. 'Everyone was just gobsmacked by his behaviour and a lot of people thought "what a prat". Especially the old guys, they just thought he was ridiculous. The late Dudley Doust was sent to interview him for the *Sunday Times*, very early in Chris's career. Dudley was American and an eccentric character himself. They'd been speaking for about 20 minutes and Dudley said to him: "Tell me, Chris, why are you still wearing your dark glasses? It's night time and you're not a rock star." And Chris said: "That's only your opinion, Mr Doust." I think he took on this Wodehousian role because it was easy to do. But I don't really know where the inspiration came from: did it come from Wodehouse? Muhammad Ali? Or was it just Chris?' Reflecting on his relationship with the British press, Eubank expressed his frustration that these pin-headed sports journalists were unable to grasp what he was desperately trying to convey. 'At any one of my press conferences, 75 per cent of what I said was philosophy,' said Eubank. 'I realise that pure philosophy can be very dry, but even when I tried to tag my theories to an event inside or outside of the ring, they still wouldn't listen.' It is redolent of David Brent's outburst in *The Office*: 'I've got stuff to say – if people would just listen but they won't.'

While Eubank liked people to think his solemn pronouncements were influenced by the world's great thinkers, Ronnie Davies says Eubank was more likely to draw inspiration from Terry-Thomas, the British comic actor who specialised in playing upper-class rogues and bounders. 'He genuinely loved all those old-school characters and comedians,' says Davies. 'We'd go and watch the old black and white films together. I used to say, "That's a lovely quote, use this one from Terry-Thomas".' In time, Davies would develop his own persona, that of a long-suffering butler to his haughty master. While some thought it an undignified role, Davies was only too happy to play along. 'We were in a lift once,' says Kevin Mitchell, 'and Eubank dropped his cane, turned round to Ronnie Davies and said: "Davith, pick up my cane." Ronnie bent down and picked up Eubank's cane and started mouthing obscenities behind Eubank's head and Eubank said: "Davith, I can see what you're saying."' 'Barry Hearn said it was the greatest double act he ever saw,' says Davies. 'I was his food tester and everything. He didn't drink, so I even had to test his trifle to make sure there was no sherry in it. I remember getting off a plane in America and Chris was wearing his cane and his monocle. He said to me: "Davith, get my bag." And this American trainer who was with us said to me: "I wouldn't carry anyone's bag." And I replied: "Listen, pal, I'm the highest-paid bag carrier in the world."'

Other people used to say to me: "He expects too much of you." And I used to say: "Listen, he's given me stuff no one else has ever given me, he gave me the opportunity to train a world champion and he was always loyal."

'I'm 20 years older than him so I suppose it was a father and son thing, but we were also great mates and we did everything together. I always made him laugh, I was always messing about, womanising, getting drunk, and he loved it. I was always there for Eubank, no matter what. I dedicated my life to that man, but he gave me so much in return. I knew the real Chris, and he knew the real Chris, so it didn't really matter what anyone said. People who called him arrogant didn't really know him. He was never the same one day to the next, you never knew what he was going to do or what he was going to come out with. But he was a lovely person, a very misunderstood man.'

Other stories suggest that at least some of Eubank's public posturing was actually carried out with tongue firmly in cheek. 'One day the gate wasn't working at his mansion in Hove,' says Davies, 'so I had to give him a leg-up over a wall. He was wearing a pair of those lovely, hand-made riding boots and I said to him: "Put your boot in my hand and I'll lift you over." And as I was lifting him over he turned to me and said: "Davith – are your handth clean?"'

'You'd be going to a boxing match in a stretch limo,' says Jim McDonnell, 'and he'd say to the driver: "Don't go down this street, there are council properties down this street, go down this street where there are million pound houses." Or he'd get a lift with someone and he'd say: "I can't be seen getting out of an Escort." It was all part of his character, he was having a joke, tongue in cheek, always on a wind-up. Deep inside he's a really nice guy. But whether you loved him or hated him, you couldn't ignore him. He'd be driving around in this Hummer and he'd park it anywhere. I used to say, "Chris, you can't park there". And he'd say, "Jimthki, the facts of the matter are simple: they can't clamp me, the wheels are too thick". And he was right, they couldn't. But he used to get tickets for fun, he was very foolish with money.'

Indeed, as early as 1992 journalists were warning that, despite Eubank's huge earning power in the ring, the money was sure to run out at some point given the extravagance of his spending. Eubank wore £90 Versace underpants, bought himself a Harley Davidson and a mock-Tudor pile in Hove, racked up huge bills on weekend shopping trips to New York, always flying Concorde, and spent £40,000 a year on a suite at London's Grosvenor House Hotel. He would pay for his barber to fly from Manchester to Gatwick, before paying for a taxi down to Brighton, every ten days. 'It costs me £320 per haircut,' boasted Eubank. His relationship with his barber was telling: where just about everyone else saw a head of bog-standard African hair that his wife could have kept kempt with a set of clippers, Eubank saw the finest head of hair in England. In 1993, Eubank won a 'best-kept head' award. Some suspected the award had been made up just so Eubank could vindicate the expenditure, all part of the smoke and mirrors that attended his every move.

If Eubank had a gift for upsetting people, luckily for him it was a lucrative one. And, my, did Eubank upset people. Not long after hiring a top PR company to improve his image, he enraged community leaders in Moss Side by offering himself as a role model to Manchester's disaffected youth. Cynics saw his visit as a thinly veiled attempt to promote an upcoming fight while others found his 'money is freedom' message crass and offensive. Who did this man think he was, strutting about in his jodhpurs and riding boots? Answering the question directly, Eubank said: 'I'm a paragon, a demi-God.' Only a demi-God? Perhaps he was learning some humility, after all. For an interview with the *Daily Mirror* at a plush Brighton hotel, Eubank turned up astride his Harley Davidson. 'Excuse me,' said the hotel receptionist. 'When you asked if you could bring your bike inside, we thought you meant a mountain bike. I'm afraid we can't have a Harley Davidson parked in the hotel foyer.' If all that wasn't enough, he suddenly became bosom buddies with Mike Tyson, who was at the time serving time for rape in an Indiana prison. Eubank told an audience of schoolgirls and mothers at Blackpool Sixth Form College: 'If any of you go to a hotel room at 2am you know sex is on the agenda. I have told him: "Mike, you are innocent."' Whatever the PR company was getting paid, it was far too much. Or maybe not.

Some, if not all, of this behaviour would have been forgiven if Eubank was delivering between the ropes. But the respect he had earned with his impossibly courageous displays against Benn and Watson began to ebb away as he reeled off a succession of underwhelming and sometimes controversial victories. Eubank's first defence of his WBO super-middleweight crown was against South Africa's Thulani 'Sugar Boy' Malinga, five months after his fight against Watson. The durable Malinga was expected to provide limited opposition but took Eubank all the way before dropping a split decision. Eubank had Malinga down in the fifth round but failed to finish the job. Sage observers saw it as evidence that Eubank's killer instinct had been significantly diminished by the tragedy of White Hart Lane. Wrote Harry Mullan: 'The fact that a man who, on his best nights, was a fierce enough competitor to stop men of the quality of Nigel Benn and Michael Watson was this time pushed to his limits by a fighter of Malinga's limited accomplishment suggests that the events of last September have left a permanent scar on this complex, spiky individual.'

'In the first Benn fight, when Benn was obviously running out of petrol, you didn't see Eubank strutting around the ring,' says Barry Hearn, 'you saw him go in there and tear his head off, finish the fight as quick as he could, get the job done. And in the second Eubank–Watson fight, when Eubank went down for the first time in his career, Watson was six, seven rounds in front at the time, he'd bashed Eubank up. But Eubank just stood there and motioned him forward as if to say: "I'm still standing, you've got to finish the job." And he hit Watson with that right uppercut, which was the perfect punch, with terrible implications. But after that fight, he never was the same fighter, I'd say he was about 50 per cent worse. Every time he had someone in trouble, he never finished the job. It wasn't from the fear of doing it to someone else again, which might make Chris sound like a nicer person, it was actually the fear of someone doing it to him.' Says Ronnie Davies: 'He never said so to me but that Watson fight took something from him. To this day, we have never mentioned that fight.'

Next was a third-round knockout of veteran American John Jarvis, a man who had fought once in the previous 20 months, before Eubank outpointed former two-time world title challenger Ron Essett in Quinta do Lago, Portugal. 'I would struggle to recall a world title fight in which the boxers showed less commitment,' said Harry Mullan. One tabloid labelled it 'The Snore on the Shore'. While it was clear that Eubank's punishing schedule was taking its toll, he ploughed on regardless. Less than three months after his win over Essett, Eubank fought the wily American Tony Thornton in Glasgow and was the beneficiary of another controversial decision. It wasn't so much that Eubank was awarded the decision that raised eyebrows, it was the fact that two of the judges had the champion winning by five and three rounds. Two months later, Eubank was back in the ring, beating Juan Carlos Gimenez on a tedious night in Manchester. Wrote Mullan: 'His road show is desperately becoming a boringly repetitive routine which is eroding the reserves of credibility Eubank accumulated so painfully against the likes of Nigel Benn and Michael Watson.'

A few sports journalists, however, enjoyed seeing the sport of boxing and its chroniclers being given the runaround by Eubank, particularly Simon Barnes of *The Times*. Barnes was, and still is, openly disdainful of boxing – 'boxing is not a metaphor, it is a death duel' – refusing to see any nobility in two men smacking each other round a ring for the pleasure of a baying audience. 'The boxing establishment tends to despise Eubank,' said Barnes, about whom the rumour was once put about that he spent the duration of a heavyweight world title bout hiding under a table, which he denies. 'He cannot be all bad, then. He has exploited boxing and the boxing writers. He has dragged them out again and again to watch him knock down the next victim for the next fat pay cheque. When they tell him his behaviour flies in the face of boxing ethics, he just laughs. Boxing ethics? An oxymoron if ever there was one.'

Barnes was right in his assessment, up to a point. There was an honesty in Eubank that made many in boxing distinctly uneasy. Whereas most boxers tended to go along with talk of the glory of the game, Eubank saw boxing only in terms of financial gain. And if there was no glory and only financial gain, then boxing, as defined by Eubank, ceased to be a sport. But if the boxing writers were so disgusted by the manner in which Eubank was carrying on, why did they continue to give him the oxygen of publicity? They did so because they had greater forces working upon them, namely the owners and editors of their respective publications and the Great British Public. Most boxing writers, and certainly grey heads such as Harry Mullan, Hugh McIlvanney and Ken Jones, did detect a certain dignity in boxing and it vexed them that Eubank brought what they loved into disrepute. Jones, in particular, railed against 'the gullibility' of the public. Furthermore, they felt let down by Eubank, whom they believed possessed genuine talent but had chosen to fritter it away on a succession of low-grade title defences. But they also knew that Eubank brought attention to their sport, sold news-papers, boosted viewing figures and put bums on seats in arenas across the land. Mullan would probably rather have been reporting on an amateur tournament in a drafty school hall than on Eubank's victory over Juan Carlos Gimenez in an arena in Manchester, but these were the commercial realities he and the rest of the boxing fraternity were dealing with.

However, when only 4000 people turned up to see Eubank easily outpoint the 35-year-old Lindell Holmes at Earls Court, it looked like the road show had finally run out of steam. Only when some sustained booing kicked in after the eighth round did a hitherto dull fight come to life and, even then, Eubank's assaults lasted barely a couple of seconds at a time. The lack-lustre nature of his latest victory had journalists asking when, if ever, Eubank would risk mixing it with the division's more exalted names from the other side of the Atlantic. More worryingly for Eubank, ITV seemed to have had enough. 'We'll certainly find enough for a big unification fight with either WBA champion Michael Nunn or the IBF's James Toney,' said ITV head of sport Bob Burrows, 'and certainly

Nigel Benn – but not for the type of fights he has been having.' Under fire, Hearn claimed he had approached Toney and Nunn but both had turned Eubank down. 'They said Eubank is too awkward,' said an irritated Hearn. 'Tell me, who do I get?' The name of exciting young American Tim Littles was thrown Hearn's way. Hearn, not surprisingly, was not sold.

Asked about Eubank, Al Braverman, an antique match-maker for Don King, was moved to recall a conversation he once had with an unnamed British promoter. 'Can he box?' said the promoter. 'Just a little bit,' said Braverman. 'Is he strong?' 'Only for a round or so.' 'Can he punch?' 'Not enough to worry you.' 'I'm not happy about it – sounds as though the fella could be dangerous.' 'What are you looking for,' sighed Braverman, 'a fighter without arms?' For his part, Eubank really wasn't bothered what anyone thought about the quality of his opposition. 'Why should I care?' said Eubank. 'I'm the richest super-middleweight on earth. I fight for money, not glory. I make no apologies for boxing people I believe I can beat.'

'Chris tried to make sure his opponents fit his style and gave him the best possible opportunity,' says David Haye, 'and as a businessman that's what you've got to do. He wouldn't have been paid much more for fighting Herol Graham than some Mexican road sweeper and would have had a far harder time doing it. What would have been the point in that? Chris Eubank wasn't shy to let his promoter know what he wanted, and in a business sense that made perfect sense. He was the boss, he was in charge, and he told Barry Hearn what was what. OK, some of his performances weren't the most spec-tacular, but it wasn't about that, it was about him. Nigel Benn was almost always in spectacular fights but the difference was

Chris Eubank did it the way he wanted to do it: if he wanted to walk around for two minutes of the round, tapping his gloves, posing and pouting, that's what he'd do. People hated it but they were captivated by it. And it took balls to go out and do some of the stuff he did.'

'Chris knew he was a decent boxer but he wasn't James Toney or Roy Jones,' says Jim McDonnell, 'and he was never going to put his arse on the line against those boys. Domestically, against Benn, Watson and Steve Collins, he felt maybe he could be in a 50–50 fight or maybe have the edge. He used to say to Barry, "I want to go into the ring knowing I'm 80–20 to win it, minimum 60–40. Never 50–50". He was getting great money from ITV, and later from Sky, so he wasn't going to risk those pay cheques by fighting people of the magnitude of Toney or Jones. It wasn't that Chris was scared, not fighting certain people had nothing to do with his courage. It was just that boxing to him was not about being brave, it was about making the most pound notes for the least risk.'

In January 1993, Herol Graham announced his retirement from the ring. In his *Boxing News* 'obituary', Harry Mullan wrote: 'It seems downright unfair that Chris Eubank, a man with the honesty to admit he wanted no part of Herol, should have won ten 'world' title fights while Graham couldn't win one. But that is the nature of this sport, which rewards its winners and punishes its losers like no other.' Graham decided he no longer had the required spark after being outpointed for a second time by Sumbu Kalambay and stopped by Bradford journeyman Frank Grant. But he was also worn down by his fruitless pursuit of Chris Eubank and Nigel Benn, which was like attempting to catch lightning in a bottle. The irony being, they would have said much the same about Graham.

'Whoever Chris was fighting, I would make sure I was there afterwards, in the same room,' says Graham. 'So people would say: "Chris, here's Herol, why don't you box him?" I'd be at the back of the room – "Chris, hello, it's Herol!" – but he'd never acknowledge me. How can you call yourself a true champion when you spend your whole career sidestepping people? Saying things like: "I don't want that fight because I'll have to work too hard. He's a mover, he's not a fighter. He's a boxer, a runner." No way would Eubank have got in with guys like Mike McCallum or Sumbu Kalambay or Julian Jackson. Look what Mike McCallum did to Michael Watson, Mike McCallum would have taken Eubank and Benn apart. How would I have beaten Chris Eubank? I would have just gone in the ring! Tap, tap, tap, move around and frustrate him, just like I did with the rest of the guys.

'I always tried to get the fight on with Nigel as well, but he would never want to know. I used to say to him: "If you're the best, I'll box you." So he made sure never to say he was the best. He'd just tell me: "You're a runner and I'm a fighter. Why would I want to box you?" I would have been Nigel Benn's worst nightmare, I would have plagued him. Big puncher he was, he would have had to come and chase me. Against a puncher, I'm off, I'm running away, I'm going to torment you like you're the cat and I'm the mouse, and I win in the end. It was too scary for them, much too scary. They knew I'd belittle them in the ring. Michael Watson was a better fighter than both Benn and Eubank but he didn't want to fight me either. He could have had the fight any time, any place, anywhere. I was the one squealing, saying: "Let's fight, and if you beat me you've shown you can beat a good, flashy guy – a matador." But he wouldn't go for it because I was too big an obstacle. The only way any of them could get rid of me was by stepping over me. Which they did, the three of them together. I didn't mind in one sense, in that I knew I was better than them anyway.'

CHAPTER ELEVEN
Somehow, I remember

While Chris Eubank was hogging the headlines, whether through his courageous feats in the ring, his outlandish outfits or his endless philosophising, Nigel Benn was rebuilding his shattered career. Not for the first time. Only this time he would do so without the help of Ambrose Mendy, with whom he had become terminally disillusioned. 'Ambrose was a great promoter and a great businessman,' says Benn. 'He could have gone far, been bigger than Frank Warren, bigger than all of them. If he'd kept his head right.' Instead, Mendy was imprisoned for fraud in May 1991, shortly after Benn's knockout of Robbie Sims, his first fight since his defeat by Eubank the previous November. Benn, who served as a character witness at Mendy's court case and claims he paid Mendy's lawyers' fees, decided it was the right time to walk away.

'It was one of the best times in my life with Ambrose,' says Benn. 'I learned a lot from him. I just wish he hadn't carried on the way he did. Sometimes people try to build their own platform and convince people they made me who I am. And people get greedy and spoil it for themselves, that's what it boiled down to. At the time, Ambrose had a big house and I was still living in my terraced house. But when I left Ambrose

I went from the three-bedroom terraced house to a six-bedroom mansion. I started lining my pockets. He was a big part of my life, but as long as I was with him I hadn't really hatched. When I left him I was able to flap my wings and take flight.'

Benn's defeat by Eubank had the press men falling over themselves to write off his career. But Benn's seventh-round knockout of Sims, a former world title contender and the half-brother of Marvin Hagler, had at least some of them believing again. 'Nigel Benn is still very much a force to be reckoned with in the world,' said *The Times*'s Srikumar Sen, who had been so scathing of Benn following his loss to Eubank. Benn, hinting at his coming split with Mendy, said: 'Let Chris Eubank be the bad boy now. I don't want to be known as the "Dark Destroyer". I have got all that aggression out of my system.' Sims, who had never been knocked out or stopped in a 42-fight professional career, no doubt disagreed. Certainly Barry Hearn thought Benn still carried enough threat to form one third of a British 'three kings', which the thrusting promoter thought could rival the Leonard-Hagler-Duran-Hearns quartet that thrilled American boxing audiences throughout the 1980s. To this end, Hearn signed Benn on a fight-by-fight agreement and promised him the winner of Eubank–Watson I and 40 per cent of a £2 million purse.

The controversial outcome of the first fight between Eubank and Watson frustrated Benn's ambitions before the tragic outcome of the second meant he would have to spend even longer lurking in the wings, away from the limelight. Either side of Eubank–Watson II, Benn forced a fourth-round stoppage of Kid Milo, against whom Eubank had toiled the previous year, before stepping up to super-middleweight to fight Lenzie Morgan, a journeyman American, whom he easily outpointed in ten. There followed third-round knock-outs of Hector Lescano and Dan Sherry, the same Dan Sherry who had given Eubank fits 12 months earlier. Hearn had promised the winner of Benn–Sherry a rematch with Eubank, but Eubank had other ideas, even though Benn was the WBO's number one contender. 'Who's to say he has really changed his spots?' said Eubank. 'All the needle pricks he has given me don't endear him to me. I don't care what Nigel Benn thinks. Public demand means nothing to me. The only thing I have to do is stay black and die.' With Eubank still refusing to budge on his ludicrous demand for a £1.65 million payday and the WBO threatening to strip him of the title, Hearn had virtually written the fight off before Benn's contest against Thulani 'Sugar Boy' Malinga. Ironically – or naturally, given Eubank's business-led approach to boxing – Benn's narrow points victory over Malinga, whom Eubank had beaten on a split decision, rather altered the landscape. 'Judged on this perform-ance,' wrote Harry Mullan, 'Benn would fit comfortably into Eubank's career strategy of handpicking opponents he knows he can beat, in order to extract maximum money for minimum pain.'

Mullan was proved right. Eubank suddenly relented and agreed to fight Benn again, with September 1992 given as the provisional date. However, when WBC title-holder Mauro Galvano agreed to give Benn a shot that same October, Benn was dropped from the WBO rankings. But a fight against Galvano in the Italian's backyard was a gamble Benn was more than willing to take. By not agreeing to a rematch earlier, Eubank seemed to have miscalculated. If Benn beat Galvano it would greatly increase his bargaining power in negotiations with Eubank, especially given that the WBC title was still far more highly regarded than Eubank's WBO crown. If Benn lost, he would surely retire, robbing Eubank of the biggest payday out there. And there were plenty of people who thought Benn would lose.

Indeed, tales of Italian shenanigans were legion in the lead-up to the fight. 'When I came to Italy with Lloyd Honeyghan and he knocked out Gianfranco Rosi, they took half a minute to count to ten,' said Benn's new trainer Jimmy Tibbs. Scottish flyweight Pat Clinton was given a set of wrongly calibrated scales before his European title challenge against Salvatore Fanni in Cagliari, thought he was 2lb over the limit and ended up weighing in 2lb under. The gym gossip was supported by the facts: of the 30 Italy v Great Britain championship clashes at either European or world level which had been settled by the judges, only two had gone the visitor's way, including Clinton's. Mickey Duff was particularly concerned, given Galvano's reputation for running: 'Beating Galvano in Italy is an impossibility,' said Duff. 'You've got more chance of beating the Pope.'

Benn was unfazed. While he publicly disowned his well-worn moniker after the split with Mendy, the satin-look 'Dark Destroyer' tracksuits were back for the Galvano fight. As was the dark destructiveness. 'He was very intimidating towards his opponents,' says Tibbs, 'and he frightened the life out of Galvano in Italy. At the doctor's meeting a couple of days before the fight Nigel jumped up out of his seat and said: "You having a go?" And Galvano was on his toes down the road. I thought, "Well, that's one round to us anyway". Nigel didn't mean anything personal by it and I didn't even know it was going to happen. But at the weigh-in, Galvano had about 20 minders around him.'

In front of 2000 rabid locals in a converted ice rink on the outskirts of Rome, the 28-year-old challenger punched Galvano from pillar to post from the opening bell, cutting the champion over the eye in the second round and persuading him, in the strongest terms, to quit before the start of the fourth. Galvano's team, true to type, lobbied for a technical draw and thought they would get it. But American referee Joe Cortez was having none of it, insisting the injury had been caused by a scything right hand from Benn. After five minutes of tense consultations, Benn was declared the winner and the WBC super-middleweight champion. When the verdict finally came, an elated Benn struggled to hold back tears, before dedicating his victory to Michael Watson. 'After Nigel beat Galvano,' says Watson, 'he came round to my house in tears and said: "This belt is yours." I love Nigel, he's a true gentleman.'

'I was one of the only British fighters to go over to Italy to win a world title,' says Benn. 'And the WBC belt was the crème de la crème. Chris was there, ringside with his wife. And he knew he had the fourth division belt. No, that's disrespectful, but the WBC was the premier belt. And once I got the WBC belt, I didn't have to go looking for him, he had to chase me.' Spying Eubank, hiding behind a pair of shades, Benn leant through the ropes and made his old rival a challenge. 'Now we can do business,' said Benn. 'Let's do it,' said Eubank, looking a little uneasy. A month later, Eubank opined: 'Benn has lost his bottle. All that's left is empty talk. I honestly believe it's off.'

Instead, Benn had signed up to fight Welshman Nicky Piper, an upright and deliberate boxer with an IQ of 153. Piper was not even in the WBC's top ten and rated fifth in Britain and 14th in Europe. But his promoter Frank Warren, never a man to let a set of pesky rankings get in the way of a lucrative domestic match-up, catapulted his man into contention. Despite Warren's machinations, there were those in the media who thought a Piper victory would be a good thing. 'British boxing is rudderless and warlord-led,' wrote Frank Keating in the *Guardian*. 'Benn's flaunting swagger and Chris Eubank's sneering strut in the face of no-hopers is allowed to continue unchecked. And much else besides, all dancing in front of the spectre of Michael Watson in his wheelchair.' The marauding Benn proved that an IQ of 153 is about as useful in a boxing match as boxing gloves made of blancmange, bludgeoning Piper to defeat in the 11th round. Three months later Benn beat Galvano in a rematch in Glasgow, outpointing the reluctant Italian after a frustrating 12 rounds.

When Eubank announced his intention to challenge America's big guns at the start of 1993, few believed he would be true to his word. 'I'm prepared to deal with James Toney, Michael Nunn and Iran Barkley,' said Eubank. 'Last year, I made it clear I would pick and choose. I have done this. Now it's time for me to prove myself number one.' A month later, Eubank toiled to victory over Lindell Holmes, who had fought once in 19 months, before signing to fight Northern Irishman Ray Close, who nobody had ever mistaken for Toney, Nunn or Barkley. Mindful of ITV's growing disgruntlement and the inconvenient fact that Benn had only one fight remaining on his Matchroom contract, Hearn began hatching a rematch between Benn and Eubank in haste. But with both fighters demanding £1 million, pulling together enough cash to make it happen was proving something of a nightmare, even by boxing's labyrinthine standards.

'I took a decent enough punt on Eubank–Benn II because I didn't have a TV deal and didn't have a venue, but I knew the fight had to be made,' says Hearn. 'But I was sitting there thinking: "I've lobbed out two million quid here, better go and find a venue. That's going to cost me another three-quarters of a million. I've then got to promote it . . ." All in all, it amounted to quite a lot of money. Anyway, the phone went and it was Don King, who said: "Congratulations on making the fight, I'm going to be your partner." And I said: "Are you really, what makes you think that?" And he said: "Well, I'm going to give you $2 million in overseas TV." Considering I had about $50,000 in overseas TV sales at the time, I thought that sounded like a bloody good idea – there was no way I could lose any money.' So far, so very convenient. According to Hearn, however, King was soon pulling in the favours. Says Hearn: 'Don phoned up and said: "Can we give my friend Frank Warren 10 per cent of the fight?" Basically, it was a hand-out. I said: "Don, I don't really care – you give him five per cent, I'll give him five per cent, Frank's a nice kid, he can do this and that for us." So Don took 45 per cent, I took 45 per cent and Frank took 10 per cent. The show was going to sell 47,000 tickets, it was going to make millions. Everybody was going to have a very nice touch indeed.'

Warren, you will not be surprised to learn, has wildly different recollections of his involvement. 'Barry Hearn is full of shit,' says Warren. 'The fact of the matter is, he could not get a British TV deal. Trevor East was ITV's deputy head of sport at the time and I met at his house over the Easter bank holiday weekend. We then had a call with Greg Dyke, who was head of ITV, and based upon the winner fighting Michael Nunn, ITV agreed a record £1 million rights fee. As a result of delivering the TV money, I received a percentage of the promotion. If I hadn't done the TV rights deal, there would not have been a promotion. Giving me a hand-out? He's got some fucking cheek.'

Contemporary newspaper reports reveal Warren was indeed

involved in the making of the fight at a far earlier stage than Hearn now likes to admit. Reluctant referee East, meanwhile, confirms Warren's version of events is the more accurate. 'Barry's recollection is unfair,' he gets carried away with himself,' says East, who followed Warren to Sky Sports in 1995 and ended up as the corporation's deputy director. 'Frank came to my house and we did a deal for the fight. Frank's relationship with ITV was as strong as anyone's and had been since 1981. And if Barry was being honest, he'd tell you that the whole Benn–Eubank–Watson shebang was my idea because I was producing the boxing on ITV at the time. Barry didn't know what to do because he couldn't deliver any credible American opponents. I remember it vividly: I was driving round Shepherd's Bush Green, talking on the phone, and I said, "Fuck the Americans, we've got enough fighters to create a massive championship between what we've got".'

Another key witness to the making of Benn–Eubank II was Andy Ayling. Ayling worked for Hearn for four years until being made redundant at the end of 1992. However, Ayling was then employed by Eubank as his publicist on a personal basis before joining forces with Warren in June 1993. Ayling, therefore, has a valuable 360-degree take on events. 'First of all, can you imagine anyone ringing you up and saying: "Can you give your closest rival 10 per cent of your business?"' says Ayling, who is now event manager for Frank Warren Promotions. 'Barry Hearn's story is complete nonsense.

'What actually happened was in late 1992, Barry and Frank, along with Barney Eastwood, announced a deal to put big fights on ITV. And around that time, people were already talking about a rematch between Benn and Eubank. In May 1993, I was doing a bit of PR work for Lennox Lewis in Vegas, for his fight against Tony Tucker. Barry and Frank were out there meeting with Don King, trying to put together Benn–Eubank II. I knew that's what they were out there for because I was working for Eubank at the time. Barry couldn't get the money from ITV that was needed to make the fight happen, so he asked Frank: "Can you speak to ITV and see what they can do?" Frank then spoke to Trevor East and the only way ITV could justify paying the sort of money needed was if Frank got Don King involved. Don brought Michael Nunn into the equation and the belief was that there would be some sort of tournament to unify the super-middleweight title. King brought on board Showtime from America, Frank got the money from ITV and the fight was split three ways.'

East introduced Hearn and Warren in the mid-1980s, when Hearn was still very much a snooker man and Warren was carving out a reputation as British boxing's promotional kingpin. By the end of the decade Warren, a former solicitor's clerk and Smithfield porter, was branching out and had founded his own venue, the London Arena. However, Warren's business empire was brought crashing to the ground when he was shot outside the Broadway Theatre in Barking in November 1989. A deal to secure the future of the London Arena consequently fell through because, Warren claims, nobody in the City particularly fancied doing business with a man who had been gunned down by a masked assailant on the streets of East London. In 1992 the London Arena went into receivership. Meanwhile, Hearn had got the Eubank bandwagon rolling. 'Hearn benefited first from me getting rid of the Mickey Duff–Terry Lawless cartel and second from me getting shot,' says Warren. 'I had to come back with something.'

Warren limped on with London featherweight Colin McMillan as his headline act but when McMillan lost his WBO title in September 1992, there was no one standing by to replace him. But in 1993, Warren got wind that Benn's contract with Hearn was about to expire, contacted Hearn about making Benn–Eubank II and negotiated the deal with ITV. Warren was back in the game. In the years since, Hearn and Warren have been best of business enemies, cautious business partners and courtroom rivals, but East believes they could have been so much more than that. 'I told them way back then, if they could get their act together, they could virtually run British sport between them,' says East. 'But Frank being Frank and Barry being Barry, they couldn't make it work. Ever since that day, never the twain shall meet. Let's just say working on Benn–Eubank II was an interesting juggling act.'

King's major concern had been the heavyweight division since his co-promotion of 'The Rumble in the Jungle' between Muhammad Ali and George Foreman in 1974. But King lost his grip on boxing's traditional blue-riband weight class when Mike Tyson was defeated by James 'Buster' Douglas in 1990, before Tyson's imprisonment for rape further dented his Machiavellian ambitions. In November 1992, King promoted Lennox Lewis's first defence of his WBC title against his own fighter, Tony Tucker, only for Lewis to foil King's plans to get his talons back in the division. Until Tyson was released, King would just have to swallow his pride, deal with the resulting indigestion, and focus his attention on the smaller men, guys like Eubank and Benn. 'Barry Hearn told me these two guys feel so badly towards each other that they would have got it on for nothing,' said King. 'I couldn't let that happen.'

King was memorably described by Tyson as 'a wretched, slimy, reptilian mother fucker – a bad man who would kill his mother for a dollar'. Larry Holmes said of King: 'The reason he wears his hair so funny is to hide the horns.' But Benn was more than willing to do business, however big the slice of the pie King would wind up getting. 'Why deal with the little rats, why not deal with the big rats?' says Benn. 'I'd rather deal with Don King because if he pays me £1 million, I'm happy. If he pays himself £20 million, I don't care. I didn't get involved in the negotiations, I just knew what I wanted and that's what I got. A lot of people in boxing get consumed with what other people are getting. But £1 million did me just fine.' Adds Hearn: 'I got Eubank and Benn together and said: "This is the deal, if you want a million quid each, Don King's going to be my partner and he wants both of you to join him, win or lose, and the winner has to fight Michael Nunn." And they both said, "Fair enough, we've had a great run together, it's been fun".'

Warren, however, says neither Benn nor Eubank were aware of the supposed clause in their contracts which stated the winner would have to fight Nunn. 'Don King's money and the involvement of American TV was all predicated on the promise that the winner would fight Michael Nunn,' says Warren. 'But when I announced the winner would be fighting Nunn, Benn's manager, Peter DeFreitas, phoned me from Tenerife and said: "What's all this about Michael Nunn? We don't know nothing about it." I said: "That's what we were told, that's what Hearn said." But Eubank knew nothing about it either. King and I challenged Hearn, who said it was nonsense, but DeFreitas was adamant and asked Hearn to produce the contract to fight Nunn. He never did.'

With the rematch that everybody wanted to see apparently done and dusted, the last thing the key brokers wanted to see was Eubank or Benn come a cropper in their respective tune-up bouts. However, it very nearly happened when Ray Close fought Eubank on 21 May 1993. Wrote Harry Mullan in the *Sunday Times*: 'If there was any justice in boxing, and we know

now there isn't, unsung Irish challenger Ray Close should have ended Chris Eubank's astonishing, and always controversial, reign as WBO super-middleweight champion.' Instead, only judge Dave Parris saw what Mullan saw, scoring the fight 116–113 for Close. Parris's fellow Englishman Roy Francis had it 115–115, while Denmark's Torben Hansen, a late replacement, had it 116–112 for Eubank. Only Eubank's 11th-round knockdown of Close had salvaged a draw.

'My man was robbed,' said the 24-year-old's manager Barney Eastwood. 'Ray is a child in comparison to Eubank's experience. He showed up Eubank as a phoney who's been fighting bums.' In an attempt to explain the often eccentric scoring of his fights, Eubank said: 'The judges unavoidably take into account charisma as well as points. You should look haughty, confident, arrogant, brave, superior.' He could have been describing Hulk Hogan. It was Eubank conceding what many had suspected, that professional boxing at the elite level, at least when Eubank was involved, had morphed into a grotesque mirror image of professional wrestling. A few days after his near-thing against Close, Eubank, apparently forgetting he was supposed to be fighting Benn, announced plans to fight an unknown 36-year-old Italian via Zaire called Mwehu Beya. To the purists, it was more proof that boxing was in complete meltdown: this wasn't WWF, it was a whole lot madder than that.

A month after Eubank's victory over Close, Benn kept his side of the bargain with a relatively straightforward knockout of South London's Lou Gent. Benn had Gent over three times in the third round and twice early in the fourth before the fight was stopped. Although Benn, as was his fashion, took a fair few lumps along the way. With the way clear for the rematch between Benn and Eubank, the phoney war started in earnest. 'We are being paid £1 million, but I under-stand Eubank is on considerably less,' announced Benn's 'advisor' Peter DeFreitas. In early July, further details of the bout were publicised. The first world title unification bout between two British fighters would take place at Old Trafford on 9 October, guaranteeing a paying audience of more than 40,000. Various television deals, including the crucial link-up with American cable network Showtime, meant more than 100 million would be watching around the globe. 'HELL'S ANGELS FIGHT OF HATE!' screamed the *Daily Mirror*. 'HIT-MEN AT WAR!' It was as if that terrible night at White Hart Lane had never happened.

At the press conference to officially announce the show – which had been given the tagline 'Judgement Day' – things turned ludicrous. Eubank, astride his gleaming Harley Davidson and decked out in cream jodhpurs, riding boots, a striped waistcoat and Biggles-style goggles, was given a police escort to the doors of London's Waldorf hotel. Once inside, he recited a pre-prepared statement, gravely announcing that he would not be engaging in any verbal jousting of an unsa-voury nature. At one point in his rambling speech, Eubank compared the agonies of a boxing match to childbirth. In an attempt to bait his rival, Benn referred to the purse split, it having been confirmed that he would be receiving £1 million to Eubank's £850,000. 'One per cent of something is better than 100 per cent of nothing,' said Eubank, cryptically. 'Contrary to what you may think, I am not a greedy man.' That Eubank was so resigned to getting the thin end of the deal seems odd, until you discover he actually earned more than Benn. 'Nigel always said he wanted more money than Chris Eubank because he felt he had the premier belt and was the bigger draw,' says Andy Ayling, 'it was always a pissing contest between them. And Nigel thought he did get more money than Chris. But what Nigel never found out was that Chris was getting his purse paid net of all the sanction fees, while he was going to be paid gross of all the sanction fees. So actually Nigel made less than Eubank.'

Having failed to rile Eubank at the press conference, Benn, apparently still hankering after the old times, took to the airwaves. 'There is hatred there, so much hatred,' said Benn in a radio interview away from the dais. 'Not for the boxer, just for the person. I will do literally anything to beat that guy – I want to punish him.' At a press conference at Old Trafford a few days later, things heated up. Eubank upbraided Benn for bringing hate into the equation and called him a 'snide' for having done so behind his back. Benn rose to his feet, pressed his face an inch away from Eubank's and said: 'I just don't like you – does that satisfy you?' Eubank, however, was sticking to the moral high ground. 'As far as I'm concerned, this is not a grudge match,' he said. 'This phrase Judgement Day . . . it's ugly. Somehow, I remember September 1991.' For once, Eubank seemed to be the only man speaking sense.

In March 1993, Michael Watson made his first public appearance since being battered into a coma by Chris Eubank. The celebrity football match at Highbury, home of Watson's beloved Arsenal, was organised by Ambrose Mendy and the *Daily Mirror*-backed Michael Watson Appeal Fund. Watson, dressed in an Arsenal shirt, a leather jacket and a baggy black beret, was wheeled onto the pitch by Gunners striker Kevin Campbell while thousands chanted his name. In the 20 months since his life had changed irrevocably, Watson had received a visit from Muhammad Ali, 15,000 get-well cards, a rosary from the Pope and thousands of pounds in donations. Eubank was also a regular visitor, although the celebrities who flocked to Watson's bedside during the early days of his recovery melted away like snow on a warm, spring day.

To the 20,000 packed into Highbury that afternoon, Watson must have appeared as a miracle: wasn't this man supposed to be good for nothing? Useless? A vegetable? So they had been told. But the miracle was far from complete. Not long after his emotional reappearance, Watson left Homerton Hospital and returned to his home in Chingford, where the darkness descended. Away from the hospital and the constant treatment and rehabilitation that gave his life purpose, Watson felt trapped in his own living room, whose walls seemed to creep ever closer as the days crawled past. 'When I went home,' says Watson, 'I had to deal with having lost everything. It was during this terrible time that I fully realised just how far I had fallen.' While Nigel Benn was pounding the rarefied mountain trails of Tenerife and Chris Eubank was engaging in war after war in his gym, Watson was climbing the stairs to his bedroom, five carers in tow. Like Edmund Hillary and his Sherpas scaling the foothills of Everest. And every bit as intrepid.

CHAPTER TWELVE
Judgement Day

The build-up to the second fight between Benn and Eubank dwarfed the first in terms of hype and hoopla, to the extent it was the most eagerly anticipated rematch in British boxing history. While only Benn's lightly regarded WBO middleweight belt was on the line for their first contest three years earlier, two world title belts were up for grabs in the return: Benn's WBC super-middleweight strap and Eubank's WBO equivalent. While the first fight was largely a domestic affair, the second fight was sold to 60 countries. Back on the home front, it was feared the all-British heavyweight world title fight between Lennox Lewis and Frank Bruno, which took place at Cardiff Arms Park the week before Benn–Eubank II, might deflect attention. But those fears proved unfounded, with an estimated £30,000 being taken at UK box offices daily and 40,000 tickets sold four days before the fight. Lewis–Bruno, meanwhile, drew a comparatively meagre 25,000 spectators. It was open to conjecture whether Benn–Eubank II would set an attendance record for a post-War boxing match in Britain – some claimed Bruce Woodcock and Lee Savold fought in front of 50,000 at White City in 1950 – but it was a monster promotion nonetheless. 'This is a grudge fight that goes beyond the realms of reality,' said Don King, never one to underplay things. 'There is bad blood, the television sets will be popping with excitement. This fight is an atomic bomb waiting to explode.'

More level heads weren't so sure. Rematches in boxing, like film sequels, rarely live up to the hype, whatever amounts of money are thrown at them. Not even Ali–Frazier II was able to come anywhere close to the sheer ferocity and intensity of their first encounter, with both fighters reluctant to tread the path of danger and unfathomable pain they had been down before and which remained scored on their respective memories. Although, to be fair to the both of them, they made up for it in the third, the brutal 'Thrilla in Manila'. In addition, many believed the rematch between Benn and Eubank was a couple of years too late and that three years of hard campaigning had dulled the edges of both fighters, particularly Eubank. Indeed, Eubank was proving to be the imponderable part of the equation. While Benn had kept his competitive instincts sharp with his rise back up through the ranks, Eubank had engaged in a succession of world title defences which were barely worthy of the name. His schedule had been relentless, but the opposition had not. 'It raises the possibility that Eubank has been so far removed from the grimmer demands of prize-fighting,' wrote Ken Jones in the *Independent*, 'that he might find it difficult to cope with Benn's swarming attacks.' Furthermore, the lacklustre nature of many of Eubank's engagements since his tragic fight against Watson strongly suggested he had not come to terms with the inner torment and that his fire had been doused.

Still, while Benn had been the red-hot favourite before their first fight, Eubank had far more backers second time around, for good reasons. Eubank, a naturally bigger man than Benn, was widely believed to be better suited to the higher weight, and given that the weigh-in was set for the evening before the fight, there was every chance Eubank would effectively enter the ring as a light-heavy. Furthermore, while Benn had continued to stop opponents as a super-middleweight, his victories had been harder earned than when he was eight pounds lighter: Benn had to grind down Nicky Piper and Mauro Galvano in their second fight, before engaging Lou Gent in a high-risk brawl. And both Galvano and Gent had wobbled him, meaning the question mark over his chin remained. 'Galvano's reputation as a puncher more or less corresponds with Switzerland's as a naval power,' wrote Ken Jones. Crucially, although some of Eubank's recent performances had left plenty to be desired, his desire had never been found wanting on the really big occasion, as anyone who had seen his first fight against Benn and his second fight against Watson would have attested to. 'When I fought Nigel last time,' said Eubank, 'I said to myself, "Never again". But I haven't got that same kick in my last seven fights. I almost relish the thought of taking one of those big punches.'

Despite the enormity of the rematch, there remained a vocal minority of boxing writers for whom Benn–Eubank II was little more than a sideshow and who were adamant the real super-middleweight champion was either IBF title-holder James Toney or WBA title-holder Michael Nunn. In addition, a poll carried out by *Boxing News* revealed that fewer than 10 per cent of its readers thought either Benn or Eubank was the real champion at 168lbs. But at a press conference in New York two months before Benn–Eubank II, nominally to announce a series of fights to unify the super-middleweight division, Eubank managed to steal the show while upsetting just about everyone present, except perhaps his promoters. First, Eubank grabbed the microphone and demanded all questions be directed to him under 'parliamentary practice', which triggered catcalls and jeers. Benn and Nunn stood up to confront Eubank, before Benn and Terry Norris, the WBC light-middleweight champion, left the dais in disgust. 'We will all need time to understand this young man,' said King.

Nevertheless, even the most sceptical commentators were able to live with the tenuous claims made by the promoters and recognise Benn–Eubank II for what it was, a potentially thrilling grudge match between Britain's two most compelling boxers of the modern age. Reflecting on the attraction of the fight for the British public, Harry Mullan wrote in *Boxing News*: 'British fight fans don't particularly care what label is stuck on a match, so long as it promises the kind of action and thrills which this pairing virtually guarantees.' Even Ken Jones was sold: 'If the contest between Nigel Benn and Chris Eubank at Old Trafford does not carry the global importance spuriously claimed by the promoters there can be no doubt that it harbours the harshest realities of professional boxing.'

Shortly before the rematch between Benn and Eubank at Old Trafford, both boxers appeared on an 'audience with' special with Jonathan Ross, tagged 'Best of Enemies'. Outside of Eubank's spectacle attachments and the presence of some of the more fringe elements of the early-to-mid '90s British celebrity scene (Windsor Davies, Linda Lusardi, Tony Slattery) the show was most notable for the appearance of James Toney, beamed via satellite from actor Mickey Rourke's gym in Los Angeles. It was left to Toney to spell out to a hitherto ignorant British public what those more knowledgeable about boxing already knew, namely that the two blokes being feted in a studio in London weren't the most dangerous fighters in their division, either in or out of the ring. 'I don't care who wins,' railed Toney as Benn and Eubank looked on, distinctly unamused, 'I'll fight either one of them. In fact, I'll fight both of them on the same night.' When Benn was moved to spell out his credentials, Toney hit back: 'Let me tell you something – I'm not Iran Barkley, I'm not Doug DeWitt, when you come over here I'll kick your ass.' When Ross asked Eubank for his comment, it appeared as if he had been turned to stone. 'I'm the best,' continued Toney. 'The WBC stands for "We Be Crooks" and the WBO, we don't even count that. When I see you I'm gonna beat you and your mamma's ass.' Eubank looked genuinely hurt. 'Don't expect me to like this,' he said, 'I can't take this.' But Toney's reflections on the episode remind us of what we spectators sometimes forget, often wilfully: that the trash-talk, the posturing and the nonsense often bears little or no resemblance to a fighter's inner thoughts.

'If I could have reached through the screen and shook them I would have done,' says Toney. 'But there was never any hatred, all that was just hype to get a fight between us. I wasn't very complimentary but I just wanted in on the action. The truth is I didn't think the WBO belt was a joke, I didn't consider any belt with the word "world" written on it a joke. I wanted every title out there, every title looks good in my belt case. So I never thought of either Benn–Eubank fight as something inferior. Believe me, I was watching that night of 18 November 1990 – is that right? – because I wanted every middle and super-middleweight belt that could come my way. I was hoping the winner of that first fight would come over to the United States or I could go over there. But it never came off that way. But I give Nigel all the credit in the world because he came over here and fought some of our good guys and blew them out. I liked his style – he came at you, he didn't dance, he didn't run from no friendly fire. And that's also why I wanted to fight him, because I knew when we got in the ring he wasn't going anywhere and I wasn't going anywhere, but I had the better chin. Chris Eubank was a pretty good boxer but more on the scary side of things. He was a very strange guy, and I'm not the only one who thought that. But Chris wasn't that brave a guy to come to America, the closest I came to fighting him was when I was hooked up to that satellite feed.'

Trash-talking aside, Toney knew what many boxing aficionados also knew but chose to ignore, namely that Benn or Eubank would be mad to get on a plane and fight him in his backyard when they could make just as much money or more on home soil for considerably less risk. 'Chris was in it for the money, nothing else,' says Ronnie Davies. 'He wasn't in it for the glory. I'm not saying he couldn't have held his own against the big American names but what was the point when he was earning the same type of money, if not more, over here? He was such a draw in his own right, he didn't need them.' Indeed, the second match between Benn and Eubank had a certain purity about it: two men fighting not for mere baubles, but because they demanded it, the public demanded it, the media demanded it and therefore the money demanded it. It was that rare thing in modern boxing, a natural fight that actually came off.

Away from the cameras, both Benn and Eubank were actually less revved up than before their first fight, it was just that the media didn't want us to know that. Far better that the public imagined them to be rabid animals tethered in their respective gyms, waiting for the order to kill. But for Benn, the overriding emotion was fear rather than anger. 'Second time round Chris had gone from being a sharp dresser to this guy who was wearing a monocle and jodhpurs,' says Benn.

'But I knew him now, knew his cards, what he was going to lay on the table. So he didn't really get to me. That said, I was a bit more apprehensive than I was the first time, because I couldn't lose to him again.'

Meanwhile, Eubank was so confident that he had his shorts embroidered with the legend: 'WBO and WBC Champion'. And he had other things apart from Nigel Benn on his mind. Recalls Ronnie Davies: 'I was with him in Jamaica and there were all these kids jumping off this huge, high cliff and he said, "I'm going to do that". He took his shirt and trousers off, walked up there in his pants and did the best swallow dive I'd ever seen. Then there was a bungee jump off the pier in Brighton and he wanted to go on it before the second Benn fight. I said to him, "Chris, you're off your head, you've got the most important fight of your life in three weeks. I'll tell Barry Hearn what you've done". We had a blazing row, but he still did it. Then at the final press conference, Chris had this leather coat on and he said to me: "Davith, how do I look?" And I walked over to him and said: "Got to win the fight, got to win the fight." Meaning, none of that mattered. And, to his credit, he said: "Davith, I take your point." But that's what he was like, he was just the same as he always was before that second Benn fight because he expected to win it. He was a lunatic like that, I called him "The Man With No Fear".'

But even when Benn failed to turn up for the final head-to-head press conference, the promoters managed to put a positive spin on it. Don King sounded like he was explaining away the absence of an apocalyptic horseman. 'Right now, Nigel Benn's frenzy is at such a state, he cannot control himself looking at Mr Eubank,' said King, who hit the headlines himself a day later when it transpired he was being investigated by the FBI over allegations he had defrauded Lloyd's of London (he was later acquitted). 'He can't stand to face this man any longer without tearing him apart. We've got a hostile situation here as in war.' When the secretary of the British Boxing Board of Control objected to King's war analogy, King replied: 'They won't be playing tiddlywinks out there.' King's blood-stained streams of consciousness must have gone down a bomb with the British press pack, because Eubank was in particularly philosophical mood. Wrote Jonathan Rendall in the *Independent*: 'Eubank put everyone else to sleep with an hour and a half's worth of public meditation on life, the universe and, particularly, his place in it.' Explaining his decision not to turn up, Benn said: 'I let Eubank have the stage all to himself because that is what he loves.' Wise move, Nigel, wise move.

In the few days before the fight, the phoney war, which had been largely underground until then because of the Lewis–Bruno show the weekend before, finally exploded onto the back pages. The *Daily Mirror* ran a story which claimed Benn was punching so hard 'he could KO a donkey'. Elsewhere in its pages, Eubank was pilloried for his latest fancy, a monocle. 'A monocle is for people whose sight is defective in one eye only,' wrote Mike Langley. 'Otherwise, it's an affectation for over-dressed coxcombs like Chris Eubank. He's a sham, a poodle-faking, posing phoney whose two-bit title and unbeaten record is owed almost entirely to a hand-picked diet of cannon-fodder.' In stark contrast to his prediction for the first fight, Colin Hart in the *Sun* picked Eubank to 'torpedo' Benn in seven. 'Nigel Benn and Chris Eubank would be happier fighting in a trench instead of a boxing ring,' said Hart. 'Because that would be the best place to settle the longest-running and most bitter feud in British fight history. Benn, despite his fitness, cannot hide from the fact he has a suspect chin.' But perhaps the most revealing quote about the fight

– and the fight game – came from Barry Hearn. Asked how much money Benn–Eubank II stood to make, Hearn replied: 'We're looking to bring in about £4 million. But then boxing's always been about bullshit.'

As well as the bookmakers, a host of boxing's biggest names thought Eubank would do a repeat job on Benn, the consensus being that he would once again be too durable and too clever for his limited rival. 'If Nigel thinks about the fight then he can settle the score,' said Mike McCallum. 'But Eubank is a little smarter, maybe the better boxer and probably the stronger man.' Said Lloyd Honeyghan: 'Eubank needs a real contest to make him fight to the limit. He'll get that from Benn and that's why I feel Chris will come through.' Added Alan Minter: 'Benn's come on a lot, he's picking his shots so much better – but I still think Eubank will be too clever for him.' Michael Watson, perhaps more in hope than anything else, was one of the few to favour Benn. 'Nigel must be the all-action man,' said Watson, who had just undergone yet another brain operation. 'If Nigel sticks to his pre-fight plan, and doesn't let himself be tricked by Eubank's image, he will stop him.'

At least Benn had a plan this time around, even though he would later claim it was the wrong one. 'After the second fight between Michael Watson and Chris Eubank, I got a phone call from Benn's people saying they'd like me to come round and see him,' says trainer Jimmy Tibbs, who was in Watson's corner that night. 'He thought there was only one man in that fight up until the 11th round, when Michael got caught with that uppercut. Nigel said: "That's the shape I want to be in." We shook on the deal there and then. Nigel was all slam, bam, wallop in the first fight but the second time we got a bit technical. He was a world champion before he got with me, but he needed to move his head a bit more and he had a habit of lifting his head up high when he jabbed. So he learned to relax, bob and weave, body and head, body and head. But there was nothing wrong with his footwork, like people said in the press. So I said to Nigel: "The way to beat this kid is keep him moving for three minutes each round – he likes to have a little rest, but you mustn't let him, you've got to stick to him as close as you can for 12 rounds."' Eubank, meanwhile, claimed he hadn't changed anything. Asked why he had added Maximo Pierret, his principle trainer from his New York days, to his camp, Eubank replied: 'It is not that I was not training properly but that I am now training correctly.' It was a line that could have come from the mouth of Lewis Carroll's Mad Hatter.

It is telling that while Benn and Eubank's autobiographies run to 700-odd pages combined, the descriptions of their second fight cover no more than a couple of paragraphs. The size of their respective egos are no doubt part of the reason, neither man wanting to admit that the other has played much more than a minor role in his life. But it's also as if they are as worn out with each other on the page as they were in the flesh. 'The atmosphere at Old Trafford was extraordinary,' says Kevin Mitchell. 'But the fight itself wasn't as brutal as the first one because they knew each other, had tasted each other's strength and therefore were more wary of each other. They'd both put themselves through so much agony in the first fight that the second was always going to be a little bit more tactical.' Colin Hart is in agreement: 'Once two fighters have experienced what they experienced in that first fight they are highly unlikely to want to do it all over again because, let's face it, it bloody well hurts.'

'That's maybe why the second fight wasn't as good as the

first fight, far from it,' says Benn. 'Forty-odd thousand people at Old Trafford, hundreds of millions watching on TV, it was just electrifying. I could hear my name being chanted when I was in the dressing room, and this was an hour before the fight. But there wasn't that same intensity once the first bell went.' Everything is relative. Viewed in isolation from their first engagement, Benn–Eubank II was a tremendous show. 'The ego has landed,' quipped ITV's Reg Gutteridge as Eubank vaulted into the ring, although Jim Rosenthal says his long-time ITV colleague loved all the razzmatazz really. 'All the monocle and cane stuff, I don't think Reg got it,' says Rosenthal. 'But he recognised Eubank's ability. Also, he was a newspaper man and anything that got his sport in the head-lines on the back pages was OK with him. He loved the big-time fights in Vegas, and these two guys were bringing Vegas to Birmingham and Manchester. In fact he loved it even more because he didn't have to get on an aeroplane.' Next, the shaven-headed WBC champion was played in by the chimes of Big Ben, before violinist Nigel Kennedy led a boozy rendi-tion of 'God Save the Queen'.

Sitting among the gods at Old Trafford that night was a pie-eyed Ricky Hatton, sucking up the atmosphere and drawing inspiration. 'I went with my Uncle Jed and I was only about 15,' recalls Hatton, who went on to win world titles at two different weights and become the most popular British boxer of the satellite age. 'As a big Man City fan it takes a lot for me to go to Old Trafford and I think I paid £75 for a ticket, it took me forever to save the money up. I was dead excited about it but ended up being right at the back of the stands, they were like two one pence pieces in the ring. But to go to a fight like that, with a crowd that big and the atmosphere that generated, was something else.

'When I first started boxing at my local gym at the age of ten, Nigel Benn, Chris Eubank and Michael Watson were on the television all the time. They were all exceptional fighters but you couldn't get a more value-for-money fighter than Nigel Benn. I couldn't get enough of him, he was one of the main reasons I got into boxing in the first place, I couldn't watch his tapes enough. He was dead exciting, every punch was a hook. He was always on the front foot, always wanting a fight. I wanted to be a world champion like Nigel Benn and a lot of my style was based on him: I never took a backward step, I was always aggressive, and I like to think people liked me for the same reasons they liked him. Chris Eubank was also a hero of mine, but I wanted Nigel to smash him to bits that night.'

Fripperies dispensed with, reality descended. Eubank shaded the first round and proceeded to saunter around the ring for 30 seconds before taking to his stool. But Benn landed the first significant blow of the fight midway through the second, a clunking left hook, and followed up with a sustained two-fisted attack in the third, before Eubank fired back with a couple of juddering lefts of his own. Benn, applying relentless pressure but in a more controlled manner than three years earlier, staggered Eubank in the fourth, only for Eubank to stiffen Benn with a thunderous left in the fifth, a round the WBO champion won easily. In the sixth, referee Larry O'Connell lost patience with Benn and docked him a point for persistent low blows, a moment that would have a crucial bearing on the outcome of the fight.

The seventh was a scrappy affair but Benn came on strong in the eighth, spearing Eubank on the ropes and trapping him in corners as Eubank struggled to tie him up on the inside. At the end of the round Eubank, ignoring the pleas of his seconds, swaggered to a neutral corner and glowered at the commenta-tors ringside, remaining rooted until a few seconds before the bell for the start of the ninth. Eubank had some success in the following three minutes, finding his mark with a couple of solid right hands, but it was Benn's round again. Benn some-how found another gear in the 10th, rocking Eubank with a big left hook, and it appeared for all the world as if revenge was about to be served. But Eubank was never knowingly defeated. In the 11th, Eubank rattled Benn with a barrage of left hooks that had him covering up on the ropes and heading into the final round the fight remained in the balance. 'The biggest round of your boxing career,' roared Jimmy Tibbs in Benn's corner, while on the opposite side of the ring Ronnie Davies told Eubank: 'You've got to win this – go out and stop him, mate. He's had it, he's more tired than you.' Davies was probably right – but Benn still had it in him to laugh after one explosive exchange. And while Eubank finished the stronger, the haunted expressions on the faces of Eubank and his connections at the final bell suggested they thought Benn had nicked it.

While the fighters waited for the verdict – Benn pacing around the ring impatiently, like a husband waiting on news of his expectant wife, Eubank looking uncharacteristically anxious in his corner – ITV's Gary Newbon fished around for predictions. Michael Nunn, who thought he would be fighting the winner, wouldn't give Newbon a definitive answer but, bizarrely, thought Benn won the last two rounds. Don King thought 'fight fans were the winners'. Barry Hearn plumped for the draw, but he didn't look convinced. Gutteridge and ITV co-commentator Jim Watt thought Benn had shaded it, but Barry McGuigan next door also thought it was draw. As the minutes ticked by, Benn seemed to grow in confidence, prematurely posing for victory shots and lapping up the generous applause of the crowd. And then the verdict came. English judge Harry Gibbs awarded the fight 115–113 to Eubank and Carol Castellano scored it 114–113 to Benn. As Chuck Hassett's scorecard was read out by Showtime's in-house MC Jimmy Lennon Jr, Benn and Eubank eyeballed each other at close range. And then it came: 114–114, making the fight a draw.

'Nigel boxed marvellous that night,' says Jimmy Tibbs. 'Chris liked it his own way all the time and Nigel certainly didn't let him have it his own way that night. We thought Nigel won it, even with that point taken away. But I haven't got any hang-ups about it, it was close and Larry O'Connell was a good referee. There you go, that's boxing.' Benn was less philosophical. 'I'm very pissed off with the decision,' he said. 'I thought I won by at least three rounds. What do I have to do to win?' Benn later accused Hearn of influencing the judges, which Hearn vigorously denied. King immediately stepped up his campaign for openly displayed scoring, while Warren lobbied for extra rounds in future to produce a winner. Eubank, meanwhile, claimed not to see what the fuss was about. 'I thought I won it on boxing ability,' he said. 'But if the judges score it that way, so be it.'

Perhaps more tellingly, sage boxing writers felt Benn's sense of grievance was misplaced. 'The crowd's reaction was more one of disappointment at the failure to find a winner than outrage,' wrote Harry Mullan in *Boxing News*, 'which suggests that the verdict was probably about right. While I thought Benn had sneaked home I have certainly seen a great many worse verdicts than this one.' Wrote Hugh McIlvanney in the *Observer*: 'If neither fighter should feel cheated, the same can be said with vehemence of the stadium crowd of more than

40,000 and the millions who watched live on TV. The conclusion should encourage both of them to dilute their notorious mutual hostility with a large injection of respect.' Wise words, but only one boxer was listening.

'All I wanted was for Nigel to give me a hug,' said Eubank, who attempted to bury the hatchet in the immediate aftermath of the fight. 'But he failed to respond and that really disappointed me. It certainly would be nice to think that one day Nigel can see sense.' Benn responded: 'He is trying to get me to stop hating him and start liking him. But that will never happen. I detest him as a man and always will.' With talk like that flying about, it seemed inevitable they would have to do it again. 'A third fight?' said Eubank. 'I don't think the public would have it any other way. This was incredible.'

CHAPTER THIRTEEN
Glory is for God

As a show, Benn–Eubank II had indeed been incredible, and Benn–Eubank III might have been even more so. But inevitable and boxing don't go. Never mind that the second fight drew 16.5 million British viewers, ITV's third highest sporting audience ever; never mind that the media was gagging for a third fight; never mind that the punters would have sold their own mothers for a ticket to see a third fight; never mind that both boxers made almost £2 million combined; never mind that Eubank claimed he wanted a third fight; never mind that Benn was livid that he wasn't awarded the decision and also claimed he wanted to do it again. Once both men retreated, the dust settled and the carnage was cleared, suddenly a third fight didn't seem to make as much sense.

'I remember Chris saying to me in the ring,' says Barry Hearn, "What does that mean, a draw?" I said: "It means we get to do it all over again, Chris." It needed to happen but, despite what he said at the time, I don't think Eubank necessarily wanted a third fight, because he felt he was fairly fortunate to get the draw in the second.' In the immediate aftermath of the rematch, fantastical figures as high as £5 million were being thrown about in relation to a third engagement. But even before his second bout with Benn, Eubank had been negotiating a barely credible deal with Sky that would earn him £10 million for eight fights over a one-year period. The still-live Benn simply didn't fit into Eubank's plan – dubbed The Chris Eubank World Tour – while almost everybody else in boxing thought the plan was simply unworkable. 'Anyone would say that this type of schedule is insane but I never said I was sane,' said Eubank. 'I'm here to prove I'm not the normal man – I'm abnormal in many ways.'

However, boxing purists were actually less worried about the potential damage to Eubank's health than the damage he was seen to be doing to the sport they loved. 'The Chris Eubank wagon train seems to be hurtling with ever increasing speed towards the fairground booth,' wrote Andrew Longmore in *The Times*. 'Roll up, roll up, fight the WBO super-middleweight champion. A snip at £10 million. And, please, ladies and gentlemen, you know the rules: No real champions need apply.' Eubank's deal effectively ruled out a third contest with ITV-backed Benn or IBF champion James Toney (Michael Nunn lost his WBA belt to Steve Little in February 1994). 'We would vacate the title rather than fight on another channel,' said Hearn, confirming what many suspected, that Eubank had effectively become the Sky Sports champion. Hearn's rival promoter Frank Maloney had more reason than most to be upset by the deal, as his charge Lennox Lewis, the newly crowned WBC heavyweight champion, had been dropped as a result. 'Calling himself Simply the Best is farcical – Simply the Best Conman is more like it,' said Maloney.

Maloney wasn't the only one who thought Sky Sports' decision-makers had taken collective leave of their senses. Before the tie-up was rubber-stamped, Eubank's previous eight fights had gone the distance, half of the decisions had been contentious and most of them were stinkers. In his first fight since the draw against Benn, Eubank had looked pretty decent in beating Germany's Graciano Rocchigiani in Berlin. But there was still controversy, with one judge awarding the fight to Eubank by the margin of 118–109. 'In more than 20 years of covering championship boxing I cannot recall a scorecard which was more out of line with what had actually happened in the ring,' said Mullan. Eubank was pelted by rolled-up programmes as he conducted his post-fight interview. Eubank then nicked a controversial split decision against luckless Irishman Ray Close. After his rematch against Close at the King's Hall in Belfast, Eubank was penned in the ring for half an hour while thousands of irate home fans chanted 'cheat' at him. 'The man who styles himself "Simply the Best" has won his share of tightrope finishes in the past,' said the *Sunday Mirror*, 'but none have been so bitterly resented as this.' Maybe Sky's executives didn't watch the fight, or maybe they did but also saw the viewing figures: a barely believable 13.1 million people had tuned in to watch Eubank's latest escape. Attempting to rationalise the Sky deal, Hearn said: 'It's soap opera with boxing gloves, isn't it?' But ITV was happy to see the back of him. 'He has done a great job for us,' said Trevor East. 'But we've had the best out of Chris Eubank.'

Sky threw everything it had at Eubank's first show, against unknown Brazilian Mauricio Amaral at London's Olympia, broadcasting trailers of their new signing strutting through clouds of smoke, in the manner of some all-action movie hero bent on destruction. Over and over and over again. Eubank, however, was promising his new employers nothing. 'Sky have built it up, not me,' he said. 'I'll turn up on the night and do the job I've been training for.' Eubank, apparently, had been training for another dismal, controversial unanimous decision.

'Chris Eubank kept his WBO super-middleweight title last night with a verdict that shamed boxing,' railed the Glasgow *Sunday Mail*. 'Frankly this was simply one of the worst calls in British boxing for years.' Wrote Ian Gibb in the *Daily Mirror*. 'If the WBO judges had been in court, they would have put the Kray Twins on probation.' The boxing correspondents of *The Times*, the *Independent*, the *Sun*, the *People* and Scotland's *Daily Record* also had Amaral either drawing or winning it, while Harry Mullan wasn't the only one who noticed the venue had been only half full. 'It may be just as well that Chris Eubank plans to take the rest of his eight-fight "world tour" on the road,' wrote Mullan in the *Independent on Sunday*, 'for he has already outstayed his welcome in London.'

A little over a month later, Eubank was back in the ring against Belfast's Sam Storey in Cardiff. 'Don't go to the show,' said Eubank beforehand. 'If you want thrills, go and watch Arnold Schwarzenegger in *True Lies*.' Quipped Harry Mullan: 'He has a point: the fight scenes in *True Lies* are much more convincing than anything Eubank has offered in recent times.' What transpired was another largely uninspiring victory for Eubank in front of another sparse crowd. A game Storey held his own in the early stages, badly sprained his ankle after being knocked down in the sixth round and was withdrawn at the start of the seventh. 'I pulled him out because he was only being paid six-round money for this,' said Storey's chief second Barney Eastwood.

Even before Eubank's win over Storey, rumours were circulating that Sky wanted out. Executives who had played no part in brokering the deal were apparently deeply unhappy with the arrangement, keen to offload Eubank and equally keen to get Lennox Lewis back on board. The Lewis situation was particularly embarrassing for Sky, because shortly after they dumped him he signed up for a world heavyweight unification match against Riddick Bowe, although the fight never came off. 'When they announced that he was going to fight eight people in 12 months, you knew he was going to have to fight the biggest bunch of stiffs ever,' says Frank Warren, 'which is why it died. Let's have it right, a lot of Eubank's fights were boring – he was crafty, but he was a boring fighter – and the opponents he was fighting weren't great and there were some terrible decisions. On his "world tour", which took in Wales, Ireland and South Africa, the halls were almost empty some of the time, but people forget all that.'

Eubank seemed oblivious to the criticism and to the furious machinations going on behind closed doors, treating himself to a £140,000 Aston Martin Volante. 'I didn't buy it for speed,' said Eubank. 'I bought it because it is class and it's about being cool doing 2 mph.' Which is presumably why he decided it didn't have enough poke and insisted on £60,000 worth of modifications. Eubank was veering further and further away from the necessarily harsh realities of boxing. And from reality itself. At an appearance at the Cambridge Union – the previous week it was the Chancellor on the economy, the following week it was Ted Heath on Europe – he declared that in another life he would have liked to have been Leonardo da Vinci or a ballet dancer. After announcing his intention to quit boxing at the end of his current Sky deal, he declared that it was his aim to lecture on 'the philosophy of life and sexology'. 'I am interested in the whole study of sex and human relationships and how they relate to life,' he added. 'It fascinates me.'

But it is Barry Hearn who tells the story that perhaps best encapsulates Eubank's beguiling arrogance. 'I got tickets for us to see Barbra Streisand at Wembley – right at the front, cost a fortune,' says Hearn. 'With five minutes to the start of the show there's no sign of Chris, but Streisand refuses to go on if there's an empty seat in the front row. A minute to go, there's a ripple of applause. I thought: "That must be him at last." But when I looked around, it's George Michael. Thirty seconds from curtain up, the roof absolutely lifts off Wembley. I thought Streisand must have come on from the back of the hall, but instead it's Eubank. He parades down the hall to the front – monocle, jodhpurs, the lot – taps the floor manager on the shoulder with his cane and says: "Inform Miss Streisand she may commence."'

The next stop on Eubank's 'world tour' was South Africa, where he was to fight 'Dangerous' Dan Schommer. During the build-up, he provided plenty more evidence that he had gone from being a knowing eccentric to a man now consumed by the character he had created. Eubank denied reports that he had insisted Nelson Mandela be ringside but he did rack up a colossal bill for his King suite in the Sun City Palace hotel, replete with baby grand piano, a sauna, a jacuzzi, a dining room and two sitting rooms. He also revealed he had a manservant called Max – a former naval officer he discovered sleeping in a doorway on Oxford Street – and told the journalist Robert Chalmers: 'Of course I'm spoilt. I'm a king in my own right and my mentality is one of kings.' Colin Hart of the *Sun* remembers the trip well. 'Eubank originally had a suite which cost about 800 quid a night,' says Hart. 'But Eubank said to the manager: "I'm not thleeping here, it'th not good enough, haven't you got thumthing better?" So the manager said: "Well, Mr Eubank, we've got the presidential suite. Will that suffice?" It was the most magnificent bloody thing, overlooking a mountain. So Eubank said: "Thith will do." And the manager said: "But Mr Eubank, this suite is £1800 a night." To which Eubank replied: "I don't care, I want it." He was there eight or nine days. He also flew in his barber from Manchester to give him a haircut. That was Eubank for you.'

The nickname of Eubank's opponent masked an inconvenient truth, namely that Schommer wasn't that dangerous at all. Unbeaten in 31 fights the American may have been, but he had fought nobody of note, nobody for nearly a year and looked like an out-of-shape business administrator. Because he was. 'I don't get a lot of press in Minnesota,' said Schommer, whose previous highest purse was reportedly $3500. 'I make more money from my job than from boxing.' Just as well, because the judges mugged him. 'The old boxing lament of "we wuz robbed" can rarely have rung truer than it did in Sun City last night,' wrote Harry Mullan. 'The three judges plumbed new depths of incompetence even by the spectacular standards of the WBO.' Eubank was given the verdict by scores of 116–114, 117–113, and 116–113, to howls of derision from the 8000 South Africans who made up the crowd. Mullan thought Schommer won 117–113. At least on this occasion Eubank had the good grace to admit he had got away with it. 'If he had got the decision I wouldn't have been complaining,' said Eubank. 'Controversy is never far from Chris Eubank.'

By this stage, Eubank seemed to have few friends left in Fleet Street. The act was funny when he was providing value for money in the ring, apparently wearying now that he wasn't. In the days following his hollow victory over Schommer, sports editors the length and breadth of Britain were baying for blood. The *People* went with 'IT'S A STEAL, CHRIS', while the *Sunday Mirror* preferred 'EU STINK'. *The Times* weighed in with 'LACKLUSTRE EUBANK'S CREDIBILITY AT NEW LOW', the *Daily Record* with 'EU'RE AN INSULT TO BOXING FANS'. But still Eubank refused to apologise. 'I fight for money and I'm taking home £1 million,' said Eubank, whom even Barry Hearn thought had lost. 'I don't feel hurt if my fights don't appeal to the crowd.' But trainer Ronnie Davies was so irked by the performance he felt some explanation was needed. 'I've had to bite my tongue for four years,' revealed Davies. 'It's heartbreaking to see Chris waste his talent by refusing to make the 12 stone limit at the proper time. Shedding so much weight a few days before fights takes away all his sharpness and conditioning.' Davies's explanation did little to placate the outraged sports writers. 'Chris Eubank needs a new theme tune to replace the hopelessly outdated and inappropriate "Simply The Best",' wrote John Dillon in the *People*. '"Nellie The Elephant" sounds ideal. And he could then pack his trunks and wave goodbye to the circus he's touting around the world in the phoney guise of competitive, professional sport.'

But behind the headlines and outraged articles were journalists still hooked on the Chris Eubank act. Even if most of his fights weren't up to much, at least Eubank provided a few laughs and something to talk about in far-flung hotel bars. 'I used to love it because you rarely get characters like Eubank to write about,' says Colin Hart. 'I liked to think I had this wonderful relationship with this nutcase, there was always this great sense of amusement whatever he did and wherever he went. Before they went to Berlin for the Rocchigiani fight, Eubank said to Ronnie Davies: "I'm taking you shopping, Davith." Ronnie said: "What for?" Eubank said: "I'm going to buy you a leather coat." Davies told him he didn't want a leather coat, but Eubank said: "You're going to have one." So he took Ronnie up the West End and fitted him out in a black leather coat that went from his neck down to his shoes. Davies, who also had a crew cut, said: "I can't wear this in Berlin, it makes me look like Field Marshal Rommel." To which Eubank replied: "Prethithely, Davith, that'th why you're going to wear it." The Germans' eyes came out of their heads when they saw him at the press conference, you've never seen anything like it. That appealed to his sense of humour. And Davies was a willing partner, he loved it.'

'The day after the fight in Berlin,' recalls ITV's Jim Rosenthal, 'the snapper wanted to do something with Eubank in front of the Brandenburg Gate, so we told him to bring his belt along for a picture. He turned up with the jodhpurs and the cane but no belt. The cameraman said: "Chris, where's the belt?" And he said: "I have a severe problem with the belt – when I looked in the mirror, it clashed with my waistcoat, so I left it in the hotel."' Adds Kevin Mitchell: 'For a lot of his career, the fans hated Chris Eubank. But many in the business, the fighters and the press, loved Eubank, because here was a guy who provided so much amusement, who was bringing the sport so much publicity and razzmatazz, bringing in lots of money. And what's wrong with that? Most boxers aren't like that, most boxers are introverted and shy, but not Chris.'

While nobody in the British media was able to uncover any concrete evidence of impropriety among WBO judges, the stream of wonky scorecards thrown up by Eubank's title defences could have been substituted for ticker-tape at a parade. Since its creation in 1988, the Puerto Rican outfit had been viewed with a mixture of suspicion, contempt and bafflement. And no wonder. In 1989, the WBO had Italy's Francesco Damiani fight South Africa's Johnny DuPlooy to decide its inaugural heavyweight title-holder. Meanwhile, back in the real world, the three major governing bodies recognised the undefeated Mike Tyson as the undisputed heavyweight champion. Eubank had become such a golden goose for the WBO

– every time he defended his title, it got 3 per cent in sanc-tioning fees – that he seemed indispensable. As such, when Eubank signed to fight Henry Wharton in Manchester, the hard-hitting Yorkshireman's manager Mickey Duff demanded approval of the officials. 'There will be no fight otherwise,' said Duff. 'No close verdict has ever gone against him.'

With everyone apart from Eubank and his connections seemingly wanting the champion knocked off, the build-up to his match against Wharton at least had a certain frisson. 'I feel like the good guy in *High Noon*,' said the 27-year-old Wharton, who had been easily outpointed by Nigel Benn ten months earlier. 'Eubank is the Gerald Ratner of boxing – all his fights are crap and he couldn't care less.' At the final head-to-head press conference, it all went off, with Duff launching a bitter verbal attack on Eubank. 'You are the lowest of the low,' said Duff. 'He has made millions and he doesn't deserve it. He's lost six fights and got the decision each time. I'm perturbed that he knocks boxing. He exploits the game like a hooker. That is behaving like scum.' While Eubank, Hearn and Davies were stunned, many among the British press pack clearly agreed with Duff's sentiments, judging by their less than impartial pre-fight scribblings. 'Boxing buffs are drooling in expectation that big mouth Chris Eubank has finally bitten off more than he can chew,' wrote Ian Gibb in the *Daily Mirror*. 'They've got the taste. And when the ticket buyers can smell blood, especially Eubank's, they come running.' And so they did, with Manchester's G-Mex arena all but sold out two days before the show.

Such was the perverse nature of Chris Eubank that with a nation's sports writers and fans wanting him to fail because he had apparently failed them so often, and with many of them thinking his opponent might have the tools to humble him, he pulled out his most convincing performance for years. Jabbing with unerring accuracy from the first bell, Eubank caused swelling under Wharton's left eye as early as the second round and thereafter kept up a furious pace, replacing his usual posturing with sustained attacks and long-forgotten combinations. A game Wharton, whose eye was fully closed by the 11th, played his part but this time there was no controversy when the verdict was announced, unanimously in favour of the champion. Journalists who had damned him beforehand were now generous with their praise. 'The WBO super-middleweight champion left me wiping more than a little egg from my face,' wrote Ian Gibb. 'Great dollops of it, in fact.' However, when asked whether he might now consider fighting newly crowned IBF champion Roy Jones Jr, who had looked so stunning in dethroning James Toney, Eubank replied: 'The man who tries to find glory is the man who ends up bitter, twisted, regretful and warped. Glory is for God. When men try and acquire glory they usually end up getting hurt.' That meant no.

According to Budd Schulberg, who had seen all the greats since 1925, Roy Jones Jr had 'the quickest hands, swiftest feet and slickest moves since Sugar Ray Robinson'. Which is exactly why Eubank didn't want a bar of him. However, Eubank always denied he ducked anyone. 'Dodging a fighter is a cardinal sin,' he said, 'and is something I can never be accused of. Unless someone was officially the recognised number one contender, I had no professional obligation to face them. With Roy Jones, he was fortunately never number one contender.' To his credit, Eubank admitted Jones was the superior fighter. But his cynical logic failed to mollify his many critics, who were of the opinion that his WBO crown meant nothing as long as he chose not to fight the best from across the pond.

Jones, who would himself be accused of taking a path of lesser resistance during his long reigns over the super-middleweight and light-heavyweight divisions, found Eubank's stance entirely understandable. 'Some of the boxing writers in the States weren't that complimentary about Eubank or Benn,' says Jones. 'But writers write and don't fight nobody. They fought whoever they had to fight, and by that I mean they only had to fight each other. I never came close to fighting Eubank because he wasn't interested in leaving his own country, he was doing just fine where he was. Chris Eubank had a very unique style and it was a style I used to love to see. He was like a UK version of me, he brought different things to the ring. But he never said he was this supernatural guy who could come over to the United States, he knew he had it made where he was and he was happy with that. He had no reason to take chances, why would he? He was making good money fighting in his own backyard.'

CHAPTER FOURTEEN
Not much showbiz

Following the second fight between Benn and Eubank, Benn decided to leave Barry Hearn for Don King and Frank Warren. However, Hearn claims King very nearly missed out on either fighter because of a bizarre contractual oversight. 'The funny thing was, at the end of the fight Don was swanning round saying, "Now I control British boxing",' says Hearn. 'And I said, "Why's that, Don?" And he said, "What about our deal?" And I replied, "I know the deal: it said win or lose you get both of the fighters – but it was a draw, so you get neither of them". It was unbelievable. He went fucking potty, didn't talk to me for two years. But I said to the fighters: "Listen, it's your choice, go where you like." So Benn went with King and Eubank stayed with me. I remember at some function after the rematch Don ushered Eubank into a corner and put his arm round him and all I could hear was Eubank saying: "Don, you're talking to the wrong nigger." Fucking great line.'

Frank Warren, who had negotiated the television deal with King and ITV to screen Benn's future fights, claims Hearn is being economical with the truth. 'That's all bullshit, but that's Barry,' says Warren. 'You only had to see what he was like on the night of the second fight to realise the ego and the bullshit of the man – when he had that microphone strapped to his head directing the show I thought they were filming a Madonna video. We were taking Barry's word that he'd got the two guys under contract and that the winner was supposed to have fought Michael Nunn. But it made no difference whether one of them won the fight or it was a draw or whatever, because they would have said: "There is nothing in my contract that says I have to fight Michael Nunn."'

Benn, who banished memories of the Eubank rematch and the subsequent verdict with an all-night party in Manchester followed by an all-day party on a Pullman bound for London, soon came to the conclusion that a third match with Eubank was not the be all and end all. 'I don't think I used the right tactics on him,' says Benn. 'I should have watched how Michael Watson fought him, kept coming forward and worked Chris's body, covered up and let Chris burn himself out. But as long as I've still got my world title and that belt around my waist, it's all right. If I'd lost I'd have been peeved, but we'd made a hell of a lot of money, made a lot of people happy and we'd made a name for ourselves.' With Benn contracted to ITV and Eubank in the process of negotiating his eight-fight deal with Sky, a rubber match that had seemed inevitable only a few weeks earlier appeared to be dead in the water. And Benn had more personal reasons for wanting to leave Hearn and rejoin Warren.

'It emerged before the second Benn–Eubank fight that the WBO sanction fee wasn't going to be paid,' says Andy Ayling. 'So while it was being billed as WBC versus WBO champion, one of them wasn't going to be on the line. Nigel Benn found out about this on the day, made Barry Hearn pay the sanction fee and then said to Frank: "I want you to walk me out tonight, I want to be with you from now on." Nigel and Frank hadn't spoken for a few years but when Nigel found out someone was batting for him, he then came over. After the fight, they had a big meeting in a hotel in Manchester, all the discrepancies about the show came out and there was a big fall-out between Barry, Frank and Don King. But Frank and Don continued their partnership for a number of fights afterwards and Barry wasn't a part of it – that tells you all you need to know.' Asked if he envisaged a third bout between Benn and Eubank ever taking place, King replied: 'Eubank and Barry Hearn are involved in trickeration.' Warren, meanwhile, vowed never to do business with Hearn again.

Benn's next engagement was against Henry Wharton and it was to prove a bittersweet night at London's Earls Court. Benn retained his WBC belt courtesy of a unanimous decision over his rugged opponent but Nunn, defending his WBA title on the same card, came a cropper against fellow American Steve Little, who hadn't fought for more than a year. Nunn's defeat scuppered a lucrative unification match but Benn was still expected to fight the former champion after his uneventful points defeat of Juan Carlos Gimenez. Uneventful except for a full-scale battle involving fans of Robert McCracken and Steve Foster, who fought in the aisles of the NEC in Birmingham with chairs and metal bars.

Meanwhile, beyond the ropes Benn's personal life was spiralling out of control. In 1993 he split from his wife Sharron and in early 1994 moved with his new partner Carolyne to Los Angeles, in order to escape the media's attentions in England. But even holed up in his luxury apartment in Marina del Rey, with its floor-to-ceiling televisions, seven-foot bed and Porsche 959 parked in the driveway, Benn remained fair game for the red tops back home. For example, former porn model Melissa Ewart told the *Daily Mirror* that Benn 'failed to go the distance in bed and liked to prance around in her frilly knickers'. Benn, who had spent the previous seven years cultivating a reputation as one of Britain's hardest men, in and out of the bedroom, was not amused. 'I'm angry about the knickers thing,' said Benn. 'People are taking the piss out of me. I like a woman to dress up in sexy lingerie but I'm not diving into her undies drawer to put them over my head while she's not looking.'

But a former porn model questioning his poke in the boudoir was the least of Benn's worries. 'I had every reason to be completely happy,' said Benn. 'But I couldn't cope with not having my kids living with me. I was completely messed up, as low as I've ever been. The pain I was going through was indescribable.' At his lowest point, Benn even considered taking his own life. And then he hooked up with celebrity hypnotist Paul McKenna, who, apparently with little more than a click of his fingers, made everything better. Said Benn: 'Paul must have been thinking, "Christ, a few months ago I saw this man on telly knocking the shit out of some guy, and now he's a dribbling mess in my office!" But I wanted to be healed so badly that when I woke up I was a different man. Paul McKenna had helped put the past behind me.'

Following his victory over Gimenez, Benn started negotiations for a fight against American Gerald McClellan, one of the most feared punchers in world boxing. In 1993, McClellan won the WBC middleweight crown with a stoppage of Julian Jackson and he had reeled off three first-round knockouts since, the last of those in a rematch against Jackson. 'What separates me from everybody else is I'm mean,' said McClellan, who was almost four years younger than Benn and had 20 first-round knockouts from 31 victories. 'Nobody can beat me.' McClellan wasn't exaggerating about the mean bit. 'The kid was violent,' said McClellan's trainer Stan Johnson. 'He loved killing shit.' Whether he was mowing down flamingos in his Hummer or taping closed the mouth of a Labrador and feeding it to his best fighting dog Deuce, McClellan did indeed love killing shit, as well as watching shit get killed. In a live link-up with ITV, McClellan explained: 'I started off with 16 pit bulls and I can't stand a loser so now they're down to three.' Asked if he had a gentler side, McClellan replied: 'Yeh, but I wouldn't show it.' So genuinely mean was McClellan that he made the 'Dark Destroyer' look frilly-knickered by comparison.

Such is the fickle nature of the media that while Eubank was being criticised from all sides for the quality of his opposition, the *Daily Mirror* dubbed Benn's fight against McClellan 'a suicide mission'. 'Nigel Benn must have a death wish – or taken leave of his senses,' the story continued. 'Because the WBC world super-middleweight champion would rather face Freeport's fearsome American Gerald McClellan, who carries napalm in both fists, than an unremarkable Frenchman who is susceptible to cuts.' The unremarkable Frenchman was Frederic Seillier, a tidy campaigner who had made two successful defences of his European crown. For all the talk of 'wanting to have a war' with the uppity Yank on British soil, the truth was that McClellan was forced on Benn by King, who had become more and more frustrated with the Englishman's refusal to co-operate in the publicising of fights. In addition, Benn stood to make far more money from fighting McClellan than he did from fighting the unremarkable Frenchman. Frank Warren, who said both fighters stood to earn more than £1 million for the bout at a sell-out London Arena, explained the fight's appeal. 'This is probably the best world title fight I have ever put on,' he said. 'It has all the ingredients of an explosive

affair. McClellan is a devastating puncher and will be the riski-
est ever opponent Benn has had in his career. But Nigel is no
stranger to a tear-up.' For once, Harry Mullan had no problem
with the promotional guff. 'The "Sudden Impact" label which
the co-promoters Frank Warren and Don King have given the
match seems for once less like hype than a statement of the
truth,' wrote Mullan.

While everybody seemed to agree that Benn's bout with
McClellan had shades of his savage one-round encounter with
Iran Barkley, this time almost nobody thought Benn would
win. Dennis Andries, the British cruiserweight and former
three-time light-heavyweight world champion, was an old
stable-mate of McClellan at the fabled Kronk gym in Detroit.
And while he questioned McClellan's stamina, he also thought
it wouldn't go more than a couple of rounds. 'I don't believe
Gerald can go more than five or six rounds,' said Andries. 'But
he's a mighty puncher. People talk about his right to the head,
but that isn't the one that does the damage – it's those little
short left hooks to the ribs that really hurt. I like Nigel, but
I'm getting my money on Gerald in the first two rounds.'
Former five-weight world champion Tommy Hearns, another
stable-mate of McClellan, called him 'devastating, dynamite
and dangerous', while Hearns and McClellan's former trainer
Emanuel Steward said Benn had 'no chance'. Added Julian
Jackson, who knew a thing or two about heavy hitting: 'I
think Gerald may have a stamina problem, but he hits so hard
that proving it is difficult.' However, Benn did have support
from the most surprising of quarters. 'Benn becomes wild and
dangerous under threat,' said his former trainer Brian Lynch,
who was in the process of suing Benn for damages at the time.
'It's the way I taught him to fight – blow them away. Clever
boys like Michael Watson and Chris Eubank beat Benn. They

survived until the time was right. I don't believe McClellan has that option.' Eubank, meanwhile, gave his old rival a better chance than most. 'If McClellan comes to bomb Nigel out,' he said, 'it's 50–50.'

But Fleet Street's boxing writers were almost unanimous in their belief that Benn would be blitzed inside a few rounds. 'If McClellan fails to become champion tonight it will be nothing short of sensational,' wrote Ken Jones in the *Independent*. 'He can be expected to complete the task quickly, perhaps as early as the second round.' Ian Gibb in the *Daily Mirror* wasn't the only one who thought Benn's decision to jettison trainer Jimmy Tibbs – they had fallen out over Tibbs's proposed fee for the fight – was a potentially catastrophic one. 'Tibbs was the man who might – just might – have come up with a game plan to combat the brutal force and fury of McClellan,' said Gibb. 'The end could come very early.' Wrote Harry Mullan in the *Independent on Sunday*: 'Benn blitzed Barkley with an all-or-nothing attack, but if he tries the same against McClellan he will surely be caught; McClellan need only connect once.'

There is a commonly held view that boxing was bigger in the old days. Always that boxing was bigger in the old days. But when you discover that the 12,000 capacity London Arena was only half-full four days before the Benn–McClellan fight, you realise this is not necessarily the case. Carl Froch's 2013 rematch against Denmark's Mikkel Kessler, in contrast, was sold out two months in advance, and the O2 Arena can accommodate 18,000 spectators. That said, there was a specific reason why Benn–McClellan proved such a hard sell, namely that Benn again refused to pull his promotional weight. In fact, it was the third fight in a row that Benn had thumbed his nose at his promoters and they were understandably furious at his lack of co-operation. 'He's behaved outrageously,' said Warren, who threatened Benn with a writ after he failed to show up for a press conference four days before the fight. Trevor East revealed he had decided against sending a film crew to Benn's training camp in Tenerife because there was no guarantee that Benn would make himself available. Indeed, Benn was fast gaining a reputation as an even bigger prima donna than Eubank. 'However difficult Chris Eubank was to deal with coming up to a fight he always came around in the end,' said East.

When Benn finally flew in, only three days before his fight with McClellan, his first engagement was with Lynch in the High Court. 'It seems like everyone wants Nigel Benn as a meal ticket, and I will not allow it,' said a smouldering Benn. The following day, Benn, who claimed he was owed £100,000 in VAT, had words with Warren at the final head-to-head press conference. 'He challenged me,' said Warren, 'but I told him to save his strength for McClellan because he's going to need it.' All told, Benn was at loggerheads with his wife, his girlfriend, two former trainers, his promoters, his television backers and tax men on both sides of the Atlantic. It didn't seem like the ideal preparation for the toughest night of his career.

But at least Benn sounded convincing when it was his turn to speak about his impending engagement with McClellan. 'If a fight's going to get me going, this is the fight to do it,' he said. 'If it goes one round or 12, it doesn't matter. The buzz he's given me is tremendous. He's banged out a lot of people, but who? I've seen it called High Noon for The Dark Destroyer. If this is High Noon, tell McClellan my guns are loaded and waiting to beat him to the draw.' Said McClellan: 'If Benn tries to have his famous tear-up with a man like me, he's committing suicide. You go to war and you win this war. Or you go to war and you die.'

McClellan didn't die, he was just left brain damaged. And blind. No more dog fighting, just fighting for life. For the rest of his life. What was left of it. McClellan loved killing shit. Nigel Benn nearly killed him. Not on purpose. But that's boxing. And to think he had been accused of quitting, as he crouched on one knee, referee standing over him, gesticulating wildly. Having soaked up 10 rounds of bestial savagery – jabs, uppercuts, hooks, crosses, elbows, heads and forearms – the commentators apparently thought he was just taking time out to wipe his brow and had forgotten about the count. McClellan didn't know it at the time, but a blood clot was growing in the cavity between the inside of his skull and his brain. In truth, he probably doesn't know about it now. Having been counted out, McClellan rose to his feet, turned to his trainer and asked: 'I lost the fight?' He then weaved towards his corner, turned so that his back was against the ring post and slid to the canvas before a stool could be placed beneath him. 'His brain is quite swollen,' said McClellan's neurosurgeon John Sutcliffe the morning after the fight. 'Just as you would expect after being punched for 10 rounds.' Ten months earlier, Sutcliffe had operated on Bradley Stone, who had been injured in a fight for the British super-bantamweight title against Richie Wenton. Stone died two days later. The omens weren't great.

As McClellan lay stricken in Whitechapel's Royal London Hospital, the merry-go-round of accusations and recriminations whirred into life. Fingers were pointed at French referee Alfred Azaro who, it was claimed, counted too slowly when Benn was battered through the ropes in the opening round. Fingers were pointed at McCellan's trainer Stan

Johnson who, it was claimed, should have picked up on his charge's unusual blinking and the fact his gumshield was hanging from his mouth as early as the third round. Fingers were pointed at Nigel Benn who, McClellan's sisters claimed, had almost killed their brother. Fingers were pointed at Gerald McClellan who, it was claimed, hadn't done the necessary work in the gym, had dived to make weight and was critically drained. Fingers were pointed at boxing fans who, it was claimed, were mentally unstable. Fingers were pointed at boxing itself which, it was claimed, was sick. Politicians inquired, journalists lectured, medical people admonished and cautioned. And in boxing gyms across the globe men carried on sparring, hitting the bag and once in a while enquiring: 'How's old Gerald McClellan?'

The Benn–McClellan fight is boxing's dirtiest secret, because it was everything most fans wanted. Except the someone nearly dying bit. And nothing has changed since. Ask anyone in the game about the prospect of the rematch between Carl Froch and Mikkel Kessler – fans, fighters and writers – and watch those grins widen and those eyes light up. 'It's gonna be a war, it's gonna be savage, it's gonna be a fight to the bitter end.' Nobody ever adds: 'I hope no one gets hurt.' Only when fighters do get hurt do people question their own blood-lust. 'When boxing is at its most thrilling and heroic, there is always the danger that the essence of its appeal, its very right to regard itself as a sport, will be called into question by a sickening injury,' wrote Hugh McIlvanney after Benn–McClellan. 'All the familiar confusion of emotions dominated by an ambivalence that teetered towards guilt crowded in again last night as the hot surge of excitement stirred by Nigel Benn's unforgettably brave victory against the odds yielded to the icy realisation

that Benn's defeated opponent, Gerald McClellan, was pros-
trate and alarmingly distressed on the canvas in his corner.'
Benn was less equivocal: 'You got what you wanted to see.'

McIlvanney had long before cemented his reputation as
boxing's eulogist-in-chief, waxing lyrical about the death in
1980 of Welsh bantamweight Johnny Owen and the injuries
suffered by Michael Watson. Owen's compatriot Eddie
Thomas, the former British and European welterweight
champion and manager of British greats Howard Winstone
and Ken Buchanan, attempted to explain why McIlvanney –
and just about everyone else – kept watching. 'It broke my
heart to see Johnny lying in his coffin and made me feel that
boxing isn't worth the candle,' said Thomas. 'But there is
something mysterious that keeps drawing you back.' In truth,
there's nothing mysterious about it at all: Gerald McClellan
wasn't the only one who liked seeing dogs fight.

That Michael Watson was sitting ringside seemed strangely to
salve the guilt: if a man who had been maimed in similar fashion
could legitimise what he had witnessed then surely it couldn't
be as awful as it seemed. In his autobiography, Watson refers to
the Benn–McClellan fight as 'one of the most amazing fights I
had ever seen . . . which I know is probably impossible for many
people to understand'. In September 1994, Watson's lawyer
issued a writ against the British Boxing Board of Control for
negligence. The Board, Watson argued, had neglected their
duties to provide the requisite medical care on the night of his
second fight against Chris Eubank. The case against the Board
gave Watson renewed focus and in 1995 a man some of the best
doctors in the land said would never stand again rose from his
wheelchair and took his first tentative steps. The Board,
however, was determined to fight tooth and nail, and it did not

matter one jot whether Watson was able to walk or not. And it did not matter, apparently, that it was Watson who had effectively saved McClellan's life: those five doctors present for Benn–McClellan, the anaesthetist, the paramedics, the two ambulances – they were all there for a reason.

At least Watson could cling to the hope, however faint, that some semblance of justice would one day be served. McClellan had no such outlet. Having woken from an induced coma after 11 days McClellan eventually returned to the United States, although there were suggestions he was flown home too soon. Back in his native Freeport, Illinois, McClellan fell into the care of his three sisters, who worked round the clock in eight-hour shifts to tend to his every need. 'He's not aware he's blind,' said sister Lisa a year after the fight. 'He thinks it's just dark or somebody's turned out the lights. He has good days. He laughs. He talks. He's happy. Then he has days where he says: "Something bad happened to me." And he wants to die.'

Various members of the McClellan family were fighting fires on various fronts. An undignified public row broke out between Lisa McClellan and Don King, with McClellan's sister denying King's claims he had paid for her brother's medical care, despite King producing receipts amounting to $226,758. She also accused King of paying Emmit McClellan, Gerald's estranged father, hush money not to talk to the media, which King and Emmit denied, and claimed she had video evidence proving her brother's mouthpiece had been spiked. Gerald's girlfriend sided with King, saying the promoter had flown her to England on Concorde and put her up for six weeks in a London hotel. King accused Lisa McClellan of being a pawn in an FBI conspiracy against him, while Emmit McClellan claimed the FBI had offered Lisa $50,000 to come forward with a statement against King, a convicted criminal the American authorities had wanted to nail for decades. Frank Warren also came out fighting, vociferously denying newspaper claims he had neglected McClellan and forcing the *Sunday Times* to print an apology. Meanwhile, back in Freeport, Illinois, McClellan sat cocooned in his own private hell. Brain damaged. And blind. Sometimes wanting to die.

'There is so much absurdity in boxing,' says Donald McRae, whose journey through the sport for his book *Dark Trade* left him with 'some of the sweetest and some of the saddest memories' of his life. 'I don't even feel it is a sport, it's something far beyond sport because of the dangers and also the psychological darkness these fighters have to face. Benn and Eubank and the fights they had are crucial to gaining insight into the darkness of boxing. They get to the heart of what boxing is about – and there's not much showbiz. It's actually about desire, emotional pain, physical agony and, ultimately, death. And Benn's fight against Gerald McClellan underlined just how dark it is.' Documents were eventually unearthed that revealed Frank Warren paid Don King £400,000 to bring McClellan to England. McClellan's purse was then whittled down to £133,000. Further deductions were made for McClellan's trainers, former trainers and sanctioning fees. Which left McClellan – brain damaged, blind, sometimes wanting to die – with £41,000.

CHAPTER FIFTEEN
Twit in a trance

An estimated 13 million British television viewers watched Nigel Benn nearly kill Gerald McClellan in London. Seven days later, an estimated 13 million British television viewers watched Naseem Hamed nearly kill Sergio Liendo in Livingston. Liendo was floored by Hamed in the second round, but the referee allowed the fight to go on. Liendo was floored again and what followed was one of the longest minutes in British boxing. The Argentine lay sprawled on the canvas, not moving, as the count was started and then abandoned. And then he suddenly stirred. Of course, it is a touch sensationalist to say Naseem Hamed nearly killed Liendo. It's just that, with the previous weekend's scenes fresh in the memory, spectators at least now realised what they were dealing with.

As a rule, super-bantamweights aren't box office. But it was his victory over gnarled veteran Liendo, who hadn't been stopped in 51 previous contests, that convinced any remaining doubters that Naseem Hamed wasn't your common or garden little man. And it wasn't just the power he carried in both fists that set him apart. It was Herol Graham's old trainer Brendan Ingle who first spotted the potential of the cocky little kid flailing away wildly in his Wincobank gym. 'Watch that little

Arab,' said Ingle to reporters, when Hamed was only seven. 'He'll be the best of the lot.' Indeed, so sure of his promise was the wily Irishman that he secured sponsorship for Hamed when he was only 13. Four wins into his pro career, an 18-year-old Hamed was already making tabloid waves, demanding a shot at the British flyweight title, despite the fact that he was three years under age. So good was he that even Barry McGuigan, who had been so wary of Chris Eubank's idiosyncrasies when he was coming through, was prepared to excuse Hamed's ceaseless showboating. 'He's flash but we can forgive him his antics because he's good,' said McGuigan.

Nine fights into his career in the paid ranks, Hamed was proclaiming: 'I will change British boxing, I will be better than anything that has gone before.' And the bosses at ITV believed it, signing Hamed up before Eubank was even out of the door. 'He can develop into a bigger cult figure than Eubank,' said Trevor East. Said Hamed: 'I fight so brilliantly as to make Eubank look deadly dull.' On his big screen debut, Hamed knocked out former Belgian champion John Miceli in one round, before wresting the European bantamweight crown from experienced Italian Vincenzo Belcastro. On his way to a one-sided points victory, which included two knock-downs, Hamed performed Ali shuffles, taunted his opponent with hands on hips and pretended to chat with reporters. 'Vincenzo does not understand what this Hamed was doing,' said Belcastro's manager. 'He thinks Hamed is a good boxer but he thinks Hamed should learn to box normally.' The grey heads in the press seats were appalled by Hamed's behaviour. 'Abolitionists who contend that boxing's ethos is hardly more elevated than that of bear-baiting,' wrote Hugh McIlvanney, 'were given a measure of encouragement as Hamed inflicted an elaborate repertoire of taunts and ridicule on Vincenzo

Belcastro. A danger is that television, swooning over the ratings engendered by all the pouting, posturing and showbiz claptrap inseparable from Chris Eubank's performances, might see Hamed's playground arrogance as a quality to emphasise in the marketplace.'

McIlvanney was to be disappointed. The Belcastro fight made Hamed a star overnight, and with Eubank having switched to Sky, ITV were going to milk Hamed's playground arrogance for all it was worth. Before the first defence of his European title, Hamed vowed to knock Antonio Picardi out in three rounds. Hamed did just that, before celebrating his win with a cartwheel across the ring. 'I have to apologise to Eubank because he is what was,' said Hamed. 'I am what is! You can forget him and Nigel Benn and all those other guys. This is my time.' On 12 October, Hamed stepped up a class and fought former two-time world title challenger Freddy Cruz, a 32-year-old who had not been stopped in 56 fights. Hamed battered Cruz from pillar to post before the referee called a halt to proceedings in the sixth round. Former light-weight world champion and ITV co-commentator Jim Watt called Hamed 'without doubt the most exciting and unique talent British boxing has seen for years'. Three days later, Eubank laboured to victory over battling businessman Dan Schommer in South Africa. It looked for all the world like Sky had backed the wrong man.

While Hamed was loath to admit it – bizarrely, he once accused Eubank of imitating him – Eubank was indeed the template for many of his moves. The overblown ring entrances, the vaulting over the ropes, the tapping together of the gloves, the statuesque posturing and staring into the middle distance, they were all well-worn Eubank staples by the time Hamed blasted onto the scene. But so it goes with boxing, where hardly anything is new and most things are merely borrowed and juiced-up to reinvigorate the flavour. In fact, and as is usually the case, Eubank's flamboyance was in turn heavily influenced by the American scene, and Puerto Rican legend Hector Camacho in particular.

When Camacho, the greatest showman of American boxing's last golden age, beat Ray Mancini to claim the WBO light-welterweight title in 1989, he made his entrance wearing a loin cloth, spangled boots and a matador's hat and cape. During his long and mostly distinguished career, Camacho variously entered the ring in a gladiator's outfit, an American Indian costume, complete with feathered headdress, a fox-fur robe and a dress. Before his fight with Sugar Ray Leonard in 1997, Camacho left the press corps and commentators gasping when he stripped down to nothing more than a smile for the live televised weigh-in. Compared to Camacho, Eubank seemed like a throwback to the sepia age. Indeed, Hamed probably had more in common with Camacho than Eubank, certainly in terms of his boundless ring-related extravagance and stupendous natural talent. No wonder, then, that Hamed didn't take a blind bit of notice when Eubank took him aside and philosophised about the dangers of comparing oneself to others. 'I quoted him a small extract from the 1692 poem "Desiderata",' says Eubank. '"*If you compare yourself with others you may become vain and bitter, for always there will be greater and lesser persons than yourself*". But he couldn't take it on and I became quite frustrated.'

Eubank recouped a large amount of respect with his victory over Henry Wharton but Sky Sports' executives were not about to throw him an easy fight as a reward. Not when Hamed was pulling up trees on the other side. When Ray Close was forced to withdraw from a third fight after he failed a brain scan, rugged Dubliner Steve Collins stepped in. Collins had paid his dues and was about as hard as they came. Having started his professional career in Boston in the same gym and with the same handlers as Marvin Hagler, he went the distance with WBA middleweight champion Mike McCallum in 1990. Collins also came up short when challenging for the vacant WBA belt in 1992, when he was narrowly beaten by Reggie Johnson, and again when he was outpointed by European champion Sumbu Kalambay. But despite these losses, Collins could easily argue his record was as impressive as Eubank's, or at least that the names on it were. And while he had never fought as a super-middleweight and had not fought at all for ten months (he had won the WBO middleweight crown from Englishman Chris Pyatt in Sheffield in his previous fight), Collins could also argue that he was infinitely fresher than the champion: during the Irishman's ten months of inactivity, Eubank had fought 55 rounds.

An ill-tempered build-up saw Eubank out-psyched for possibly the only time in his career. 'Benn couldn't work Eubank out,' says Colin Hart, 'very few people could work Eubank out. In fact, the only man who could really work him out was Steve Collins. Collins spooked Eubank before their first fight, he really got into Eubank's head.' At the press conference to announce the fight, which was set for the small Cork village of Millstreet, Collins sent Eubank into a rage by claiming he was betraying his African roots by carrying on like an English gentleman. To hammer home his point, Collins conducted some of the press conference in Gaelic. 'I have never been so insulted,' railed Eubank, 'they were totally racist remarks. Collins will pay for what he said and did today. This has changed everything – this means a fight to the death.' The Benn–McClellan fight would take place three weeks later, but

Eubank's ill-chosen words stirred memories of the passing of Bradley Stone and his own ill-fated victory over Michael Watson. To make things worse, Eubank swore at the mayor of Dublin, who had suggested a tour of the city's sights.

Collins's provocation had the desired effect. Not only did they work his opponent into a lather, they also ensured the 6,000-capacity Green Glens Arena was sold out within two hours of the tickets going on sale. But even away from the dais, the home favourite was making plenty of confident noises. 'Eubank's OK, he's just not in touch with reality,' said Collins. 'I'm going to do him a big favour and bring him down to earth. Eubank is going to make me a rich man.' But the fight almost came apart at the weigh-in when Collins announced he was regularly being hypnotised as part of his preparation. It was a pretty cheap trick but Eubank fell for it a treat. 'Chris was on the verge of pulling out because he felt the hypnosis would give Collins an advantage,' said Ronnie Davies. 'I think it is a sham.' It was only after crisis talks with Barry Hearn, who also handled Collins, that Eubank relented. Perhaps the knowledge that two of the three judges for the fight would be Puerto Rican helped ease Eubank's fears: nine times Puerto Rican judges had sat in judgement in Eubank's seven previous world title contests and not one had decided against him.

Despite Collins's shenanigans, most boxing writers thought Eubank would have too much for the challenger. But it wasn't to be. In a rocking Green Glens Arena, Collins survived a 10th-round knockdown to claim a unanimous points decision, with one of the two Puerto Rican judges giving it to the challenger by a margin of 115–111. Eubank's ten-year unbeaten run was over, his 43-fight winning streak was over, his 19-fight reign as a world champion was over.

And how the tabloids gloated. 'ON EUR BIKE!' screamed the *People*, referring to Eubank's ring entrance astride a Harley Davidson; 'TWIT IN A TRANCE! DEFEAT AT LAST!' roared the *Sunday Mirror*, as if trumpeting the downfall of a great dictator; 'EU HAD IT COMING!' raged Scotland's *Daily Record*, which had never forgiven him for the controversial draw against Ray Close in Glasgow or the iffy verdict against Tony Thornton.

More sober publications paid tribute to Eubank's courage and grace in defeat, although some wondered why he had been allowed to get away with fighting so many journeymen for so long. 'There are legions who are convinced that his unbeaten record was a fake anyway,' wrote Ian Chadband in the *Sunday Times*, 'so the sight of Collins winning a unanimous points decision to take his WBO super-middleweight crown will be hailed as long overdue.' For Eubank's connections, the real worry wasn't that he had lost his belt and his unbeaten record, it was that the defeat seemed to offer incontrovertible proof that he had lost his killer instinct. 'Eubank gave his title away,' said Ronnie Davies. 'He had Collins down for nine in the 10th round and virtually out.' 'I was waving him forward,' says Hearn, 'but he just stood there posing and preening. No fighter does that, you get the job done.' Explaining his failure to finish Collins off when he had him wounded, Eubank said: 'I didn't want what became of Watson to happen again, so I froze.' It should also be remembered that the fight took place only three weeks after Benn–McClellan.

After the Collins defeat, few would have been surprised if the 28-year-old Eubank had walked away from boxing. After all, it was a sport he professed to hate, a sport he had vowed to escape from before the age of 30, with his faculties intact and millions in the bank. And he did have millions in the bank.

Surely? Actually, far from it. The shocking truth was, despite – or more correctly because of – the mansion in Hove, the souped-up Aston Martin with the 6.3-litre engine and the white hide upholstery, the Harley Davidson, the block book-ings at The Dorchester, the weekend shopping trips to New York, the globe-trotting barber, the walk-in wardrobe contain-ing his vast collection of riding boots and rack upon rack of Savile Row suits and the little Louis Vuitton case he liked to travel with, which he claimed contained £100,000 worth of jewellery, he was £2 million in hock to the taxman. 'I'm not annoyed with myself because I have lived,' said Eubank. 'It's been like a fantasy world for the last four years. I've lived like the Sultan of Brunei's son, and I could quite easily live out the rest of my life reminiscing about the past four years.' And so Eubank announced his intention to retire 'as soon as my family is financially secure'. Which looked like being a fair few years and lots and lots of lumps and bumps away.

As the weeks went by Eubank's initial grace in defeat curdled to bitterness. 'Collins now says he wasn't really hypnotised,' said Eubank, 'but he gave interviews that said he was. Did he beat me? No, he cheated. He won the fight, but the methods he used were not ones he can openly tell his grandchildren he used.' Meanwhile, the posters for his next fight against Argentina's Bruno Godoy in Belfast betrayed the doubts that had seeped into the Eubank camp: 'Simply the Best?' went the legend, the question mark telling. The press labelled it a cross-roads fight, one that would tell us if Eubank was all rusted up or still had a bit of poke under the bonnet. Eubank promised fight fans 'a little more ruthlessness and a little less chivalry'. Fans, press and Eubank were all to be frustrated. A clash of heads in the first round opened up a nasty wound over Godoy's left eye and the contest was stopped after only two minutes and 45 seconds. Robbed of a vital workout before a proposed rematch with Collins, Eubank launched another stinging attack on the Irishman, calling him 'a cheat, a sly creep, a gouger, disgusting and deplorable'. And after a 55-second knockout of Spain's Jose Ignacio Barruetabena in Whitley Bay – a finger injury to Collins had pushed the rematch back from July to September 1995 – Eubank said: 'Next time I face Collins it will not be my fault if he loses his life. There will be no more kindness. I will show no mercy.' Michael Watson was probably watching. Gerald McClellan might have been, only he was now brain damaged and blind.

It was around this time that Eubank and Barry Hearn parted ways. The problem between them, as always in boxing, was money: Eubank thought he should have been making more from gate receipts while Hearn claimed there simply wasn't enough coming in from Eubank's 'world tour' to grease the many gears and cogs of his business. Reflecting on their mutually beneficial relationship, Hearn readily admits it was Eubank who made it so wildly successful and not the other way round. 'My whole life has been one succession of amazing pieces of luck,' says Hearn. 'I started out in snooker in 1974 and Steve Davis turned up in 1975, an 18-year-old with his arse hanging out of his trousers, and ended up being the greatest snooker player in the world. I started getting involved with boxing and suddenly Eubank walked into my office and ended up being the biggest box-office sensation of the 1990s. When I first met Eubank he wasn't fully formed but he had a natural confidence and swagger. Boxing is weird, it's the only sport where the competitors are told to go out and sell most of the tickets for an event. Can you imagine me turning round to Steve Davis and saying: "Good luck at the Crucible, son – here's 500 tickets, here's your posters, off you go"? So Eubank used to look down his nose – expansive nose that it was – and say: "You're the promoter, you sell the tickets. I'm the fighter, I'll do the fighting." That's really how it should be, but no one else really did it like that. But what I did do is draw out this natural confidence and swagger and enhance it.

'It's correct to say that promoters and trainers are only great if their fighters are great. You can be the worst promoter in the world but you can be the biggest promoter if you've got the best fighters. The number one promoter in Europe at the moment is my son Eddie because he has Carl Froch, David Haye, Ricky Burns and Kell Brook, all world-class fighters. They make him a world-class promoter. Although, if you're going to deliver your fighters the money, you've really got to be good as well. That said, I've been so lucky, I sometimes think I'll get run over by a lorry or something. Although God did balance it out a little bit by giving me Leyton Orient to look after.'

Eubank's return fight against Collins was promoted by Don King and Frank Warren, who was turning the tide in his ongoing battle against Hearn. 'Barry Hearn should have started worrying about getting hand-outs when I kept winning purse bids for his fighters,' says Warren. 'And they all left him to join me: Chris Eubank, Nigel Benn, Steve Collins, Chris Pyatt, Herbie Hide . . .' Eubank–Collins II was set for Pairc Ui Chaoimh, a Gaelic football stadium in Cork, for 9 September 1995. The British Boxing Board of Control fined Eubank £5,000 for his ill-chosen words about Collins, but Eubank remained unrepentant, telling the champion at the weigh-in: 'My career is more important than your life.' Collins replied: 'Having beaten Eubank once, there are no terrors left. His threats have made me more determined to beat him.'

In front of 20,000 raucous fans at a rain-soaked Pairc Ui

Chaoimh, Collins did indeed prevail again. A hyped-up Collins started in ferocious fashion, literally running out of his corner at the sound of the first bell and taking most of the earlier rounds on work-rate alone. Eubank belatedly came to life in the sixth before a clash of heads in the seventh opened up a cut next to Collins's right eye. But Collins withstood the now customary Eubank rally down the stretch and was handed the verdict on a split decision, although most observers thought the champion, who bullied Eubank at times, won by four or five rounds. Eubank skipped the post-fight press conference but others were there to fill in the blanks. 'I don't know what he will do now,' said Ronnie Davies, 'and I'm closer to him than anyone apart from his wife. There are no excuses, he got beaten by a better man.' Barry McGuigan, who knew better than most how difficult it was to accept what everybody else saw and give up the ghost, was less equivocal. 'It's sadly the end of a long and illustrious career,' said McGuigan. 'Chris Eubank has got nowhere else to go.'

Eubank's second defeat by Collins was a devastating blow, and not just to the Englishman's ego. There had been tentative talk of a third instalment against Benn, potentially worth as much as £3 million, but this now seemed like a pipe dream. Indeed, the most natural fight, in light of Eubank's latest defeat, was Benn versus Collins. Sky deal over and his earning potential decimated, most agreed Eubank would be sensible to retire. Granted, Eubank could feel the hot breath of the tax man on his well-starched collar but did he have the desire and the humility required to claw his way back up to the top of the mangled, bloodied ranks? A month after the rematch against Collins, the British public got their answer. Eubank invited the media to his home in Hove and, after holding a minute's silence for Scottish bantamweight James Murray, who had died a few days earlier after challenging for the British title, he announced he had bowed to the inevitable. 'I have invested wisely and I am secure for life,' said Eubank. 'There is life outside the ring. I've been boxing since I was 16 and it's a hard life. I won't be coming back.' Eubank claimed he had been offered 'millions of pounds' to return by competing television channels, but the truth was rather different: ITV was only prepared to take him back at a drastically reduced rate and Sky, which had taken on Frank Warren's burgeoning stable of fighters, including Naseem Hamed and Nigel Benn, was relieved to be shot of him. Even so, almost everybody expected him to return. Eubank claimed to hate boxing, but the enduring tragedy of the man was that boxing was what defined him. And since when did Eubank ever do anything sensible?

Shortly after announcing his retirement, Eubank was interviewed by Mrs Merton on her spoof chat show. It was Eubank's chance to show the world that everything before had been an act, a persona he had tailored merely to further his boxing career. But in an excruciating piece of television, Caroline Aherne, aka Mrs Merton, appeared to be the only one in character. Eubank sat in virtual silence as Aherne took him to the cleaners, making a mockery of Eubank's oft-repeated claim that he was almost anybody's intellectual equal, a man who could 'show off, charm, communicate with people who have PhDs in philosophy and make them feel intimidated'. 'Were you surprised, as we all were,' said Merton, referring to Eubank's defeat by Collins, 'when he came from behind and licked you in the ring?' Eubank clearly didn't get the joke, but Aherne ploughed on undeterred. 'Did he say: "Come on over here if you think you're hard enough?"' If Eubank got the joke now, he certainly didn't show it.

THE HATE GAME

The Mrs Merton interview only confirmed what many already suspected, that Eubank was Alan Partridge made real: socially awkward, narcissistic, obsessed by status, insensitive to social norms, prone to one-upmanship and embarrassing social faux pas. The scene on Brighton seafront on New Year's Eve 1995 would have slotted into Partridge's sitcom seamlessly. While having dinner with his family in the Thistle Hotel, Eubank spotted a little boy looking down in the dumps. Some might have told him a joke, others might have tried a card trick. Eubank drove home to his house in Hove, loaded up his Range Rover with £4,000 worth of industrial fireworks and set up an impromptu display on the seafront. Of course, it all went horribly wrong. Revellers were sent running for cover, the windows of pubs and restaurants were rattled by the explosions and two women were seriously burned and had to be treated in hospital. 'I was only trying to cheer that kid up and give my family a nice night out,' said Eubank, who was sentenced to 200 hours of community service.

Things got even weirder. Despite his well-documented money problems, Eubank claimed he had made an offer of £38 million to buy Brighton pier. He then bought a title for £45,000. 'With my dress code and being the Lord of the Manor of Brighton,' said Eubank, 'hopefully in 300 years they will speak about me in the same way as they speak of other trailblazers.' Then there was Eubank's beloved American Peterbilt rig, of which he spoke of in almost mystical terms: 'Chrome. Midnight blue. Beautiful. It's beautiful, this truck. A beautiful monstrosity.' 'Chris was on holiday in Florida,' says Colin Hart, 'and Ronnie Davies was with him, because Davies went everywhere, on family holidays, the lot. Suddenly this bleedin' great truck went past and Eubank said to Davies: "I want one of those." Davies said: "What the fuck are you talking

251

about?" But Chris found out the name of the truck, bought one and had it shipped back to Britain. He drove around in it, but just the cabin.' The truck – 12 ft high, 32 ft long, weighing eight tons, with ten wheels and 13 gears – cost £150,000 and a further £22,000 to ship home, despite Eubank not having a licence to drive it. Eubank passed his HGV test at the fourth attempt and promptly set himself up as a human tourist attraction, driving up and down Brighton seafront, honking the horn. Heading nowhere, because he had nowhere to go now his training ring had been dismantled.

In Eubank's mind he was a great British eccentric and philanthropist, bringing fun and wonder to the humdrum lives of the simple folk of Sussex. 'The truck lifts people,' he said, 'it inspires them. When I go to the grocery store for some milk, people literally stop in the street and stare! It's great fun, a good buzz. It never ceases to raise me.' In reality, a lot of people thought Eubank and his truck were a bloody nuisance: parking it wherever he fancied, clogging up streets, annoying people with his horn, Eubank cut a tragicomic figure. 'The noise is driving me mad,' said local resident Keith Ball. 'You can hear him morning, noon and night.' Battling Siki walked his pet lion down the Champs-Élysées, Chris Eubank drove his truck down Brighton seafront. For Siki, things didn't turn out well.

CHAPTER SIXTEEN
That's fucking it

In June 1995, Nigel Benn signed up for a title defence against Italian Vincenzo Nardiello. The venue? The London Arena, where he had wreaked such awful havoc on the life of Gerald McClellan only four months earlier. Benn described his beating at the once heavy hands of McClellan as 'worse than being hit with a pickaxe handle' and told how he had been too weak to lift his baby daughter for days. The last time he had seen McClellan was at the Royal London Hospital, where they were treated in adjoining cubicles immediately after the fight. According to others present, McClellan briefly regained consciousness and shook his rival's hand before Benn ducked out: two men bidding farewell at the crossroads – one fork leading to the light, the other into darkness. While many wondered how a man who had plumbed such perilous physical and emotional depths could fight on, Benn merely claimed the McClellan bout 'put the animal back in me'. Although there were less melodramatic and more prosaic reasons to continue. 'You can't go in with the attitude that you can't give it your all any more,' says Benn. 'If that's how you feel, get out of this brutal sport. I never had that attitude, even after the McClellan fight. I probably should have retired but I wasn't financially secure. I didn't have time to think about what happened to Gerald because I had to think about my family.'

Before Benn's contest against Nardiello, Orlin Norris was stretchered from the ring with an oxygen mask strapped to his face having been knocked out by fellow American cruiser-weight Nate Miller. Norris was whisked through the same doors McClellan was whisked through, travelled the same roads McClellan travelled and ended up at the very same crossroads. But Norris was luckier than McClellan and found to be suffering from nothing more serious than severe heat exhaustion. The fans in the London Arena weren't to know this as Benn and Nardiello stood nose to nose before the open-ing bell, ready to do damage. But still they roared their hero in, like banshees on a battlefield. Nardiello was sent sprawling six times before his father threw in the towel in the eighth round. 'Same arena, different man, same hurt game,' said Benn. 'Since "that" fight other people say I should quit but I think people should just keep their noses out of my business. I know what is best for Nigel Benn.'

At the post-fight press conference, Frank Warren, who had made Chris Eubank an offer to join him in the wake of his first defeat by Steve Collins, looked disconsolate as Benn made it clear the only fight that interested him now was Roy Jones Jr. 'The taxman might be looking for him, not me,' said Benn. 'He ain't got nothing I want, except his Harley.' However, boxing politics seemed destined to prevent the fight against Jones from ever happening: Benn fought on American televi-sion network Showtime; Jones, who had vowed never to fight on a King show, on HBO. Not that King seemed deterred. 'We are going to travel down the yellow brick road to the city of Oz,' said King, 'dodge the Scarecrow, Tin Man and the Lion and bring back Roy Jones.' King claimed a Benn–Jones match could be worth $50 million but, in truth, the road to the city of Oz was even more treacherous than he made out. Only it wasn't scarecrows, tin men and lions he had to dodge, it was rival managers, promoters and television executives. Meanwhile, Benn stayed on course with a seventh-round stoppage of American Danny Perez on the undercard of Frank Bruno's world title triumph over Oliver McCall at Wembley. On an emotional night, Benn vowed to donate $1 million of his purse for fighting Jones to Jones's close friend McClellan. But as the days turned into weeks turned into months the city of Oz seemed to get no closer.

While Warren and King schemed behind the scenes, rival challenges came in from Collins and Yorkshire warhorse Henry Wharton. Jones, meanwhile, threatened to quit boxing and become a basketball player if the Benn fight failed to come off. Benn's connections claimed Jones was asking for the lion's share of the purse and that Benn wanted at least a 50–50 split. Instead, Benn signed up for a mandatory defence against Thulani 'Sugar Boy' Malinga, the South African he had only just shaded almost four years earlier. With a unification match against Collins virtually in the bag, few countenanced a Benn defeat but it quickly became apparent he had nothing left in the well. Malinga jabbed his head off for most of the fight and the split decision verdict in favour of the challenger was generous to Benn in the extreme. Benn promptly announced his retirement, before proposing to girlfriend Carolyne in the ring. Blood, sweat, tears and kisses, the evening summed up Benn to a tee.

Two days later, Benn announced his intention to continue fighting. 'I don't think I am shot or punch-drunk,' he said. 'I needed a kick up the backside. I don't want to go out like this. I was mentally unprepared. I thought it was going to be an easy night. I just did not have the fear factor which is what I need to perform at my best.' Benn could have been reading from a boxer's handbook, entitled: *101 Ways to Convince Yourself You've Still Got It (when everyone else can see you haven't)*. Desperately seeking positives, Benn said the defeat to Malinga provided him with the chance to become a three-time world champion and so Jones entered the frame again. Telephone numbers were quoted, claims and counter-claims were made before Jones, tiring of the wearisome soap opera, decided to make a personal entreaty.

'I called him and asked him if he wanted the fight and he said it was something he'd definitely entertain,' says Jones. 'But at the time he was caught up in a divorce so I didn't bother him any more after that. But Nigel Benn was a wonderful fighter, people didn't give him the credit he deserved. Benn beat a very good friend of mine, Gerald McClellan, so you can't say that those guys, Benn and Eubank, weren't great fighters or just as good as the top fighters in the United States at the time. Benn was everything they said he was, his nickname was perfect: he was a true Dark Destroyer. What people didn't understand was, it's very difficult to go in the ring and knock somebody out and he knocked nearly everybody out, including some of the top American fighters. And they were action-packed fights, wars. But I thought I would have outboxed and outfought him. The mistake McClellan made against Benn is he went out and slugged with him and that was Benn's favourite thing. So I wasn't going to slug with him, I was going to box him, soften him up, get some of that power out of his system and then step in for the kill. Like Michael Watson did.'

Barely a month after the Malinga fight, it was announced that Benn would challenge Collins for the Irishman's WBO super-middleweight crown. 'I feel naked without my belt,' said Benn. 'People ask for my autograph and I have to put "former champion".' Two days later, the *Sunday Mirror* reported that Eubank was coming back as well and was already in light training. Suddenly, it felt like Benn–Eubank III was just round the corner. Reports soon began to emerge that Eubank was in negotiations for a comeback fight in Cairo, reports that turned out to be true. Eubank had been approached by an Arab consortium, which was keen to stage the first ever professional bout in Egypt. Eubank said he saw himself as a pioneer for the sport of boxing, but it was the reported £1 million purse that probably clinched the deal. 'I was treated like a king out there,' said Eubank. 'Being made to feel wanted and being treated in such a special way never hurts the ego.' It's certainly better for the ego than being moaned at for honking the horn on your big truck.

When Benn lost to Collins in curious fashion in July 1996, it looked like any chance of Benn–Eubank III happening was gone. For all of 30 minutes. Having retired in the fourth round after twisting his right ankle when falling through the ropes, Benn grabbed the microphone and announced: 'I honestly think this is it for me.' But at the post-fight press conference, Benn performed a dramatic U-turn: 'There is still a lot of fighting left in me. I know I can beat Steve.' Ringside conspirators thought Benn resigned himself to defeat a bit too readily and most who saw the fight believed Benn's bestial spirit was tamed. 'The public who still flock to his fights realise it,' wrote John Sadler in the *Sun*. 'Those who stage them suspect it too. And Benn, himself, knows he should hang up the gloves. It is simply a matter of not being able to stick to the judgment made honestly and sensibly in the aftermath of the action that has confirmed his body can no longer support the ambitions in his mind.' The next day, a rematch between Benn and Collins was announced for November.

But first was Eubank's fight in Cairo, dubbed 'Style on the Nile' by Eubank and 'Carry on up the Nile' by the *Guardian*'s Kevin Mitchell. Eubank boasted he had been lured out of retirement by Middle Eastern royalty and some Cairo newspapers claimed his second coming was at the request of Prime Minister John Major and the Queen. The truth was he had teamed up with an alleged Sudanese princess from Devon, who had been acquitted three years earlier of a multi-million-pound property fraud. Barry Hearn attempted to talk Eubank out of the deal but Eubank's pride would not allow it. Eubank found out exactly how valuable Hearn had been to him down the years when it came to negotiating with television executives. At a meeting with an ITV delegation – at the Dorchester, naturally – Eubank demanded £1 million. By the end of some vigorous discussions, the ITV executives had knocked the figure down to £8000. Eurosport offered in the region of £20,000 to show the fight three days after the event, while Sky offered nothing. Said one senior British television executive: 'It was looking more like the "Fumble in the Jumble Sale" than the "Rumble in the Jungle".' In an attempt to recoup their losses, Eubank and his 'royal' connections priced ringside seats at £675. Other seats were priced at between £75 and £150, despite the fact that wages were so low in Egypt that tickets at football matches went for £1 or less. As a result, the arena was full of army personnel on the night of the fight, presumably watching for free. Eubank, who beat little-known Argentine Luis Dionisio Barrera in five rounds, remained unbowed and frighteningly deluded: 'I am becoming more and more aware of the keen interest heads of state are showing in me,' he said.

'Omar Sharif was supposed to be there, Mohamed Al-Fayed,

the King of Jordan, it was just the biggest scam of all time,' says Mitchell. 'We got to Cairo and nobody even knew the fight was on. Then, when we got to the arena on the outskirts of town, it was like we were under attack, there were all these military vehicles rolling up full of navy cadets, soldiers and policemen. And there was no sign of Omar Sharif. Because they couldn't sell it, Chris spun it into this grand Middle Eastern project, claimed they were taking boxing to dusty Egypt. He said that in the future there'd be all these Arab kids boxing all over the place, which I'm pretty sure hasn't happened. But that fight says a lot about the man: we were prepared to follow him to Cairo even though we knew it was complete nonsense from start to finish. I'd even written a story beforehand saying what a load of nonsense the fight was – and that's why we ended up going, because it was a load of nonsense. No one else in the world could have persuaded us to follow such a ridiculous cause. It wasn't a contest of any sort, but with Eubank you went for the adventure.'

Over in Tenerife, Nigel Benn was telling clubbers at his DJ sets in Playa de las Américas that 'the fuse is lit'. But most thought it would fizzle out before long. 'I've been in with Eubank, McClellan, Watson, Barkley and DeWitt,' said Benn. 'The last person I worry about is Steve Collins.' Replied Collins: 'What I see is a man under pressure. And everyone knows about his chin, it's made of glass. Unless he has grown another arm, he knows he's in big trouble.' 'When I fought Steve the second time I knew I was kind of gone,' admits Benn now, 'but I still bet £100,000 I'd beat him, because I wanted to convince myself.' At a packed-out Nynex Arena in Manchester, Benn gave everything he had until his corner pulled him out before the start of the seventh round. Benn threw his gloves into the crowd, grabbed the microphone and announced his intention to quit – again. 'I can't go on,' said Benn. 'Since 1987 I have been trying to do everything to please the British public. There might be another Dark Destroyer but that's fucking it for me.' Benn's speech was drowned out by jeers and catcalls, from punters who felt let down. Punters Benn had entertained for the best part of a decade. Punters whose lust for blood Benn had sated. Punters Benn had maimed for. Punters Benn had almost killed for. How quickly they forget, these men who smell of cigarettes and pubs, men who think they are hard but have never laced up gloves. 'Give him his due,' said Collins, 'he is the greatest fighter Britain has ever produced.' And still they jeered and catcalled.

Benn's indignity didn't end there. At the post-fight press conference, Naseem Hamed, who fought on the same card, admonished Benn for quitting. 'I would not have sat down on my stool like that,' said Hamed. 'You can break my legs and rip my arms off, but I would still have come out fighting.' Benn growled back: 'You've still got a lot to do before you become a legend or match what I've achieved in boxing.' Chris Eubank, meanwhile, was strutting behind the dais like a peacock, shooting his cuffs and inspecting his gold-topped cane. 'What have you come back for?' sneered Hamed. But to everybody's surprise, Benn jumped up and embraced his old rival: sworn enemies turned brothers in arms against this nasty little interloper. 'Nigel bumped into Naz at an awards ceremony shortly after that and wanted to tear his head off,' says Kevin Mitchell. 'He was so angry that anybody, let alone a fellow boxer, would say that about him. The reality was he gave as much as he had left that night.'

Benn's rollocking ring career appeared to be over, but Eubank boxed on. There was talk of a long overdue match against

Herol Graham, who had returned to action after a four-year sabbatical (Graham lost a third world title challenge in 1998 when he was stopped by Charles Brewer, having dropped the American twice). There was talk of Eubank challenging European light-heavyweight champion Crawford Ashley. Instead, Eubank fought a Colombian journeyman called Camilo Alarcon at a tennis club in Dubai. In his autobiography, Eubank covers the fight in two paragraphs, the first of which focuses on the £148 glass of brandy he bought a friend in a hotel bar. On the night of the fight, Eubank arrived on a crane before knocking out his opponent in the fourth round. But behind the scenes, all was not well. Eubank, once again displaying a spectacular lack of business acumen, failed to sign contracts with his co-promoters and when Ronnie Davies tried to intervene, Eubank took umbrage. 'I run my business,' says Eubank, 'I always did. He worked for me, whether he liked that or not.' Once again Eubank's pride had got the better of him, because Davies turned out to be right. Eubank received nothing for the fight and Davies would never work his corner again.

Meanwhile, Barry Hearn appeared to be finished as a big-time promoter. In the space of 13 months, Hearn had lost six world titles: Eubank, Herbie Hide, Eamonn Loughran and Paul Weir were beaten, Paul 'Silky' Jones was stripped of his crown and Steve Collins parted in acrimonious circumstances. Worse, Eubank, Hide and Collins ended up with Frank Warren. 'I shall always wear that big smile on my face and I will ignore all the back-stabbing and the rumours,' said Hearn. His smile looked more than a little bit forced when one of his few remaining headline acts, Mark Delaney, was stopped in five rounds by Welsh sensation Joe Calzaghe in April 1996.

'The Benn–Eubank fight was one of the main reasons Sky

offered Frank a fortune to take his stable to them,' says Trevor East, who became head of ITV Sport in 1995 before following Warren to Sky. 'Frank was at the peak of his powers, while Sky had got totally pissed off with the shit Barry had sold them – eight meaningless Eubank fights against stiffs. They couldn't wait to get out of the deal and decided Warren was the man to back instead.' Warren, who was almost on his knees only five years earlier, seemed to have seen his arch rival off. 'Barry's not a boxing man, he dips in and out of the sport,' says Warren. 'I outbid Barry Hearn for the second Eubank–Close fight, I outbid Hearn for the second Eubank–Collins fight. In fact I never lost a purse bid against Barry Hearn. And Barry and Eubank got dumped by Sky and then Hearn got dumped by ITV. And who did Eubank come to at the end of his career? Me.'

In September 1997, Eubank and Warren announced their new alliance at a press conference in Piccadilly Circus, during which the former champion claimed all that stuff about him hating boxing wasn't actually true. 'I love boxing,' said Eubank, 'I'm here for fun.' Eubank's first fight under Warren's promotional banner was meant to be a light-heavyweight contest against Londoner Mark Prince. But when Collins pulled out of his scheduled fight against Calzaghe for a third time and was stripped of his WBO super-middleweight title, Eubank stepped in at 11 days' notice. Eubank called Collins, who said he had a leg injury, a 'bottler'. Collins, furious at being bumped, promptly quit the sport, continued his protracted and expensive court battle with Hearn and never returned. Meanwhile, boxing folk were scandalised by the decision to have Eubank fight Calzaghe for the vacant title when he had waged two insignificant fights in the desert since losing his second fight to Collins and was dangerously above the 12 stone super-middleweight limit.

Most people expected Calzaghe, who was six years younger than Eubank, a former three-time ABA champion and unbeaten in 22 professional fights, to be too fresh and too fast, including Ronnie Davies. Davies was officially sacked as Eubank's trainer a week before the fight, although told he could still be part of Eubank's court in the diminished role of 'companion'. 'I loved Chris to death and we were as close as brothers,' said Davies, who had been a trainer, butler and confidant to Eubank for ten years. 'Out of the blue Chris decided he wanted to bring in an American trainer and I strongly objected. He then rounded on me and said: "In that case I am going to punish you."' Davies claimed that from that moment on Eubank banned him from eating with him, talking to him or even being in the same room as him. 'I put up with a lot from Chris down the years,' added Davies. 'He would treat me like a servant in front of the media and I went along with it for a laugh. But even that got out of hand, it was "get me this, get me that" until it drove me mad.'

For Calzaghe, being caught up in the Eubank circus proved a bewildering experience. 'Benn and Eubank were the big dogs for me,' says Calzaghe. 'I was massive fans of both of them when I was coming through, they were the two most exciting fighters in the country. I was 19 or 20, an ABA champion when they first fought and I was thinking: "I'm going to turn pro one day and take these guys on. I want to be in these big arenas with them, have millions of people watching us on TV." I remember seeing Eubank's fight against Sam Storey in Cardiff and while it wasn't a great fight to watch, the atmosphere when he walked to the ring to "Simply the Best" was unreal. I remember thinking: "This is what it's all about, what an adrenaline rush." I really liked the way Eubank carried himself. Sometimes his fights were disappointing but he had such huge charisma, you had to see his fights. The way he spoke and some of the stuff that used to come out of his mouth, I used to love it, it was show business, man, he captured the imagination and brought money into the game. It's weird to think that a few years later I was going to be boxing him.

'The first time I met Chris was at the Grosvenor Hotel in London for a press conference. I looked over at him and he came towards me and said: "Hello – and you are?" He knew exactly who I was, but I thought it was quite charming. I said: "Chris, you'll know exactly who I am after we fight." He gave me a wry smile, a very firm handshake and then he was off. It was all very surreal for a Valley boy. I was very brash, very cocky, knocking everybody out in the first couple of rounds, and I had no real respect for him. I thought I was going to knock this guy out as well. But I'll never forget what he came out with at the weigh-in. He looked me straight in the eyes and said: "You're not going to knock me out and I'm going to take you to one place you've never been before – the trenches." I didn't know where the trenches were until I fought Chris.'

According to the posters, the headline act at the Sheffield Arena was Naseem Hamed, who was making the eighth defence of his WBO featherweight crown, against Puerto Rico's Jose Badillo. But if anyone could upstage the local hero in his own backyard, Eubank could. 'No doubt many of the paying public and millions watching on television will get the greatest kick out of seeing whether it is Eubank or Hamed who makes the silliest or the most spectacular entrance into the ring,' wrote Colin Hart in the *Sun*. 'But when it comes down to the serious business of boxing, the fight fraternity will be far more fascinated by Eubank's battle with Calzaghe.' But if Eubank needed a reminder of his diminished status in the game, he was provided with one by Frank Warren a couple of days before the fight. When Eubank demanded a helicopter to fly him from Brighton to Sheffield and a chauffeur-driven Mercedes on arrival, Warren told him to get lost, or words to that effect. Eubank hired his own helicopter instead, paying £4000 for the privilege, but strong winds prevented it from taking off on time and he missed the final pre-fight press conference.

Calzaghe claimed to be disappointed he wasn't facing Collins but he was actually being disingenuous. 'I knew when Eubank stepped in for Collins that he'd be a tougher fight,' says Calzaghe. 'At least with Collins you knew what you were going to get, but with Eubank that wasn't the case. He wasn't the best fighter but he was very strong and very clever.' Hamed having toiled to a seventh-round victory over Badillo, Eubank appeared in silhouette behind a curtain of smoke at just after midnight before making his customary entrance into the ring: striking a pose of jaw-jutting defiance on the ring apron, vaulting over the ropes, pedalling backwards across the canvas. No one had gone home.

At the sound of the first bell, Calzaghe rushed Eubank and Eubank let fly with a howitzer right hand, which the Welshman did well to duck inside. But 20 seconds later, Eubank was on his backside having shipped a flashing left hand. 'After I knocked him down I looked at my dad and said: "This is easy, man, I'm gonna knock this guy out in the first round!"' But Eubank was up at two and smiling sheepishly all the way through the mandatory eight count. 'I threw everything and the kitchen sink at him in the first round,' says Calzaghe, who was so confident of victory he also threw in a couple of Ali shuffles. 'It was the same in the second round, the third round, the fourth round and after five rounds I was absolutely exhausted. I remember sitting on my stool in the corner, looking out and seeing him strutting round the ring. It was surreal. It was then I realised it was going to be a hard night and I soon found out where the trenches were.' Calzaghe continued raining blows down on Eubank but the old warhorse kept coming. And coming. And coming. But Calzaghe, who had been the distance only once in the paid ranks, showed he had the heart, stomach and whiskers to match his flawless footwork and dazzling hand speed.

'He was by far the toughest fight I ever had,' says Calzaghe, who was awarded a one-sided unanimous decision. 'Chris was a very dangerous character when his back was against the wall, that's when you saw the best Chris Eubank. You saw it against Benn, you saw it twice against Watson, you saw it against Henry Wharton. I was all over him but he was so determined, he wanted to win so badly that he pushed me to the brink. Every time I see Chris I thank him for giving me the best education so early in my career, I couldn't have had a better learning fight.' Verdict announced, a strange thing happened: when MC Michael Buffer asked for a round of applause for Eubank, the crowd rose to their feet as one and raised the roof. A chuffed-looking Eubank walked to the middle of the ring and gave an understated bow before returning to his corner. This is what respect felt like and it clearly humbled him. 'If I had got out sooner the public would never have known I was capable of taking punishment,' said Eubank, 'losing and accepting it like a gentleman.' Hamed was now the only clown in town, but how Eubank loved being the straight man.

The Monday after Eubank's thrilling bouts against Nigel Benn and Michael Watson, work places across the land would have been abuzz with boxing-related conversation. Young and old, male and female, blue collar and white collar, boxing buffs and general sports fans, millions would have poured forth on what they had witnessed on the box the previous weekend. What a violent man that Benn is, what an idiot that Eubank is, how the hell did Watson lose *that*? As late as 1994, boxing provided three of ITV's top five sports audience ratings, all in excess of ten million. But, just like that, the sport disappeared from most people's living rooms. In April 1995, Frank Warren left ITV for Sky Sports and took with him a clutch of household names, including Benn, Naseem Hamed and Frank Bruno. Warren's close relationship with Don King also gave Sky access to the biggest draw in boxing, Mike Tyson, who had just been released from prison and was set to return to the ring soon. For the second time in less than a year, a promoter ITV had shown great loyalty to and whose fighters it had built into superstars – Barry Hearn and Eubank joined Sky in 1994 – had left for more lucrative shores. Subsequently, ITV executives decided the time was right to walk away from the sport. The BBC, meanwhile, had been on the margins for years and had neither the money nor the inclination to jump back in.

'Up until the mid-1990s, boxing was an essential part of terrestrial television's fabric,' says former ITV boxing presenter Jim Rosenthal. 'Heads of ITV Sport like John Bromley and Bob Burrows bought into boxing and could live with the fact that it can be messy at times, you can lose an opponent the night before a fight, a fight might last 18 seconds or you might get 12 horrible rounds. They understood that was all part of the fascination of boxing. So it was an absolutely key pillar at ITV, the numbers we used to do on a Saturday night for *The Big Fight Live* were enormous – you're talking 15–20 million people, which satisfied the commercial people as well as the sporting people. After the second Benn–Eubank fight, ITV conjured a one and half a hour-long programme on the Sunday night to tell the story of how the fight was scored. We just cleared the schedules. To do that nowadays, to get two successive nights on the same weekend, it would never happen with any sport.

'Sadly there were tragedies in the ring – including Michael Watson and Gerald McClellan – and executives turned away from boxing because they didn't want those things happening in millions of living rooms on a Saturday night. And if I'm honest, even I was uneasy about the Benn–McClellan fight. That was pitched as Britain against America, which created an atmosphere like I've never been a part of, before or since. I imagine it must have been like the old bear-baiting and cock-fighting days, it was that frightening. It worried me deeply. So after that amazing period in the early-to mid-1990s, ITV executives washed their hands of boxing, which was very damaging to the sport in terms of reaching that wider audience.'

However, Trevor East, who became head of ITV Sport in 1995 before following Warren to Sky, contends ITV's decision to walk away was motivated more by business than moral concerns. 'Of course, when someone gets badly injured people start wondering why they're covering this sport,' says East. 'But as a TV man, boxing is the most time-consuming and difficult sport to run. And ITV loses patience with any sport unless it delivers on a consistent basis and it knows exactly what it's going to get. And with boxing, you never know what you're going to get. The highs are fantastic but the lows can be awful. It can deliver great, great nights of entertainment, deliver huge audiences and commercial revenues, but other times it can stink the place out or you might lose your main fight the night before because someone's injured himself in training. Sponsors and advertisers don't quite know what to do with it – they'd love to get involved but they're always wary of boxing for those reasons.'

So while Naseem Hamed's last fight on ITV was watched in 11 million homes, the largest audience he attracted on Sky in 1997 was 831,000, which was 300,000 more than the satellite channel's next best boxing audience. Bizarrely, the biggest UK television audience for boxing in 1997 was for a Commonwealth title fight between Sheffield middleweight Paul 'Silky' Jones and South African Johnson Tshuma, which was aired on a delayed basis by BBC One and pulled in 2.5 million viewers. Almost overnight, boxing's television viewership had been decimated and over the next decade boxing would go from being a mass-appeal sport to a trade sport, largely for die-hards and aficionados.

Eubank would later claim that Calzaghe's failure to capture the public's imagination in the same way as he and Benn had was purely down to the Welshman's lack of a sense of theatre. 'Unfortunately, the nature of the modern game demands that to be gifted, disciplined and technically skilled is not necessarily enough,' said Eubank. 'You must have character, charisma and personality as well.' This is unfair to Calzaghe, who retired as an undefeated former two-weight world champion in 2009 and is a strong contender for greatest British boxer of all time. Granted, Calzaghe lacked Eubank's magnetism out of the ring but he was a superior fighter, and many would argue a more exciting one. Rather, it was Calzaghe's misfortune to come along at a time when boxing had been shunted to the fringes of the media.

It tended to follow that if a certain sport was not shown on terrestrial television then newspapers were less inclined to write about it, because, the argument went, not enough people knew who, and what, you were writing about. And so the cycle continued. Although, given that more and more sport is being gobbled up by various satellite networks, the emergence of the internet and the fact that a satellite subscription is no longer the luxury it was, this trend is changing out of necessity. Nevertheless, Calzaghe's major breakthrough fight did not happen until 2006, when he gave one of the finest performances in a British ring in destroying American hope Jeff Lacy. The channel? ITV, which had recently returned to boxing after years on the sidelines. Before that bout, you could have said to a London cabbie: 'What about that Calzaghe fight last night?' And the chances are he'd look blankly at you in his mirror and reply: 'Didn't see it, mate. Used to love boxing but it's not on TV any more, is it?'

And so the cruel truth for Eubank was that far fewer people witnessed his transformation from Brighton Braggart to 'brave and gracious' loser than he would have liked. Although he probably would have related to that famous Gloria Swanson quote from *Sunset Boulevard*: 'I *am* big – it's the *pictures* that got small.' But while Eubank apparently hoped to manage his withdrawal from boxing in a dignified fashion, far more people would have read about his alleged punch-up with Hamed at Heathrow Airport than watched his courageous display against Calzaghe a week or so earlier. 'Naz was taunting and goading me and he got my goat,' said Eubank. 'I grabbed the belts and threw them to the floor. Next thing he's swung at me. He missed. It was all very ungentlemanly.' Hamed later ridiculed Eubank for the size of his nostrils, while Eubank made it clear he would not stoop so low as to accuse Hamed of having big ears. Eubank, who looked upon Hamed's progress as a 'scientific social experiment', developed something of an obsession with British boxing's new superstar. The old master seemed utterly astonished that a fellow boxer – and a young upstart at that – could treat him in such a way, apparently forgetting that it wasn't that long ago that he was calling Nigel Benn a coward and a fraud.

In March 1998, Eubank announced he was moving up two weight divisions to challenge Manchester's WBO cruiserweight champion Carl Thompson. Judging by his pre-fight utterances, Eubank seemed to be revelling in his new-found status as seemingly hopeless underdog. 'The only way you get into the legendary ranks is when you do what the critics say you can't,' said Eubank, who admitted to being inspired by Benn's upset of Gerald McClellan. True, Eubank had been written off before, but this time he was fighting a stone and a half above his customary super-middleweight limit against a man who had finished 11 of his previous 14 opponents inside the distance. Eubank, who had lost his last three world championship encounters, portrayed himself as a man testing the bounds of reality. Others thought he had developed a death wish. The reality was, the arch-egotist was terrified of losing his grip on fame and status. 'I've been to a film premiere and the cameras did not want me,' said Eubank. 'I did not like it. It made me feel bad. But as a champion, they have no option but to pick up the cameras and click. Fame is really a fantastic thing.'

Eubank flew into the pre-fight press conference from his training base in Cornwall on a private jet and swanned in 35 minutes late wearing a tweed suit, plus fours and twirling a cane. But Naseem Hamed's trainer Brendan Ingle was less than impressed. 'He's a phoney and a double-eyed dealing fella,' said Ingle, whose charge was topping the bill against Puerto Rican Wilfredo Vazquez at Manchester's Nynex Arena. 'Look what he's done to Ronnie Davies. That fella sweated

blood for him, looked after him and wiped his bleedin' nostrils
– but he's elbowed him. He walks past Ronnie as if he was
something on his shoe.' Ingle, in an echo of Mickey Duff's
furious attack a few years before, went on to accuse Eubank of
picking on Hamed, stealing his act, being shown up in sparring by Herol Graham many moons earlier and underpaying
him when he worked his corner against Dan Sherry. Eubank
was aghast. 'If I was a weaker man, a more emotional man, I'd
cry,' he said.

Eubank, as almost everybody had predicted, came up short
against the teak-tough Thompson. But there was glory in the
manner of his defeat. 'Eubank proved beyond any shadow of a
doubt what a courageous fighter he was against Thompson,'
says Colin Hart. 'He was the much smaller man and he took a
terrible hiding, but he kept coming and kept coming. Beneath
all that bullshit was a brave, brave fighter.' Says Kevin Mitchell:
'Chris had one of the biggest hearts I've ever seen in boxing.
That man had unbelievable courage and never was it more
evident than against Carl Thompson. That's why Ronnie
Davies always said Chris was the man he'd have beside him in
a dark alley, the hardest man he ever met.' 'Very few people
gave Eubank the credit he deserved,' says Frank Maloney, 'but
they did after that Thompson fight. To beat Eubank, you had
to nail him to the canvas and then go back and put a sword
through his heart, just to make certain. He never knew when
he was beaten.'

Eubank was forced to negotiate a labyrinth's worth of dark
alleys against Thompson and when he eventually emerged, it
was with only one eye blinking at the light. But it was every
bit as rough for Thompson, who took several diversions onto
Queer Street and was floored by a trademark Eubank uppercut in the fourth round. And how the crowd roared when that

happened: 'EUUUU-BANK! EUUUU-BANK!' If this was what it took to be accepted, if this was what it took to hang on to fame, these were the grim depths Eubank was willing to descend to. Even Ingle was moved to say: 'Have you ever seen such guts?'

After the fight, Eubank, his face a grotesque mask of lumps and bruises, was rushed to hospital, where he was held for two days. As the medical men and women prodded and poked him he must have looked for all the world like just another hapless boxer who had vowed and failed to beat the game. In the wake of the Thompson fight boxing folk queued up to tell him to stop. The referee for the Thompson fight, Roy Francis, said he felt like weeping when he attempted to halt the fight, only to be told by Eubank that he wanted to box on. Said Frank Warren: 'I would like to see Chris Eubank retire now, he has nothing left to prove. But we all know he has problems financially and, unfortunately, boxing is his way of earning a living.' Ronnie Davies, still bitter at his treatment but still in love with the man, made a heartfelt plea. 'If he does carry on, he's likely to be walking round the streets of Brighton and not even know he is in Brighton,' said Davies. 'He is doing something he said he would never do, and that is to fight on far too long.' Eubank swept out of the Manchester Royal Infirmary in the back of a limousine wearing a newly delivered Armani suit. Of course he was going to continue.

But it wasn't just pig-headedness and a lust for fame that drove Eubank back to the ring. Or at least that's what he claimed. 'When I was winning I expected to be liked, but people didn't react like that,' said Eubank. 'The higher one soars the less people can see who can't fly. If I'm soaring, the man in the street doesn't care and doesn't understand and that's why I don't want to win again.' In defeat, Eubank proclaimed, he had discovered an empathy with the common people. It was redolent of the Queen Mother's famous quote during World War II, after Buckingham Palace had taken a few hits from the Luftwaffe: 'I'm glad we've been bombed. It makes me feel I can look the East End in the face.' Even when attempting to convey his new-found humility Eubank could not help portraying himself as something like a deity.

Having been roared into the ring for his inevitable rematch with Thompson, Eubank struggled to hold back the tears. These very same men who had showered him with hate down the years – men who smelt of cigarettes and pubs, men who thought they were hard but had never laced up gloves, who had called Eubank a bastard and a cunt – now prostrated themselves in his presence. Again, Eubank was magnificent. For seven rounds, the challenger was more than the champion's equal, befuddling Thompson with snappy combinations, landing with trademark right hands and rocking him with a savage left in the seventh. But Thompson came rolling and thundering forward. By the end of the seventh, Eubank's left eye was almost closed and by the end of the ninth he was once again half-blind. The doctor had a look, the challenger protested, but the referee decided everyone had had their fill of Chris Eubank. 'You win some, you lose some,' said Eubank, who was ahead on two scorecards when the end came. 'But I can't seem to win any these days.' After nearly 13 years, 52 fights and 400 rounds of the hardest game, the time had come to walk away.

CHAPTER SEVENTEEN
So bloody noisy

As far back as the middle of the 1950s, the venerable chronicler of boxing A. J. Liebling considered that he was covering a sport in terminal decline. 'There exist certain generalised conditions today,' wrote Liebling, 'like full employment and a late school leaving age, that militate against the development of first-rate professional boxers.' Furthermore, Liebling deplored the commercialisation and sanitisation of the sport and detested the growing influence of television, which he held responsible for falling gates, the closure of small boxing clubs and the subsequent decline in the quality of boxers. Liebling died before he had the chance to sink his teeth into Cassius Clay, but he did manage to sneak a look. 'Just when the sweet science appears to lie like a painted ship upon a painted ocean,' wrote Liebling, having seen Clay training before his fight against Sonny Banks in 1962, 'a new Hero, as Pierce Egan would term him, comes along like a Moran to pull it out of the doldrums.' Who knows what words Liebling might have employed to describe the boxing scene of today but as elegant as they would undoubtedly have been, they would not have been as hopeful as when he was writing about the future Muhammad Ali. Waiting for boxing's Hero in 2013 is like waiting for Godot.

Neither Nigel Benn nor Chris Eubank was a hero in the sense that Liebling meant it. Both were fine fighters, better than most, but few would consider them to be genuine all-time greats. Indeed, most would place the two men that came directly in their wake, Naseem Hamed and Joe Calzaghe, above them in a list of top British fighters. But there exist certain generalised conditions today, as Liebling might have put it, that make Benn and Eubank seem greater. 'That period had lots of great fighters and big matches and great nights, one after another,' says Kevin Mitchell. 'We had this great rivalry between Benn and Eubank, with Michael Watson and Steve Collins thrown in as well. There were trips to America, to the Middle East, South Africa, boxing was all over the papers, it was on free-to-air television, so everyone knew who these guys were. You didn't have to say "Nigel Benn, the boxer", people knew who he was, even if they weren't remotely interested in boxing. And the same went for Chris Eubank. Every press conference would be packed, and it didn't matter what the fight was, whether it was for a British title or a world title. Boxing correspondents don't go to British title fights any more because those stories don't get in the papers. Boxing has been overrun by football, like every other sport. It was a special time, an exciting time. And just so bloody noisy.'

'That was certainly the last golden age of British boxing,' says Colin Hart. 'You had that little group of Eubank, Benn, Collins and Watson and I feel privileged to have known these fighters and covered their fights. I was very fortunate, I was working for a newspaper that was increasing in circulation, that was sold on sport maybe even more than tits. Before that I'd had ten years round the world with Ali, Foreman, Norton and Holmes, and then I had Leonard, Hagler, Hearns and

Duran. Maybe I look at modern boxing with something of a jaundiced eye because I was so spoilt. But Benn and Eubank was one of the greatest rivalries I covered, British or otherwise. They were larger than life.'

You can argue the toss as to whether terrestrial television washed its hands of boxing or boxing washed its hands of terrestrial television but the effect was much the same. Without regular exposure in millions of living rooms across the UK, boxing receded to the fringes of the collective consciousness of British sports fans. When Joe Calzaghe crossed over into the mainstream with his victory over Jeff Lacy on ITV, he had already been a world champion for more than eight years. Nottingham's Carl Froch, the latest in a long line of world title-winning British super-middleweights, had similar problems breaking through. Indeed, it wasn't until his switch to Barry Hearn's Matchroom promotional outfit in 2011 and his championing by Sky Sports that he became anything like a crossover star. 'People should have been talking about me as the next big thing,' said Froch, who had already had five world title fights when he made the move. 'I've gone over and above the call of duty in my fights to warrant being a household name.' But even now, having established a reputation as one of the bravest and most exciting fighters in world boxing, his fame doesn't come close to that achieved by Benn and Eubank in the 1990s.

A big part of this is down to personality. While both Calzaghe and Froch are intelligent and can be engaging and eloquent, they lack the charisma that Benn and Eubank brought to the game. And while you could argue that had Calzaghe and Froch ever met in the ring on terrestrial television they, too, would have been greater than the sum of their parts, this is only true to a certain extent. Because while the

26-year-old Benn was a newly crowned world champion when he met the 24-year-old Eubank, Calzaghe was a long-established world title-holder and already well into his thirties when Froch started calling him out. Why would Calzaghe fight the unheralded Froch when he could fight Roy Jones Jr and Bernard Hopkins? 'Now I think I could have fought all those guys and made ten times more money,' said Calzaghe, referring to Benn, Eubank and Collins. And when Calzaghe finally slipped into retirement and Froch finally began to get his due, he felt much the same about Calzaghe.

'It's a shame for Joe Calzaghe,' says Ricky Hatton, 'because he's arguably the best British fighter there's ever been. But unfortunately he didn't have a Chris Eubank or a Nigel Benn in his era. Carl Froch is very similar, he's doing the country very proud but he hasn't got a domestic rival. I don't think I could be a bigger Carl Froch fan, he's everything I like about boxing – I've never known a British boxer to fight so many champions consecutively – but he won't end up as popular or well known as Benn or Eubank because he didn't have that rivalry to make him. Benn and Eubank made each other. Every British boxer sits around hoping they get their own Nigel Benn or Chris Eubank, a domestic rival in their division.'

So at the same time as highlighting the many deficiencies of modern boxing, we should remember that the Benn–Eubank rivalry was a special case. And we should also remember that despite the many problems boxing has – its lack of visibility, the proliferation of titles that makes it impossible for the casual fan to follow with any certainty, promoters, sanctioning bodies and television networks all protecting their interests and seeing to it that the best fighters rarely meet in the ring – the sport, at least in Britain, continues to thrive. Indeed, Hatton is proof that, armed with a few wisecracks, a bit of earthy banter and plenty of talent, a fighter can still be a superstar in the post-terrestrial age.

'There is still that appeal,' says Jim Rosenthal, 'it's just that terrestrial television has decided not to be part of the party. Ever since Cain and Able, although I'm not sure who got the verdict in that one, it's been part of us and it makes me really sad the way the BBC has opted out of professional boxing completely and ITV dips its toe in periodically and then walks away. It's opened the way for Sky and stations like BoxNation [Frank Warren's boxing subscription channel] who have realised there is that appeal and always will be that appeal for boxing. It's part of our national fabric and always will be but the sport has plenty to complain about in terms of the shameful lack of exposure the terrestrial channels give it at the moment. I'm always an optimist and I always prefer to look forward rather than looking back and I hope there are golden ages around the corner. But that era of Benn and Eubank will take some beating. They were two incredible characters getting together at the right time and going eyeball to eyeball and stopping the nation. Could that happen again? It would take some doing, even if terrestrial channels commit to the sport in the future.'

Eddie Hearn, who has taken over the boxing arm of Matchroom Sport from father Barry, is optimistic about the future but agrees that the fight game is suffering from a chronic shortage of stardust. 'It's the same sport, there's the same politics, the same rivalry between promoters,' says Hearn, who now handles the career of Froch. 'Not a lot has changed, we just don't have the personalities we had back then. But also, fighters haven't been promoted properly, sold to the public, as fighters and as people. Benn was a warrior, there were no real gimmicks, he went in and he had a war, that was Nigel Benn, the "Dark Destroyer". Carl Froch is the same sort of thing, he goes in and he has a war. But he didn't have a broadcast partner for most of his professional career and you can't get a message out without a broadcast partner. You need people constantly saying: "Watch Carl Froch, watch his fights, he's unbelievable."'

'The Lucian Bute fight [Froch destroyed his Canadian opponent to reclaim a portion of the world super-middle-weight crown in 2012] was the crossover fight, where people went: "Fucking hell!" And now he's a pay-per-view star on Sky. You've got to have the right broadcast partner, you've got to have the right personality and you've got to have the right promoter. And Eubank was a promoter's dream – a pain in the arse, but a promoter's dream. And what hasn't changed is, when you've got a great product, it sells very well. When you've got an average product, it sells average. It's not rocket science. You do Carl Froch versus Mikkel Kessler and it does 18,000 sales in two hours, with expensive tickets. People find the money if they want to go to a great event. It's about giving fans value for money and creating a fan experience. If you can create a great atmosphere and a great night of boxing, the punters will leave and think: "I bloody love boxing – it's good, innit?"'

One man who believes we should all remove our rose-tinted spectacles is Frank Warren – one-time sparring partner of Barry Hearn, who now has a fresh sparring partner in spring-heeled Eddie. 'I don't agree it was the last golden age of British boxing,' says Warren. 'It wasn't a golden era at all. Naseem Hamed did much more business than they could ever dream of doing and was involved in some great fights. Hatton put more bums on seats than they ever did and we got more people go to Joe Calzaghe against Mikkel Kessler than ever went to see those two – 50,000 in the Millennium Stadium against 40,000 in Old Trafford. People get caught up in all this stuff but the difference with Calzaghe and Naz is they fought almost everybody who was around, Eubank and Benn never. They didn't fight Michael Nunn, they didn't fight James Toney, they didn't fight Roy Jones. Benn went to America and he beat Gerald McClellan, but was Eubank a great fighter? I don't even put him in my British top ten. You can't have it both ways, you're either a great fighter or you're not – the great fighters fight the best that are around and Eubank never did that.'

Barry Hearn having withdrawn from boxing in order to concentrate on darts, snooker and his beloved Leyton Orient – not forgetting fishing and poker – Warren is now involved in a battle for the heart and soul of the British fight game with the chip off the old Hearn block. Which might help explain what Trevor East contends is Barry's 'skewed recollection of events' surrounding the making of Benn–Eubank II. 'Barry thinks Matchroom has got Frank on the back foot,' says East, 'and he's trying to stick the knife in.' At the time of writing Eddie Hearn has an exclusive deal with Sky while Warren's promotional company is making big losses. Although, by the time you read this, it might be the other way round, such is the capricious nature of boxing. And while Warren's BoxNation subscription channel, which specialises in top-quality, international boxing, is still churning over, his promotional stable has been leaking boxers at an alarming rate, and has been for some time.

In 2005, Warren lost Ricky Hatton, having delivered him the IBF light-welterweight title; in 2008, Warren lost

Joe Calzaghe, having been with him for 12 years; in 2010, Warren lost Amir Khan, having guided him to the WBA light-welterweight title. To lose one world champion may be regarded as a misfortune, to lose three such household names looks like you've lost your touch in a big, big way. 'Boxing can be heartbreaking,' says Warren, 'because you can get very close to people, and that's sometimes a lack of professionalism. You trust what someone says, maybe on the back of a handshake, and you do feel let down. I don't deal with that too well. Maybe it's something lacking in me, I don't know.'

Despite these high-profile losses, Warren soldiered on, always regenerating. In 2008, he signed a trio of British Olympians, including gold medallist James DeGale and in 2012 he promoted the two biggest shows in Britain, David Haye's fight against Dereck Chisora and Ricky Burns's fight against Kevin Mitchell (not to be confused with the journalist of the same name). 'What we do is invest,' says Warren. 'We lose money and we make money and hopefully we make more than we lose. But we're prepared to take the loss. Eddie Hearn has said without Sky TV we wouldn't be doing boxing, he wouldn't be interested. That's the difference. I promoted without TV companies – when Setanta went bust [Warren had a short-lived partnership with the Irish broadcaster before its British arm went under], I signed those Olympian kids and we put the shows on elsewhere. I don't care what anyone else does, it doesn't interest me. All I've ever focused on is what I do, and what I do is deliver more world champions than anyone and develop them. I don't nick them from somebody, I put the money in from day one.'

However, in more recent times many of Britain's top boxers have found the lure of Sky allied with Eddie Hearn's megawatt smile difficult to resist. In quick succession, British light-heavyweight champion Tony Bellew, super-middleweight prospect George Groves and WBO lightweight champion Ricky Burns defected from Warren to Hearn. In addition, Hearn snapped up Olympic gold medallist Luke Campbell and former GB team-mates Tom Stalker and Kal Yafai. Hearn's one-sided barrage continued with the signings of David Haye, probably still the biggest draw in British boxing and back on the trail of the world heavyweight title, and Olympic super-heavyweight champion Anthony Joshua. And Warren appeared dangerously exposed when Nathan Cleverly, his last genuine headline act, lost his WBO light-heavyweight title in August 2013. Although, if Hearn needed a reminder that Warren was far from finished, he got one when Belfast super-bantam-weight Carl Frampton defected the other way.

'I have no real feelings towards Frank Warren,' says Eddie Hearn. 'I always said to my dad: "Do you hate Frank Warren?" And he always said: "No, socially he's a nice geezer, but he's a rival." If Frank Warren wasn't around now I don't know what I'd do, because I wouldn't be getting out of bed with the same ambition every morning. You've got to have someone to compete with, someone you want to be bigger than, have a better team than. We are head and shoulders above anyone else in the country now. He's still got Cleverly and Chisora and Billy Joe Saunders, but we've got Carl Froch, David Haye, Ricky Burns, Kell Brook, Tony Bellew, Lee Selby, George Groves, Darren Barker, Anthony Joshua, Tom Stalker, Luke Campbell, it's non-stop.

'Frank's still very much alive and you've got to always think about what he's doing. But I don't get obsessive about it. He's always having a pop, but I take that as a compliment. I've only been a licensed promoter for two years but I've got to him, and I think that's quite funny. He rants and raves and goes mad about it whereas I just smile and think, "This is good fun". Deep down he can see in me a little bit of what he was doing all those years ago, when he blew open the Mickey Duff-led promotional cartel. But he's now one of the older lot, just trying to keep up and stay in the game.'

CHAPTER EIGHTEEN
People still stare

There almost wasn't a British fight game for Warren and Eddie Hearn to fight over, at least not as they had known it. Michael Watson's battle for justice went on for the best part of a decade and when the High Court finally ruled that the British Boxing Board of Control had been in breach of its duty of care on that fateful night of 21 September 1991, it was ordered to pay substantial damages. The problem being, the Board was flat broke, having not been insured, and shelled out something in the region of £500,000 in legal costs. Subsequently, lawyers advised the Board that it had no legal liability to Watson and it appealed. The battle rumbled on and in December 2000 the Court of Appeal ignored the Board's argument that it was merely a regulatory body, did not organise fights and that Watson was injured as a result of 'willingly accepting a risk' and upheld the original decision. The problem being, the Board was now even more broke than before, having entered administration the previous year. Not for the first time in boxing's long and chequered history, Watson was fighting for money that didn't actually exist. The Board fought on, applying to the House of Lords, at which point Warren had seen enough.

'It was a tragedy for the sport and more importantly for

Michael Watson,' says Warren. 'The Board was badly advised, they should have settled with Michael Watson, it was due to their negligence. So I sat down with the Board and Michael Watson's people, having never promoted him, and we brokered a deal.' Warren advised the Board to settle, threatening not to pay any more licence fees if it refused to do so. The Board reluctantly agreed to sell its headquarters on Borough High Street, where it had been based since 1929, and reversed its decision to take its appeal to the House of Lords. More importantly for Watson, it eventually agreed to pay him £400,000 in compensation. Warren also organised a charity night, which raised a further £180,000. At the event at the Grosvenor House Hotel, Watson was feted by hundreds of fellow fighters, including a 70-year-old Jake LaMotta, still going strong despite taking far more punishment in his five fights against Sugar Ray Robinson than Watson ever did. At one point during the evening, Watson climbed into the ring with Chris Eubank and Lennox Lewis and his arm was raised in victory one last time.

'I've forgiven the Board of Control,' says Watson. 'I showed mercy on them in the court case – I could have shut them down but I let them continue. It's just a shame the fighters can't receive the benefit for all their hard work. Boxers should be in charge of the Board of Control, not old men who have never put on a pair of trainers in their lives. They don't know nothing about the fight game. I was sent to give boxing a wake-up call, protect other fighters. Now I've no regrets, everything works out for a reason. If I had beaten Eubank that night, God knows where I would be now. I probably would have had the wrong people around me, but I've been protected, prevented from going down the wrong path in life. The path of darkness. I'm 100 per cent a better person, I have God in my life now. I'm connected to the true source.'

Safe in the belief he had God in his corner, Watson stunned the world when he announced his intention to take part in the 2003 London Marathon, in aid of the Brain and Spine Foundation. 'Michael has no business walking to the end of the road, never mind taking on the marathon,' said Peter Hamlyn, the neurosurgeon who saved Watson's life. 'He is an extraordinary individual. Extraordinary for surviving, extraordinary for recovering his mind and extraordinary for learning to walk again.' At 12.12 p.m. on Saturday 19 April, almost a week after most of the 32,745 entrants had completed the course, Watson stopped just before the finishing tape, flashed that winning grin and threw out a flurry of punches, before dragging his left leg across the line. Eubank was present to see his old adversary perform a miracle, which he said made him feel 'ashamed but at the same time inspired'. In the weeks and months immediately after his accident, even Watson's own neurosurgeon thought he might be in a vegetative state for the rest of his life. Some vegetable he turned out to be. And an even greater fighter than we thought he was.

In the early hours of a summer morning in 1998, Nigel Benn drove from his mansion in Beckenham, Kent, to Streatham Common in South London. He parked his car and began chugging down sleeping pills, each one washed down with a gargle of cheap white wine. As men solicited for business all around him, Benn remembered all the people he had hurt – his wife, his children, his loving parents – and, consumed by self-loathing, took the next step. Still in control of his senses, he climbed out of his car, pulled a length of hose from the boot and attached it to the exhaust, before feeding the other end through the window. And then he turned the key. Three times the hose was blown off and after the third time he dissolved into tears and gave up. 'I was hurting the woman I loved and didn't know why,' says Benn. 'I suffered depression, nervous breakdowns, I just wanted to end it all. All that money but there was something missing.' As with Watson, that something was God. Inspired by his long-suffering partner Carolyne, Benn began attending church, soaking up the words of the Bible and following Watson down the fork that leads to the light. 'There were two places I was going to end up,' says Benn, 'a mental hospital or six feet under. And then I read the word of God, Mark 8:36: "What does it profit a man to gain the whole world and forfeit your own soul?" Now I'm not chasing anything and my life is splendid.'

Benn was not the only boxer from the era who found himself befuddled on leaving the highly exhilarating and simultaneously chaotic and regimented world of professional boxing. Having failed for a third time to win a world title when he was stopped by Charles Brewer in Atlantic City in 1998, Herol Graham slowly descended into darkness. 'It's so difficult to be up in the spotlight for so long,' says Graham, 'and to find that someone then turns the light out. And when they did I felt lost, abandoned and saddened.' His marriage having disintegrated and unable to provide for his gaggle of children because of a cavalier approach to money and a string of poor investments, Graham spent night after night on his own, staring at a television set that no longer worked. Waiting for phone calls, from old mates in the game he had given so much to. Perhaps offering him a job teaching boxing to kids, perhaps offering him a chance to shine in the commentary box. Phone calls that never came. And so one night in December 2007, Graham took a bottle of brandy and a knife to his bedroom, said some prayers and began hacking at his wrists. But, like Benn, he was unable to finish the job. In 2008, Graham, the man many believed could have stood Benn and Eubank on their heads, was sectioned. While Watson and Benn were saved by God, Graham was saved by an old girlfriend called Karen. Under Karen's wing Graham slowly rebuilt his life and found meaning again. Putting out the bins, bringing in the milk, all those things that seem so natural to us everyday folk and so emasculating to ex-boxers. No thrills in bins and milk.

The dazzling Michael Nunn was earmarked as the next Sugar Ray Leonard during his days in the amateur ranks. And while Nunn never quite attained true greatness, he didn't have a bad career: world titles at two different weights, 58 wins from 62 professional fights, $6 million in purses. Handsome, with a fleet of sports cars and celebrity friends, Nunn seemed to have it all. In truth, he never really had a grasp on anything. When Nunn lost his IBF middleweight title to James Toney in 1991, he fell into a familiar downward spiral and in the following years was cited dozens of times by police for charges ranging from driving without a licence to assault. When Nunn lost his WBA super-middleweight belt to Steve Little in 1994 the purses shrank still further, the desperation grew and he was forced to file for bankruptcy. In 2002, Nunn was arrested in a hotel in his home town of Davenport, Iowa after paying an undercover officer $200 for a kilogram of cocaine and is currently serving a 24-year prison sentence for trafficking. 'That life,' says Nunn, 'it's over with. But I'm a two-time world champion, you can't *ever* take that away from me.'

As these words are written, Steve Collins, now 48, is pursuing a fight with Roy Jones Jr, now 44. 'I'm not coming back for a pay day,' says Collins, 'this is a grudge match.' A grudge match that pretty much nobody wants to see apart from Collins – the same Collins who decided against a comeback 14 years ago because he suffered a blackout in training. Jones was voted best fighter of the 1990s by the Boxing Writers Association of America and in 2003 became the first former middleweight to win a heavyweight world title for 106 years when he easily outpointed John Ruiz. That was the time to bow out. Instead, the man Budd Schulberg described as being 'almost as hard to hit as Will-o'-the-Wisp Willie Pep' carried on and started getting hit an awful lot. Jones has lost seven of his last 14 fights but, whether the Collins fight comes off or not, the 'Pensacola Pinwheel' has no intention of retiring. 'I've got nothing left to prove in the sport but I want to win a cruiserweight title before I leave,' says Jones, 'so I've won every title available from middleweight to heavyweight. If I can get the cruiserweight title, I'm done, I'm out of here. If that's the goal I set I, of all people, deserve the right to go for that goal because of all I did for boxing.'

James Toney is difficult to understand. Literally. From his home in California he slurs down his telephone that he wants to fight on and that nobody has the right to tell him he shouldn't. In April 2013, a blubbery, wheezing Toney was taken apart by an unknown Australian called Lucas Browne in Melbourne. When concerned journalists asked why Toney was having trouble speaking, his connections blamed jetlag. 'He's not going to quit fighting,' his father and corner man John assured them. In 2010 it was reported that Iran Barkley was broke and homeless. 'I was hanging out with Eddie Murphy,' says Barkley, 'I had to keep up.' In 2012, Barkley announced his intention to return to boxing. Fat, 51, blind in one eye, still dreaming of one last shot. Doug DeWitt assures you life is good – owns a couple of homes in New York, trades stocks, runs a stable of white collar fighters, occasionally treads the boards. But then he gets all gloomy and wonders what could have been. 'I screwed up,' says DeWitt. 'I didn't reach my potential in boxing and I have to live with that. The WBO title is not Doug DeWitt fulfilling his potential, Doug DeWitt fulfilling his potential was knocking out Tommy Hearns and beating Marvin Hagler on a decision. And not even being in the Nigel Benn fight. I have a little bit of a sour taste from boxing.' Turns out, Doug, you're not the only one.

In 2007 Benn met Gerald McClellan for the first time since they bade farewell at the crossroads 12 years earlier. As it turned out, neither fork led to the light but only Benn had emerged from the darkness. Before a fund-raising dinner at the Grosvenor Hotel in London, Benn knelt next to McClellan's wheelchair, grasped his hand and was told by his old foe: 'This man almost took my life.' McClellan then turned to his sister and said: 'Lisa – he looks sad?' Benn reeled away, took refuge behind a pillar and dissolved into tears. 'I had never dealt with it,' said Benn, 'never talked about it to anybody in 12 years. Not my mum and dad, not my friends, not my Bible teacher. When I saw his family, when I saw Lisa, what it had done to her life, there was a whole new emotion there. But I feel as if I can deal with it now, as if I have been forgiven.'

Five years before his gut-wrenching reunion with McClellan, Benn had moved his family to Majorca and begun preaching the Word of God, as well as offering a sideline in marriage counselling. 'When he said that he would change, he meant it,' says Carolyne Benn. 'It has been amazing to witness the transformation in his life and the desire he has to bring the good news about Jesus.' Says Michael Watson: 'He was a true gentleman and he still is: a good family man, an ideal husband and a good role model. To see the way he is makes me proud, he's very content and very humble.' 'I was Satan's right-hand man before God said He wanted me,' says Benn. 'He said: "I have plans for you." He said He wanted the "Dark Destroyer". He knew that people would sit up and listen to me.' Once upon a time it took a crunching left hook, now all it takes to get the congregation on his side are a few lines of Gospel. But the born-again Benn never forgot what his old life in boxing had given him.

Benn became an ambassador for British Military Martial Arts, training kids in gyms around the country, petrifying them by telling them he was 'going to take them to places they've never been'. Where Watson, Eubank, Barkley, McClellan and Collins went, and where it wasn't a nice place to be. He also gave exhibitions and talks on the game he still loved, never forgetting the punters who put money in his pocket and made him who he was. 'I wish they'd had pay-per-view back then,' says Benn. 'Cor, I tell you what mate, if Chris and me had been American we'd have been absolutely caked. But I'm happy with what I came out with. I managed to retire at 32, out of the game quick. It just seemed like I was around for a long time because whenever you picked up a paper I was in there and we were fighting on terrestrial TV. People would have a party, get the beers in and watch the fight for free. I was over in Majorca and two old women walked past, they must have been about 80, and one of them said: "Don't he look like Nigel Benn?" I was like, "But it is me!" Me and my wife were laughing because even these old grannies knew who I was!

'When I do exhibitions I have all these old people around me, taking pictures, laughing and joking. These are the people who made me and I never forgot that, I always tried to stay close. I am who I am and if people want a picture with me, I'll give them a picture. Whereas Chris would be like, "Don't touch me". Me and Eubank did one show but he can't take criticism. People take the mickey out of me and it's like water off a duck's back. I'm able to banter with people but he can't do it. And now he wants to start doing them with me but it's too late. I've been doing them since 1997, I've done over 400 of these Q&A sessions. We could have made millions together in that time, he could have made a pot load of money but he was never able to come down off his perch and realise the people you're dealing with are salt of the earth folk. A lot of people said it was a mask but that was the only side I ever saw of Eubank. That persona can take over, it can become your life. I was watching him on the telly only the other day and he was still exactly the same. But we need people like Chris in the game, he was a great showman. He had class, he really did. There will only be one Chris Eubank, no one will ever come close.'

Michael Watson can't find it in him to be charitable about Eubank, a man he believes remains stranded at the crossroads. 'Chris still doesn't know which path to take,' says Watson. 'I feel sorry for him, he needs peace. He doesn't know what he's talking about, he's going round in circles. He was born that way, it's in his nature. But the rest of it, it's all an act. Before we fought for the second time, I'd walk down the road in Brixton and they'd all be calling me champ. They all knew he was false, false to the max. He's too haywire, he's all over the place, he needs to find himself. People know Chris better than he knows himself. He's been sussed. And he knows that, and he's ashamed of it. He needs to be real, that's the problem he's suffering with.'

Of Britain's four middleweight kings of the early 1990s – Eubank, Benn, Graham and Watson – it is Eubank who emerged from the carnage as the most tragic figure, in the classical sense. Having been ensnared, defined and eventually defeated by a sport he claimed to hate, in retirement Eubank became cannibalised by the persona he created. 'Fighters can be taken over by their personas,' says Eddie Hearn, 'no doubt about it. People ask me about Adrien Broner all the time: "Is that what he's really like?" The answer is "yes". When I was in Atlantic City recently,

I was in the hotel spa and I saw him sitting in a jacuzzi on his own with his sunglasses on, surrounded by five security guards. And he was yelling at the top of his voice: "Yeh man, I am the greatest!" And I was thinking: "What the fucking hell are you doing? There's no one in there with you apart from your security." It's as if he'd forgotten who he was.

'But Broner is just brash and arrogant, and anyone can do that. Eubank is more extreme, he has this nutty streak in him. To be sat at home one day and think to yourself: "I know, I'll start wearing a monocle and jodhpurs and get myself a cane and I'll drive up and down Brighton seafront all day honking the horn in my big truck" – that's slightly mad. I used to imagine Eubank walking through the door of his house, taking off his monocle and jodhpurs – like Superman taking off his cape and boots – grabbing a beer from the fridge, falling into his armchair and saying to his wife: "I'm absolutely exhausted, love, I'm not sure how much longer I can keep this up." But I never saw the mask slip.'

While Eubank was still fighting, this persona served a purpose, namely to secure him big fights, big purses and big television deals. But in retirement, it made him a figure of fun: without his feats in the ring to buttress his regal pretensions, Eubank just seemed ridiculous. Tom Fordyce, chief sports writer for BBC Sport, tells a story about Eubank that captures the former boxer's state of mind as he receded from the limelight. 'I interviewed him in 1999, for a big piece in the now defunct *Total Sport*,' says Fordyce. 'So there we were, the photographer and I, waiting in the vast eight-storey, glass-topped atrium of London's Landmark Hotel, while all around us coiffured and polished businessmen sipped lattes and made deals and waistcoated flunkies glided between the palm trees. And suddenly the background hum of chatter and slurp dropped away and we noticed everyone was staring up at the wide balcony that overlooked the entire ground floor. There, wearing nothing but the tiniest pair of white briefs, stood Eubank – locked in a muscle-clenched pose, peering out over the sea of upturned faces. With slow deliberation, he turned on his heel and began stepping down the wide staircase that swept into the room. No one spoke. Espresso cups slipped through fingers. Fearing some sort of diplomatic incident, keen to break the voodoo spell, I dashed over and offered my hand. "You see?" murmured Eubank, as he regarded his onlookers imperiously, ignoring my palm. "People still stare at me. People still know who I am.'"

Even more tragic was the gaping chasm between how Eubank thought the British public perceived him and how it actually did. For example, Eubank saw his appearance on *Celebrity Big Brother* in 2001 as a roaring success on a personal level – 'I had been given the opportunity to show the public the real me, without media distortion' – but he was mocked by his fellow inmates and first out the door, losing a head-to-head phone vote to Anthea Turner, whose own popularity was at an all-time low. Eubank also appeared on the BBC panel show *They Think It's All Over*, during which he was called an 'ill-dressed twat with a speech impediment'. When Eubank complained about his treatment, host Nick Hancock railed: "'Oh my God! I'm the centre of attention!", said the man with a tea cosy on his head.' The same year, Eubank submitted himself to 45 days' filming with Louis Theroux for a fly-on-the-wall documentary. 'All I want is for people to say Chris Eubank is an all-right guy,' said Eubank. In fairness to Eubank, he came across as an all-right guy and viewers were particularly struck by the normalness of his wife Karron and their four children.

The programme was essentially a sparring session for the series *At Home with the Eubanks*, which was broadcast in 2003. Again, behind the posturing, the weird clothes and the torrent of malapropisms – 'I love my wife. I love my woman. I'm lucky to be in this predicament' – Eubank seemed like an all-right guy. But people wondered why this essentially private, socially awkward man allowed himself to be scrutinised in this way. And there was an underlying sadness to the experiment: while Eubank came across as a loving husband and dad, he also came across as a 36-year-old man at a loose end in life, a spare part, rattling around his mansion being ridiculed by his own wife and children. 'Christopher got in late, about 2.30,' said the long-suffering Karron Eubank at one point in the series. 'And I pretended to be asleep because I thought he was going to bore me with some poetry.' 'While I thought he came across great,' says Colin Hart, 'I noticed his kids were always taking the piss out of him. They knew him and they had sussed him.'

Indeed, it was particularly painful viewing for those who claimed to know the real Eubank, whom they maintained was a man of integrity, humility and nobility. 'When I had throat cancer 20-odd years ago,' says Hart, 'Chris got to hear about it and rang me to wish me well. I knew a lot of fighters and he was the only one who got in touch.' 'I know Nigel Benn was a soldier,' says Jim McDonnell, 'but if you were deep in the trenches, you'd want Eubank by your side. He was a great person and if you were ever in trouble, he'd be there for you. As a friend he's loyal, he's honest, his integrity is fantastic.' 'He's a sweet man, a gentle man and he's been very kind to me over the years,' says Gary Stretch. 'He's a very different person to what a lot of people think he is. I think he is quite lonely in his own way and he has a real soft spot that he doesn't show a lot of people. Boxing was show business for him but he is actually quite a humble man, so far removed from how he was in the ring. He asks a lot of questions, he's very inquisitive, he's got a thirst for knowledge. He often says to me: "I've got such respect for what you've done since fighting."'

Stretch was one of the lucky ones. Blessed with good looks, charisma, a sharp mind and a vigorous work ethic, the working-class kid from St Helens found success as an actor in Hollywood. Eubank, too, wanted to be a 'thethpian' after he retired from boxing but it was a fanciful ambition for a man who had been playing the role of Chris Eubank for half his life. 'He could have gone and played himself in a movie, but you only get away with that once or twice,' says Stretch. 'To have any kind of a career with longevity you've got to do a lot of work but if all you're doing is playing yourself you're never going to do it. For 99 per cent of fighters it's very difficult to have been in the business and then to wake up one day and realise it's over. Most guys don't have any other kinds of skills and they're suddenly no longer managed or making decent money and they're pretty lost, they don't have anything to fall back on.'

'I did a bit of commentary with him on Talksport when Lennox Lewis fought Evander Holyfield,' says Jim Rosenthal. 'It was one of my more interesting broadcasting experiences. He'd give answers that were way too long and a more unsuitable co-commentator you couldn't really think of. We sat down and had lunch and I said to him: "There are two ways of doing this. The first being, I'll talk for three minutes of each round and you talk for one. The second being, I'll talk and pause and then you say something. But that's the hardest way because you're not the quickest speaker and silence doesn't really work on radio." There was one of those big, long silences and eventually he said: "So, by your first method you talk for three minutes and I talk for one? I don't think I like that. But I also have a problem with your second method because when I try to talk fast my lisp gets worse." It was a tough night's work.' Still searching for meaning in a life without boxing, Eubank was arrested in 2003 after staging a one-man protest against Britain's military presence in Iraq. Eubank, who converted to Islam in 1997, had backed his truck outside Downing Street and sounded its horn for a minute, before reversing into a delivery van. When a policeman merely issued Eubank with a ticket, Eubank railed: 'But officer, you must use your power as a man of the law to arrest me!'

Meanwhile, Eubank's lavish spending was beginning to engulf him. Indeed, that he was willing to tread the celebrity route was probably more down to his mounting debts than any desire to change the public's perception of him. 'Nigel had the last laugh,' says Barry Hearn, 'because he put all his money into sensible things like property and Chris spunked all his on things like giant trucks.' In 2005 Eubank declared himself bankrupt and the following year he was forced to sell off hand-stitched suits, riding breeches, canes and boots via an online auction. You could have picked up a monocle for £400. And then his wife Karron filed for divorce, moved out and took their four kids with her. 'I think my character has taken its toll on her,' said Eubank. In 2006 his two mansions in Hove were demolished to make way for flats and the fixtures and fittings put up for sale on the lawns. When Eubank turned up at a boxing writers' dinner in a jacket and tie but no shirt, fellow guests suspected it was an indication of his precarious financial position and state of mind. Eubank insisted it was actually an esoteric fashion statement. His tongue was presumably in his cheek, only nobody was quite sure any more.

In 2006 Eubank packed his sons Chris Jr and Sebastian off

to the United States. According to Irene Hutton, a single mother from Las Vegas, Eubank introduced himself in a Paris bar with the words: 'Hello, I am Christopher Livingstone Eubank – I am an ambassador.' Nine months later he turned up on her doorstep with his two sons in tow. Within six weeks Hutton was their legal guardian. While the wild, young Eubank had been packed off to New York's South Bronx – 'a place of nightmares' – by his father, Eubank decided the rather more refined streets of Brighton and Hove were too nightmarish for his two wild, young sons and left them in Vegas instead. As ever with the Eubank narrative, nothing seemed to make sense. However, as it had done with Eubank, the bizarre arrangement paid off.

'It was my dad saying: "You say you want to be a fighter? Experience what it truly is to be a fighter",' says Chris Jr, who attended the prestigious Brighton College but whose headmaster at Johnny Tocco's gym in Vegas was the great Mike McCallum. '"If you can survive out there, then you'll know if you truly want to become a professional fighter or not." I don't see it as a mug's game, I see it as one of the purest sports. But the greatest thing I can learn from him is to believe in yourself. At one point in his career he was hated. People said he was no good, a show-off and that he wasn't going to make it. But even though people were saying all these bad things and coming to see him lose, he knew he was going to make it and get these people on his side. He deserves it, he's a great guy. For all the work he put in, everything he achieved and all the entertainment he provided, he didn't deserve to be hated.'

Chris Jr turned pro in 2011 and, at the time of writing, has racked up nine wins against no losses. But there are plenty in the game who worry about the extent of his father's influence. 'It's very worrying because he has a lot to live up to,' says

Benn. 'If he jumps into the ring like his dad and has the same entrance music, then he better perform like his dad. Chris was a great fighter, so his son is going to have so much pressure on him.' 'I helped get Chris's son get a professional contract,' says Ambrose Mendy, who received a six-year jail sentence for fraud in 1995, having been locked up for a similar conspiracy in 1991. 'Pretty much as soon as the deal was done, he said: "I'd like you to be in the background, I want to be up front." I said: "That's a bit dangerous, you don't even know what you're doing." He's still banging the same old drum.' Given the disastrous results when Eubank briefly attempted to navigate his own path through professional boxing's choppy waters, Mendy appears to have a point.

For Michael Watson, Eubank's championing of Chris Jr is further evidence of a confused mind. 'He called boxing a mug's game, now he's helping promote his own son,' says Watson. 'The man is all over the place.' Explaining his motives, Eubank admitted to harbouring doubts about allowing his son to follow his own treacherous path. But then Eubank saw something he admired in his offspring. Namely, himself. 'When Christopher told me he wanted to be a boxer, I didn't listen to him,' said Eubank. 'I felt the price was too high. I regret what happened to Michael Watson and I didn't want that to happen to my son. What convinced me to let him get in the ring was his truth and his persistence. You can be the most talented person in the world, but without truth, without persistence, you will end up with nothing. My name is in the history books, I know the world of boxing, so please allow me to have an opinion: he is 40 per cent better than any other boxer in this country.' Ronnie Davies, now reconciled with Eubank, has been tasked with building the chip into something resembling the old block. 'I must be bloody mad,' says

Davies. 'I said to Chris: "You can't put me through all that again." And Chris said: "By giving you my boy I'll put another ten years on your life." He's got a lot of similarities to his old man, even though he's his own person. He's got great focus, great self-belief and I firmly believe he'll be a world champion.'

'I wouldn't say my dad's pushy,' says Chris Jr, who has already demonstrated a very Eubankian knack of riling potential rivals. 'He's never tried to force me to do anything I didn't want to do. But I trust him 100 per cent, if he tells me something I'm going to do it. He's my mentor, he's controlling everything, making sure I've got the right people around me, inputting a lot into my training, always on the phone telling me what to do. But there's no pressure at all. That ring entrance and how I am in the ring, that's all entertainment. I'm here to put on a show and bring excitement back to British boxing and that's the best way I see to do it. A lot of things he used to do have rubbed off on me but everything I do is natural. I'm his son, I've got his DNA. I've got royal blood running through my veins.' However, don't expect Chris Jr to be sporting the English gentleman look any time soon. 'I need to start getting a few more suits,' says Chris Jr. 'I'm a bit too casual at the moment. That's what he tells me anyway. That would certainly get people going, though, if I started wearing a monocle. Maybe one day I'll try it out, just to see what happens.'

When he's not steering the boxing careers of his two sons – his second son Sebastian is a heavyweight in the amateur ranks – Eubank devotes his time to charitable causes and human rights issues. He was arrested four times for protesting against Britain's military involvement in Iraq, while he also became involved in the News International phone-hacking scandal. Eubank rejected News International's 'derisory offer' of £21,000 and told the High Court the organisation's actions destroyed his marriage. The judge told him to sit down and stop grandstanding. At the London Olympics, Eubank was in charge of the Angolan boxing team. Eubank had one boxer to look after, a heavyweight called Tumba Silva. However, when Silva failed to turn up for the weigh-in he was thrown out of the Games without throwing a punch. 'The athlete was inconsolable and cried like a child when I told him,' said the head of Angola's Olympic team. 'He had put his whole life into this fight and is inconsolable. That plonker of a coach . . .' So it goes.

Fans of sport love to while away the hours ranking a particular sport's greatest practitioners. But it is easier done in some sports than others. Tennis, for example, has Grand Slam tournaments as yardsticks, so that we know incontrovertibly that Novak Djokovic (six Grand Slam titles) is a greater player than Andy Murray (two), at least as it stands. Of course, it isn't always this simple. Is Roger Federer a greater tennis player than Rafa Nadal because he has won 17 Grand Slam titles to 12, or is Nadal greater because he has five years on Federer and leads 21–10 in head-to-head encounters? Perhaps only time will tell. Then there is the thorny issue of historical comparison. Is Jack Nicklaus (18 major titles) a greater golfer than Tiger Woods (14) or is Woods greater because he achieved his feats in a more competitive era? Is Michael Schumacher (seven Formula 1 championships) a greater racing driver than Jackie Stewart (three) or was he simply in a superior car, relatively speaking, for most of his career? Was Sachin Tendulkar (15,837 Test runs at an average of 53.86) a greater batsman than Brian Lara (11,953 at 52.88) or is Lara greater because he scored tougher runs and was more aesthetically pleasing?

Throw in the evolution of rules, conditions and technology and it's no wonder these arguments can get so heated.

Then there is boxing, in which the internecine politics that characterises the sport in its modern form sometimes makes comparison virtually impossible, even between fighters of the same era. As I write, three British and one Irish fighter have fought for versions of the middleweight world title in the past two years – Birmingham's Matt Macklin (three times), Martin Murray of St Helens (twice), London's Darren Barker and Limerick's Andy Lee – yet none of them has fought each other. 'They go on about wanting to fight each other,' says Brian Lynch, 'but it's all crap. If you're a middleweight and I'm a middleweight, you're not going to fight me if I'm any good. It's ridiculous. It never used to be like that – someone used to put the money up and the fight would take place. They call this geezer the champion, this other one the champion, you don't know who the champion is nowadays. It's gone mad, no one knows what's going on and that's why people aren't interested. That's why I like Carl Froch so much. He'll fight anyone – he don't care where it is, what it's for, he'll fight them. I wouldn't pay to see many fighters nowadays but I'd pay to see Carl Froch. He's value for money and he's got a heart like a lion.'

As we have seen, ducking and diving has always been prevalent in boxing, but at least Benn, Eubank and Watson got it on. However, even when there seems to exist concrete proof that one fighter is better than another fighter, there is often evidence to the contrary. 'People say to me: "Eubank, what a great world champion"', says Jim McDonnell. 'And I say: "Who did he beat in his career? Name one world-class fighter." And they can't. He was an enigma, a good fighter but purely domestic. He was Eubank the showman, Eubank the businessman and he made a lot of money. Granted, Eubank beat Benn and they drew the second fight. But Benn proved himself in America, beat Iran Barkley, beat Gerald McClellan, proved himself against some real top boys. Eubank never did that, which is why you've got to take your hat off to Benn.'

Then there are the endless arguments over 'who made whom'. 'Eubank made that rivalry what it was because he instigated all that hatred,' contests David Haye. 'If he had the same personality as Nigel Benn and was just about going in the ring and getting the job done, it wouldn't have been what it was. It was because Eubank was such an off-the-wall character that those fights were so huge.' 'In truth, if there had been no Nigel Benn, there could never have been a Chris Eubank,' says Ambrose Mendy. 'But if there had been no Chris Eubank, there would always have been a Nigel Benn. Chris was very lucky Nigel came into his life because, without being overly critical, Chris was totally domestic whereas Nigel was international.' 'They lived off each other, they made each other,' says Kevin Mitchell. 'It's almost impossible to imagine Benn without Eubank, and vice versa. But Nigel made Chris to a greater extent because Chris had to dig so deep in those two fights and they ended up defining him. Chris was in a handful of great fights and also in lots of pretty ordinary fights that he got away with because of his posing and showmanship. But many other fighters inspired Nigel to do amazing things, most notably Iran Barkley and Gerald McClellan. Chris often only did just as much as he had to; Nigel always did as much as he possibly could. Invariably it was good enough and even when it wasn't, as against Chris in their first fight, he never left anything in the ring.'

Meanwhile, some believe too much time is spent assessing the relative merits of Benn and Eubank when they weren't even the two best British fighters in and around their weight class in that era. Indeed, such is the perverse nature of boxing that Herol Graham and Michael Watson, who never won a world title between them, are widely regarded as having been superior. 'Benn was the most exciting, Eubank was the most charismatic, Graham was the most enigmatic but Watson was the most talented,' says Frank Maloney. 'Benn was a wrecking ball, he was England's answer to Tommy Hearns. Chris Eubank would have been better off in a circus than in a boxing ring – and I mean that in a nice way, he was the ultimate showman. But if you took Benn and Eubank and put them together they still wouldn't have amounted to Watson.'

However you rank the individual fighters, it says much about the vibrancy of the Benn–Eubank era that we are able to have these evidence-based arguments at all. Too often nowadays boxing debates have a hollow ring because there are too few fighters going about their business in the mainstream, in turn because there are too few genuinely great fighters, in turn because the fighters who aspire to greatness too often refuse to fight each other, when fighting other aspirant greats remains the only sure-fire route to greatness. 'In hindsight,' says Donald McRae, 'those two Benn–Eubank fights highlight what boxing is lacking now. The show business element, the contrasts between them, meant Benn and Eubank made a huge amount of money. But those fighters remain ingrained on the minds of everyone who saw them because of what happened between them in the ring. So many fighters today, whether it's Floyd Mayweather, Andre Ward or David Haye, lack that rival that can push them to the limit, define them and authenticate their greatness. That's when things start to become really fascinating, when you become totally absorbed in boxing.'

★ ★ ★

A third meeting between Nigel Benn and Chris Eubank might have gone some way to settling who was indeed the better fighter. Although there's a good chance they would have served up another draw anyway. And it is to the chagrin of many involved with the two fighters' careers that it never happened. 'That's one of the very few sadnesses and regrets in my life,' says Barry Hearn. 'Because if we'd done a third fight properly we would have launched pay-per-view in this country, set a huge, record figure and rewarded both of them. That fight could have been worth £20 million.' But there was a third fight, after all. Not at the Birmingham NEC, not at Old Trafford in Manchester, but in an amphitheatre in Rome. Not with boxing gloves, but with shields and swords. Not in shorts and boxing boots, but in armour and sandals. It seemed like a ludicrous pretence – more *Up Pompeii* than *Gladiator* – but it served as a reminder, however faint, of what made their rivalry so great. As with the unearthing of a Roman mosaic, the colours had faded but the outlines remained.

Eubank turned up to the 2000-year-old gladiatorial training camp wearing a pinstripe suit, a bowler hat and twirling a cane. It was 32 degrees. And when he saw a cast of characters standing among the ruins in Roman costumes he suspected the whole thing was a wind-up. 'Chris was a little bit upset to begin with,' says Dan Shadrake, head of the Britannia re-enactment society. 'His initial reaction was, "What the bloody hell am I doing here?" And at first I thought the same, it's one of the oddest things I've ever worked on.' Once Eubank had been convinced that he wasn't the victim of the most elaborate practical joke in history he was thrown a sackcloth to wear and given the name Maximo, meaning 'The Best'. Benn, meanwhile, was called Eradico, meaning 'Destroy'. Then things got serious and from behind the absurdity emerged certain deep-seated truths.

Eubank bickered with his trainer, an ex-squaddie and stunt-man whom the programme makers mischievously called Spartacus. 'Taking orders from unaccomplished men is very tough,' said Eubank, who was made to do press-ups for being late. Benn, the former army man, bonded with his trainer immediately. 'He's the boss,' said Benn, 'anything he tells me I'll do.' Benn didn't complain when he was told that all there was for dinner was gruel and water. At the opposite end of the table, Eubank looked like he wanted to be sick. 'I went there to play a game, stay in the best hotels and have a good time with my wife,' he said. 'But I walked into the most gruelling, terrifying situation I've ever been in.'

'I don't want him beating me in anything I do,' said Benn. 'He's done it once already and that really hurt . . .'

'He's bubbling, he wants to erupt,' said Eubank. 'He doesn't just want to win, he needs to . . .'

'No way on God's green earth can I handle another defeat from this man. I will not be able to live it down . . .'

'He's not a talker, he's a brawler. He'd rather kick it off physically than engage psychologically . . .'

'This brings me back to where I thought I'd never be again . . .'

'I've moved on. He hasn't. He's exactly where he was in 1990 . . .'

Benn threw himself into training with frightening gusto. It turned out he had actually been training for three months. Eubank was in pieces after ten minutes. After one challenge Eubank accused Benn of cheating, after another Eubank gloated among some ruins. 'I wiped the floor with him,' said Eubank, chuckling. 'Things are good.' 'I just thought they'd turn up and think it was a bit of a laugh,' says Shadrake. 'But the rivalry was still there, they were very professional. It was quite intense. Even when the cameras were off the trainers had both boxers doing push-ups and carrying bags of sand round the ruins, they were on the go constantly. And while Chris was playing it for laughs a little bit, Nigel put 100 per cent into it. He was very, very focused and dedicated on every tiny little aspect. After day one I thought to myself: "Wow, this is serious."'

When Eubank took his gloating too far they almost came to blows and had to be separated by their trainers. This wasn't in the script. 'It wasn't staged, I can tell you,' says Shadrake, 'they really did go at each other. The programme makers told us at the start: "If it does kick off, do not get in the way or try to calm things down because they are prize fighters and you'll get your head smashed off." They didn't have to tell me twice.' 'Can I just make a point?' said Eubank to Spartacus after the melee had died down. 'I didn't start it and he struck me first.' 'That's two points,' said Spartacus, 'give me 20 press-ups.' When they finally made their peace, Benn clutched Eubank's head to his own and looked like he was going to bite him. 'Only you can do this to me,' growled Benn. 'You know that? Only you can do this to me.' 'This is far more serious than it was supposed to be,' said a puzzled-looking Eubank.

On their day off, Eubank wandered the surrounding hills and recited poetry. Benn spent it training. When it came to the actual sword fight, Benn gave Eubank such a going over that his rival emerged with a cut chin. Eubank thought he had won it. Everyone else thought Benn had destroyed him. In the second fight, Eubank snapped a mace over Benn's legs. The crowd booed. Benn was awarded the overall victory and a wooden sword as a trophy. He looked genuinely thrilled. 'Wow. Crazy. Unbelievable. Thank you, Chris.'

EPILOGUE
You never know

A week before the manuscript of the book you have just read was handed to my publishers I attended the rematch between Carl Froch and Mikkel Kessler at London's O2 Arena. And as I sat ringside, directly behind the *Guardian*'s Kevin Mitchell, I was reminded of his simple yet evocative summary of the Benn–Eubank era: 'Just so bloody noisy.' Froch is sometimes referred to as a throwback fighter. Indeed, few fighters in the history of British boxing – if any – have engaged in such a gruelling succession of elite-level contests. Beginning with the night he slugged it out with and eventually outpointed Jean Pascal to claim the WBC super-middleweight title, on to a last-gasp stoppage of Jermain Taylor that defied belief, not forgetting his glorious defeat against Kessler first time around and his manful but ultimately futile effort against the brilliant Andre Ward, culminating in his wrecking-ball demolition of Lucian Bute, Froch had served as a glorious reminder of how magnificent the sport of boxing can be when one man is willing to fight anyone, anytime, anywhere.

As the rounds ticked by – each one grimmer than the last – the butterflies in my stomach turned to seagulls, the goose bumps reached places other sports are unable to make them reach and the lump that had been lodged in my throat from the sound of the first bell began to feel like a golf ball. This is what it feels like when boxing gets it right. This is what boxing can still be. This is what so many former boxing fans are missing out on. And it was only a nagging sense of professional integrity that stopped me from tapping Mitchell on the shoulder and whispering in his ear: 'Is this what it was like when Eubank fought Benn?' But I'm almost certain what the answer would have been.

It is an hour into my interview with Nigel Benn and I can tell he is a little bit bored. As far as Benn is concerned he's said it all before a thousand times and probably can't understand why anyone would want to hear him say it again. So Benn tells his boy to fetch the iPad from the hotel room so that he can show me something of the new breed. Benn fires the machine up and suddenly we're watching Conor working the pads. And you can feel the old man beam. 'I didn't want him to fight but now I've seen what he can do,' says Benn Sr. 'I've sparred with him, did his nose in, chipped his tooth, because I wanted to say: "Son, this is what it's all about and I want to see how much you've got." And it turns out he's got power, he's got speed, he's got it all. He's certainly better than me. Two weeks ago I suddenly started welling up. I was crying, my wife was crying, Nanny started crying, we all started crying. Because we knew he had it in him.' Conor looks at me as if he knows what's coming. 'How about Benn–Eubank III?' A slight pause, a little smile. 'You never know . . .'

Acknowledgements

This book is a tribute to the monumental feats performed by some of the bravest, most charismatic sportsmen of our age; and to the duckers and the divers, the dreamers and the schemers, the much-maligned characters who gave these sportsmen a stage. In particular it is intended as a paean to a lost era and to the two boxers who underpinned that era, Chris Eubank and Nigel Benn. As such I extend huge thanks to Nigel for being generous with his time at a busy time in his life – a few days after we met in a Liverpool hotel he moved with his family to Sydney, no doubt in part because he wanted to get away from people like me. It was heartening that Nigel seemed so healthy and content. During the writing of this book I was often asked: 'How are you getting on with Eubank?' And they would chuckle knowingly when I told them I was having trouble pinning him down but that I'd get him eventually. I tried and tried and tried and God knows I offered him a few quid. But he beat me in the end. However, Chris being Chris, he still managed to steal the show from everybody. My long and revealing lunch at the Blue Legume cafe in Crouch End with Michael Watson and his good friend and carer Len Ballack opened up many new paths – some leading to the light, some into darkness – and to both I am grateful. I am glad to report that Michael's appetite is monstrous – carrot cake for starter and ravioli for dessert? – and he looks and sounds a treat. Herol Graham always made me laugh when I was a kid and it was nice to hear him back on form and giggling again. I hope the fact that almost everyone I spoke to reckoned he was the best of the lot gives him – and his family – some satisfaction.

Jim McDonnell proved a very adept sketch writer and his stories about his old stable-mate Eubank managed to be both funny and revealing. Gary Stretch, too, managed to transform Eubank from the cartoon character he hated being portrayed as into a real person. Doug DeWitt, still dreaming of the night he coulda knocked out Tommy Hearns in a ball park, provided a glimpse into the mind of an unfulfilled fighter – which, let's face it, most of them are. Errol Christie and Lloyd Honeyghan were excellent on the bad old days and can both claim to be pioneers. Roy Jones and James Toney got round to fighting each other – Jones won handily in 1994 – but they never got round to fighting Eubank or Benn. Nevertheless, it was nice to hear the reasons why and that there are no hard feelings really. Joe Calzaghe still sounded genuinely captivated by Eubank all these years after they fought, while Ricky Hatton and David Haye still sounded in awe of Benn. It was lovely to hear gnarled old pros speak about their own childhood heroes in such a wide-eyed manner. Thanks also to Carl Froch for inspiring the epilogue, and to referee Richard Steele, perhaps the most intimate witness of them all.

Barry Hearn loves chatting about the old times, he tells his stories beautifully and his enthusiasm is infectious. Certainly his equally articulate son Eddie is riddled with it. Frank Warren took some pinning down but I must thank him for being unstintingly polite, even during our 30th telephone conversation. Ambrose Mendy was brilliant and it was our (very) long telephone conversation that first convinced me this book would be achievable. If I had to choose one man who encapsulated the madness of the fight game during that era, it might be him. Thank you, too, to those other movers and shakers Frank Maloney, Andy Ayling and Trevor East and to perhaps the most venerable men in all of boxing, the trainers: Ronnie Davies, Brian Lynch and Jimmy Tibbs.

When I was an awkward, young(er) journalist trying to break into boxing one bloke who was always scrupulously polite and generous with his time was BBC commentator Mike Costello. A boxing man through and through, hugely knowledgeable about the sport and always happy to impart his wisdom, I am honoured that his words appear before mine at the start of this book. He is almost as good a writer as he is a commentator – which is to say a bloody good one. Perhaps this will inspire him to take up the pen as well as the microphone. British boxing is lucky to have had so many magnificent journalists cover it down the years and I was always aware during the writing of this book that I was perched on the shoulders of giants. In Kevin Mitchell, Colin Hart and Donald McRae I found three passionate and eloquent witnesses, and Mitchell and McRae have already written fine books which cover aspects of the Benn–Eubank era. Written primary source material was provided by most of the national newspapers of the day – thank the boxing gods for the British Library newspaper archive and Manchester City Council's online newspaper archive – but two journalists I am particularly grateful to are the late, great Harry Mullan and the recently departed Jonathan Rendall, whose interviews with Eubank before he was famous and following his first fight against Benn were particularly instructive. And not forgetting my old BBC mucker Tom Fordyce, who told perhaps the most revealing story of all – in more ways than one. Cheers, too, to Nick Owen and Jim Rosenthal for their very personal takes and to Sky's Ed Robinson for making the latter interview possible.

Others I am indebted to are Tris Dixon and John Dennen from *Boxing News*, Chris Eubank Jr, Conor Benn, Benn's agent Kevin Lueshing, Watson's publicist Geraldine Davies, Lenny DeJesus for demonstrating that Chris Eubank hasn't always been Chris Eubank, Captain John O'Grady for demonstrating that Nigel Benn has always been Nigel Benn, Jessie Mullan for being so understanding, Karen Graham, Sarah for being so patient and supportive, Lorna for keeping me out of the pub, Elliot Worsell, Richard Maynard and Dan Shadrake for proving that the Benn–Eubank rivalry will never truly die. And last but certainly not least, a huge thank you to my publishers, Simon & Schuster – in particular Ian Marshall for recognising the book's potential and Jo Whitford for putting up with my constant badgering – and my always upbeat and encouraging agent, David Luxton, for making it all happen. It was a blast writing this thing – a slog at times, but a blast none-theless – I only hope you enjoyed reading it.

Sources

Chapter One. Having a good whack

p. 10 'his chin sets questions': *The Times*, 7 November 1985.

p. 11 'I get worried when a guy goes down': *The Times*, 27 November 1987.

'Nigel will need three guys': ibid.

'disenchanted with the business of boxing': *Guardian*, 27 January 1988.

'I don't want to fight any more Mexican roadsweepers': *The Times*, 27 November 1987.

p. 12 'Benn's slam-bang tactics': *The Times*, 20 April 1988.

'in the business of creating monsters': *Daily Telegraph*, 3 December 2005.

p. 14 'I loved him more than any other person': Nigel Benn, *Nigel Benn* (Blake Publishing, 1999).

p. 15 'I got involved in a street fight': *Guardian*, 28 October 1988.

p. 16 'one-round job': *The Times*, 30 March 1989.

'It's war, I don't think it will go more than six rounds': *The Times*, 14 March 1989.

'You'll stay quiet': *The Times*, 16 May 1989.

'You seem like a very nice man': ibid.

'I'm in the hurt business': ibid.

'You are not going to beat me, son': ibid.

p. 17 'When a fighter has a 22–0 record': *San Francisco Chronicle*, 20 May 1989.

'His stamina was running out against Miller': *Independent*, 29 April 1990.

p. 18 'Logan hasn't won since Benn beat him': *Independent*, 20 May 1989.

'Benn has sparred only 12 rounds in training': Nigel Benn, *Nigel Benn*.

'I don't give a damn what others think': *Observer*, 17 April 1988.

p. 19 'stark raving bonkers': *The Times*, 23 May 1988.

'In the fifth, I heard my trainer call out': Nigel Benn, *Nigel Benn*.

p. 20 'I became so slant-eyed': Nigel Benn, *Nigel Benn*.

'When he did manage to land': Budd Schulberg, *Ringside: A Treasury of Boxing Reportage* (Ivan R. Dee Inc., 2006).

Chapter Two. Love at first sight

p. 24 'His prickly arrogance': *Boxing News*, 31 August 1990.

p. 25 'This is difficult, I am not used to seeing white men': *Independent*, 30 January 1994.

p. 26 'While all this was going on': SaddoBoxing.com, 23 August 2007.

'Nigel Benn is a coward and a fraud': *Boxing News*, 1 December 1988.

'for a plate of fish and chips': *Independent*, 30 September 1990.

p. 28 'mental midget . . . pugilistic pygmy': *Independent*, 7 May 1993.

'He just chucks money around': *Observer*, 25 November 1990.

'He's the only man I know': *Sun*, 8 November 1990.

p. 31 'The problem for my opponent': Chris Eubank, *Eubank: The Autobiography* (Willow, 2003).

'Before, in the good old days': *Clash of the Titans: Benn v Eubank*, BBC TV, 1999.

p. 32 'Where is there a fighter': *Independent*, 1 August 1990.

p. 34 'I turned pro in 1986': *Sunday Times*, 12 April 1992.

'In any poll for the fighters' fighter': *Observer*, 18 November 1990.

Chapter Three. Two minds, miles apart?

p. 37 'Boxing and Christianity are not much different': Harry Mullan, *Fighting Words* (Colebridge Associates, 1993).

p. 38 'If it comes down to a fight of will': *Independent*, 30 September 1990.

p. 39 'wealth, education and to marry a prominent woman': *Chicago Tribune*, 1 November 1987.

'There's something I want cleared up': *Sports Illustrated*, 27 March 1967.

p. 41 'I haven't invented myself': *The Times*, 2 September 1995.

'I earned very good money': Harry Mullan, *Fighting Words*.

'It was bliss': *Sunday Times*, 12 April 1992.

p. 42 'lived like a king': *Sunday Times*, 12 April 1992.

'a place of nightmares': *Boxing Monthly*, June 1989.

p. 43 'the fly-by-nights, the triers, the posers': Chris Eubank, *Eubank: The Autobiography* (Willow, 2003).

p. 45 'The sparring was more than real': eastsideboxing.com, 12 July 2011.

'He had a beautiful soul': *The Times*, 2 September 1995.

p. 46 'It is like two minds': *Sunday Times*, 17 January 1993.

'I wanted to be like my idol': Nigel Benn, *Nigel Benn* (Blake Publishing, 1999).

p. 47 'I would have bashed him up as well': Nigel Benn, *Nigel Benn*.

'Kicking ass was a way of life': *The Times*, 22 October 1988.

p. 49 'I can take discipline': *Daily Mirror*, 28 February 1995.

'I'm not ashamed to admit': ibid.

p.50 'It was the army that taught me about attitude': *Observer*, 11 June 1995.

Chapter Four. A monk's life

p. 51 'There are people in boxing': *Independent*, 20 May 1989.

'Watson will steer a course': *Guardian*, 20 May 1989.

'In the end, Benn surrendered': *Sunday Times*, 28 May 1989.

p. 52 'live a monk's life': *Guardian*, 26 July 1989.

'I boxed a round with a guy': *The Times*, 26 July 1989.

p. 53 'In the States I get hurt': *Sunday Times*, 18 November 1990.

'There was a very good club scene': Nigel Benn, *Nigel Benn* (Blake Publishing, 1999).

'sensitive parts of her body': *Sunday Mirror*, 18 September 1994.

p. 56 'One idiot tried to arrest Nigel': *Independent*, 26 January 1989.

p. 58 'glorifying the truth': *Observer*, 31 March 1991.

p. 62 'boxing's equivalent of the Zenith Data Systems Cup': *Sunday Times*, 22 April 1990.

p. 63 'an eye that stinks': *The Times*, 17 August 1990.

'If he was made to stop boxing now': *The Times*, 17 August 1990.

p. 64 'Boxing is a business where an honest man': Budd Schulberg, *Ringside: A Treasury of Boxing Reportage* (Ivan R. Dee Inc., 2006).

p. 65 'Whatever the long-term judgement': *Guardian*, 20 August 1990.

'the best English fighter ever': *The Times*, 20 August 1990.

Chapter Five. A festering volcano

p. 68 '[Eubank] has talked himself': *Guardian*, 17 November 1990.

'He remains a dedicated non-conformist': Harry Mullan, *Fighting Words* (Colebridge Associates, 1993).

p. 71 'When the good times rolled': Nigel Benn, *Nigel Benn* (Blake Publishing, 1999).

p. 72 'For God's sake, the bastard': John Duncan, *In the Red Corner: A Journey into Cuban Boxing* (Yellow Jersey Press, 2000).

p. 73 'I'm in prison and I am loaded': *USA Today*, 21 March 2012.

p. 74 'When you are a famous personality': Bob Lonkhurst, *Terry Spinks MBE: Life Was a Roller-Coaster* (B L Associates, 2012).

p. 75 'We don't consider him a risk': *Guardian*, 12 September 1990.

'He spends much of each round': *The Times*, 6 September 1990.

'It is no longer enough': *Guardian*, 7 September 1990.

p. 76 'Mendy talks in very big noughts': *The Times*, 7 September 1990.

'Benn is capable of only knocking out a man': *The Times*, 12 September 1990.

p. 79 'Benn proved to me he was a coward': *Sun*, 13 November 1990.

'He is a loudmouth': *Guardian*, 17 November 1990.

Chapter Six. Two shining stars

p. 82 'The national honour was at stake': Grantland.com, 26 January 2012.

'the darkey... the nigger... the terrible black': ibid.

'felt somewhat alarmed': ibid.

p. 83 'Any fighter who'd get into the ring': Geoffrey C. Ward, *Unforgivable Blackness: The Rise and Fall of Jack Johnson* (Knopf, 2004).

p. 84 'Citizens who have never prayed before': Ward, *Unforgivable Blackness*.

'The fight with Johnson': ibid.

'Jeffries must emerge from his alfalfa farm': ibid.

p. 85 'It was a concern': *The Times*, 12 October 1990.

'You should play down hate': *The Times*, 12 October 1990.

'I am not letting any black man': *Sports Illustrated*, 6 October 1980.

p. 86 'promoters shall not advertise a tournament': Oliver Jarratt, *The Gifted One: Kirkland Laing Through the Eyes of Others* (Oliver Jarratt, 2009).

p. 87 'The boxers themselves': Harry Mullan, *Fighting Words* (Colebridge Associates, 1993).

p. 88 'lots of nasty letters': Jarratt, *The Gifted One*.

p. 89 'In the 1960s it was virtually unheard of': *Daily Mirror*, 10 April 2002.

'My manager told me in strong terms': Jarratt, *The Gifted One*.

p. 90 'It's no longer enough to have speed': Kasia Boddy, *Boxing: A Cultural History* (Reaktion Books, 2008).

'The modern pugilist is last of all a fighter': ibid.

'Bruce Jenner, the decathlon winner': Sugar Ray Leonard, *The Big Fight: My Autobiography* (Viking Books, 2011).

p. 92 'He's everything that we are': *The Times*, 22 May 1991.

p. 93 'When I came into boxing': *Guardian*, 24 October 2005.

'I would not do pantomime': *The Times*, 9 October 1993.

p. 94 'Pridefully coiffured and sumptuously groomed': *Guardian*, 15 September 1990.

Chapter Seven. Ghosts at the feast

p. 97 'a tough club of guys-ya-want-no-part-of': Budd Schulberg, *Ringside: A Treasury of Boxing Reportage* (Ivan R. Dee Inc., 2006).

'If it had been tennis': ibid.

p. 98 'It'll be a shot in the arm': Budd Schulberg, *Ringside*.

p. 99 'most sports fans would not spend a dime': *Sports Illustrated*, 18 December 1989.

'Who the hell wants to see Whitaker': *New York Times*, 13 April 1997.

p. 101 'I hate the sight of blood': *Sunday Times*, 15 October 1989.

'He had all the boxing techniques wrong': *Guardian*, 23 November 1990.

'Graham's style is seen by some': *Boxing News*, 23 November 1990.

p.102 'Celebrations of non-violence': Harry Mullan, *Fighting Words* (Colebridge Associates, 1993).

'I have never had such a frustrating night': *The Times*, 5 November 1986.

p. 103 'Graham has turned defensive boxing': *Boxing News*, 23 November 1990.

p. 104 'They have tried to turn him into a fighter': *Boxing News*, 23 November 1990.

'He promised me the world': *The Times*, 5 September 1988.

'I came to bust him up': *Sunday Times*, 7 May 1989.

p. 105 'Herol Graham was such an inspiration': Sky Sports website, 18 January 2013.

'I can send Mike out to do any job': *The Times*, 10 May 1989.

'Your Herol's a classy boxer': *Guardian*, 23 November 1990.

'bewildering': ibid.

p. 107 'I went to the gym but I was a timid': *Boxing News*, 28 February 2011.

'I boxed his head off': *Boxing News*, 28 February 2011.

'That defeat made me realise': *Boxing News*, 22 July 1988.

p. 108 'Watson showed talent and determination': *Boxing News*, 22 July 1988.

'While Benn opted for the high-profile': *Sunday Times*, 28 May 1989.

p. 109 'Smooth Mover with a Hoover': Michael Watson, *The Biggest Fight: Michael Watson's Story* (Time Warner Books, 2004).

'I think my record compares': *Boxing News*, 22 July 1988.

p. 110 'He was going to America': Watson, *The Biggest Fight*.

p. 113 'It seemed like a bad joke': Watson, *The Biggest Fight*.

p. 114 'Nigel Benn and Chris Eubank come together': *Guardian*, 17 November 1990.

'WBO champions are still': *Boxing News*, 16 November 1990.

'Herol would stand the pair of them': *Observer*, 18 November 1990.

Chapter Eight. Who's Fooling Who?

p. 119 'Eubank can punch': *Observer*, 18 November 1990.

'Benn will win inside the distance': ibid.

'Concerning all the boxing writers': *Boxing News*, 12 October 1990.

p. 120 'Nigel Benn will do Britain's close boxing family': *Sun*, 17 November 1990.

p. 122 'You're fighting for the championship': *Independent*, 25 November 1990.

'I was proud to be spoken to': ibid.

p. 125 'about 40 or so up from Brighton': Chris Eubank, *Eubank: The Autobiography* (Willow, 2003).

'I stood in the ring': *Independent*, 25 November 1990.

p. 126 'In the lead-up to the fight': *Independent*, 25 November 1990.

p. 128 'Benn entered the ring like an uncaged tiger': Eubank, *Eubank*.

p. 129 'That was a mistake': *Independent*, 25 November 1990.

p. 130 'I came out and threw the right hand': *Independent*, 25 November 1990.

p. 132 'The pace was hot': *Independent*, 25 November 1990.

p. 133 'We were in a clinch': Eubank, *Eubank*.

p. 135 'I have almost no recollection': Eubank, *Eubank*.

p. 138 'I'd broken his spirit': *Independent*, 25 November 1990.

'I closed my eyes and roared': ibid.

p. 140 'The championship belt was': *Boxing News*, 23 November 1990.

'It was one of the great British contests': *The Times*, 19 November 1990.

'the fight had all the mayhem and drama': *Guardian*, 19 November 1990.

'It was a thrilling contest': *Independent*, 20 November 1990.

'I FORGIVE EU, COLIN': *Sun*, 20 November 1990.

p. 141 'One day someone': *Independent*, 25 November 1990.

p. 142 'His credibility as a world class performer': *Boxing News*, 23 November 1990.

Chapter Nine. Seeing dogs fight

p. 145 'You've heard this one before': *Boxing News*, 23 November 1990.

p. 146 'Two world title losses in a year': Herol Graham, *Bomber: Behind the Laughter* (T H Media, 2011).

'no way am I getting back in the ring': *The Times*, 20 November 1990.

p. 147 'Nunn is 6ft 2in and a southpaw': *Independent*, 20 November 1990.

'Chris is his own man': ibid.

p. 148 'rather die than lose': *Sunday Times*, 29 September 1991.

'I am a misunderstood champion': *The Times*, 20 April 1991.

'What can McCallum bring?': *The Times*, 24 June 1991.

p. 149 'Britain's most disliked world champion': Chris Eubank, *Eubank: The Autobiography* (Willow, 2003).

'Eubank refuses to show respect': *Guardian*, 16 June 1991.

'To some, he is a fraud': *Sunday Times*, 16 June 1991.

p. 151 'The reason I earn the most money': Donald McRae, *Dark Trade: Lost in Boxing* (Mainstream Publishing, 1996).

p. 153 'In the three wins Watson has scored': *Guardian*, 16 June 1991.

'Mentally, Eubank will destroy Watson': *The Times*, 22 June 1991.

'I think Eubank may have to': ibid.

'Watson's appearance gave the impression': *Guardian*, 16 June 1991.

'Most of the 11,500 watchers': *Observer*, 23 June 1991.

p. 154 'it was a good fight for the third division': *The Times*, 24 June 1991.

'I was regarded as the villain': Chris Eubank, *Eubank*.

'yet another bastard weight class': George Kimball, *Four Kings: Leonard, Hagler, Hearns, Duran and the Last Great Era of Boxing* (McBooks Press, 2008).

p. 155 'I want Chris Eubank': McRae, *Dark Trade*.

p. 156 'You make me sick': *The Times*, 18 July 1991.

'The sport has to be resurrected': ibid.

'I have a lot of contempt for this man': *The Times*, 21 September 1991.

p. 157 'I came back to my corner': *Daily Telegraph*, 29 April 2006.

'I knew from round six': *The Times*, 23 September 1991.

'I remember thinking of Watson': Eubank, *Eubank*.

'I suppose I was enjoying beating him': Michael Watson, *The Biggest Fight: Michael Watson's Story* (Time Warner Books, 2004).

p. 158 'the greatest round': Michael Watson, *The Biggest Fight*.

'When I put Chris down': *The Times*, 19 September 2011.

'My nervous system shorted': *Daily Telegraph*, 29 April 2006.

p. 159 'I got up for the last': *The Times*, 19 September 2011.

'I wanted to keep going': ibid.

p. 160 'Michael was closer to death': *Independent*, 11 September 2011.

p. 161 'How much mileage is left': *Observer*, 29 September 1991.

'I knew that eleventh-round punch': McRae, *Dark Trade*.

p. 162 'It is a throwback to the days': *The Times*, 23 September 1991.

'In modern-day Britain': ibid.

p. 163 'Those of us who defend': Scripps Howard News Service, 25 September 1991.

'Boxing is not a safe activity': *Guardian*, 27 September 1991.

'I thought of calling the show off': *The Times*, 25 September 1991.

Chapter Ten. So beneath me

p. 165 'By producing a move of such quality': *Sunday Times*, 29 September 1991.

'I remember thinking of Watson': Chris Eubank, *Eubank: The Autobiography* (Willow, 2003).

p. 166 'For years afterwards': *Daily Mirror*, 11 September 2011.

'For anyone who says': *The Times*, 2 September 1995.

'Boy, you're pretty. But I'm prettier than you': Michael Watson, *The Biggest Fight: Michael Watson's Story* (Time Warner Books, 2004).

'I never thought I could inflict such damage': *The Times*, 30 October 1991.

'My view of boxing has not changed': ibid.

p. 167 'The topics that average people talk about': *Independent*, 23 April 1992.

p. 168 'they've transformed me into': *Al-Ahram* (Egypt), 23 October 1996.

'The media sees me as a commodity': ibid.

'What did you think it was?': *Sunday Telegraph Magazine*, 11 February 1996.

p. 169 'I'm trying to get into Cambridge University': *Sunday Times*, 20 December 1992.

'*Thus Spake Zarathustra*': *Observer*, 21 August 1994.

'This is almost certainly true': ibid.

p. 170 'At any one of my press conferences': Chris Eubank, *Eubank*.

p. 172 'It costs me £320 per haircut': *Sunday Telegraph Magazine*, 11 February 1996.

p. 173 'I'm a paragon, a demi-God': *Guardian*, 10 May 1993.

'Excuse me. When you asked': *Daily Mirror*, 3 February 1993.

'If any of you go to a hotel room': *Daily Mirror*, 10 December 1993.

'The fact that a man who': *Sunday Times*, 2 February 1992.

p. 174 'I would struggle to recall': *Sunday Times*, 28 June 1992.

'The Snore on the Shore': *The Times*, 15 September 1992.

p. 175 'His road show is desperately': *Sunday Times*, 29 November 1992.

'boxing is not a metaphor': Simon Barnes, *The Meaning of Sport* (Short Books, 2006).

'The boxing establishment': *The Times*, 9 October 1993.

p. 176 'the gullibility': *Independent*, 9 October 1993.

'We'll certainly find enough': *Daily Mirror*, 22 February 1993.

p. 177 'They said Eubank is too awkward': *The Times*, 22 February 1993.

'Can he box?': *Independent*, 3 December 1992.

'Why should I care?': *Sunday Mirror*, 13 September 1992.

p. 178 'It seems downright unfair': *Boxing News*, 15 January 1993.

Chapter Eleven. Somehow, I remember

p. 182 'Nigel Benn is still very much a force': *The Times*, 4 April 1991.

'Let Chris Eubank be the bad boy': *The Times*, 5 April 1991.

p. 183 'Who's to say he has really': *The Times*, 25 February 1992.

'Judged on this performance': *Sunday Times*, 24 May 1992.

p. 184 'When I came to Italy': *The Times*, 3 October 1992.

'Beating Galvano in Italy': ibid.

p. 185 'Benn has lost his bottle': *Sunday Mirror*, 22 November 1992.

p. 186 'British boxing is rudderless': *Guardian*, 12 December 1992.

'I'm prepared to deal with James Toney': *The Times*, 6 January 1993.

p. 189 'Hearn benefited first': *Sunday Times*, 19 February 1995.

p. 190 'Barry Hearn told me': *Independent*, 6 October 1993.

'The reason he wears his hair': *Sydney Morning Herald*, 24 June 2008.

p. 191 'If there was any justice': *Sunday Times*, 16 May 1993.

p. 192 'My man was robbed': *Guardian*, 17 May 1993.

'The judges unavoidably take into account charisma': Chris Eubank,
Eubank: The Autobiography (Willow, 2003).

p. 193 'We are being paid £1 million': *Sunday Mirror*, 20 January 1993.

'HELL'S ANGELS FIGHT OF HATE!': *Daily Mirror*, 13 July 1993.

'One per cent of something': ibid.

p. 194 'There is hatred there': *Daily Mirror*, 13 July 1993.

'snide': *Daily Mirror*, 17 July 1993.

'I just don't like you': ibid.

'As far as I'm concerned': *People*, 18 July 1993.

p. 195 'When I went home': Michael Watson, *The Biggest Fight:
Michael Watson's Story* (Time Warner Books, 2004).

Chapter Twelve. Judgement Day

p. 197 'This is a grudge fight': *The Times*, 6 October 1993.

p. 198 'It raises the possibility': *Independent*, 9 October 1993.

p. 199 'Galvano's reputation as a puncher': *Independent*, 9 October
1993.

'When I fought Nigel last time': *Mail on Sunday*, 3 October 1993.

p. 200 'parliamentary practice': *Independent*, 13 August 1993.

'We will all need time': ibid.

'British fight fans don't particularly care': *Boxing News*, 8 October
1993.

'If the contest between Nigel Benn': *Independent*, 9 October 1993.

p. 203 'Right now, Nigel Benn's frenzy': *The Times*, 7 October 1993.

'They won't be playing tiddlywinks': *Independent*, 7 October 1993.

p. 204 'Eubank put everyone else to sleep': *Independent*, 7 October 1993.

'I let Eubank have the stage': *Sun*, 9 October 1993.

'he could KO a donkey': *Daily Mirror*, 8 October 1993.

'A monocle is for people': *Daily Mirror*, 8 October 1993.

'Nigel Benn and Chris Eubank would be happier': *Sun*, 9 October 1993.

p. 205 'We're looking to bring in about £4 million': *Sun*, 8 October 1993.

'If Nigel thinks about the fight': *Daily Mirror*, 9 October 1993.

'Eubank needs a real contest': ibid.

'Benn's come on a lot': ibid.

'Nigel must be the all-action man': ibid.

p. 206 'It is not that I was not training properly': *Independent*, 7 October 1993.

p. 210 'I'm very pissed off': *Sun*, 11 October 1993.

'I thought I won it': *Mail on Sunday*, 10 October 1993.

'The crowd's reaction': *Boxing News*, 15 October 1993.

p. 211 'All I wanted was for Nigel': *Sun*, 11 October 1993.

'He is trying to get me': ibid.

'A third fight?': *Sunday Times*, 10 October 1993.

Chapter Thirteen. Glory is for God

p. 214 'Anyone would say that this type of schedule': *Daily Mirror*, 24 May 1994.

'The Chris Eubank wagon train': *The Times*, 24 May 1994.

'We would vacate the title': ibid.

'Calling himself Simply the Best': *Daily Mirror*, 27 May 1994.

p. 215 'In more than 20 years': *Sunday Times*, 6 February 1994.

'The man who styles himself': *Sunday Mirror*, 22 May 1994.

'It's soap opera with boxing gloves': *The Times*, 24 May 1994.

'He has done a great job': *Daily Mirror*, 23 May 1994.

'Sky have built it up': *Daily Mirror*, 9 July 1994.

p. 216 'Chris Eubank kept his WBO super-middleweight title': *Sunday Mail* (Glasgow), 10 July 1994.

'If the WBO judges had been in court': *Daily Mirror*, 11 July 1994.

'It may be just as well': *Independent on Sunday*, 10 July 1994.

'Don't go to the show': *Independent on Sunday*, 28 August 1994.

'He has a point': ibid.

'I pulled him out because': ibid.

p. 217 'I didn't buy it for speed': *Sun*, 2 August 1994.

'the philosophy of life and sexology': *Sunday Mirror*, 21 August 1994.

'I got tickets for us to see Barbra Streisand': *Independent on Sunday*, 15 May 1994.

p. 218 'Of course I'm spoilt': *Observer*, 21 August 1994.

p. 219 'I don't get a lot of press': *The Times*, 14 October 1994.

'The old boxing lament': *Independent on Sunday*, 16 October 1994.

'If he had got the decision': *Sunday Mirror*, 16 October 1994.

'IT'S A STEAL, CHRIS': *People*, 16 October 1994.

'EU STINK': *Sunday Mirror*, 16 October 1994.

'LACKLUSTRE EUBANK'S CREDIBILITY': *The Times*, 17 October 1994.

'EU'RE AN INSULT': *Daily Record*, 17 October 1994.

p. 220 'I fight for money': *Daily Mirror*, 17 October 1994.

'I've had to bite my tongue': *Daily Mirror*, 17 October 1994.

'Chris Eubank needs a new theme tune': *People*, 23 October 1994.

p. 222 'There will be no fight otherwise': *Sunday Mirror*, 23 October 1994.

'I feel like the good guy': *Sunday Mirror*, 4 December 1994.

'You are the lowest of the low': *Independent*, 10 December 1994.

'Boxing buffs are drooling': *Daily Mirror*, 8 December 1994.

p. 223 'The WBO super-middleweight champion': *Daily Mirror*, 12 December 1994.

'The man who tries to find glory': ibid.

'the quickest hands, swiftest feet': Budd Schulberg, *Ringside: A Treasury of Boxing Reportage* (Ivan R. Dee Inc., 2006).

'Dodging a fighter': Chris Eubank, *Eubank: The Autobiography* (Willow, 2003).

Chapter Fourteen. Not much showbiz

p. 227 'Eubank and Barry Hearn are involved in trickeration': *Independent*, 28 February 1994.

p. 227 'failed to go the distance in bed': *Daily Mirror*, 11 November 1994.

p. 288 'I'm angry about the knickers': *Daily Mirror*, 11 November 1994.

'I had every reason': Nigel Benn, *Nigel Benn* (Blake Publishing, 1999).

'Paul must have been thinking': ibid.

'What separates me': *Guardian*, 27 February 1995.

p. 229 'The kid was violent': *Observer Sport Monthly*, 4 November 2001.

'I started off with 16 pit bulls': *Daily Mirror*, 7 February 1995.

'a suicide mission': *Daily Mirror*, 20 December 1994.

'This is probably the best': *Independent*, 5 January 1995.

p. 230 'The "Sudden Impact" label': *Independent on Sunday*, 19 February 1995.

'I don't believe Gerald': ibid.

'devastating, dynamite and dangerous': ibid.

'I think Gerald may have': *Independent*, 25 February 1995.

'Benn becomes wild and dangerous': *Sunday Mirror*, 19 February 1995.

p. 231 'If McClellan comes to bomb': *Sunday Mirror*, 19 February 1995.

'If McClellan fails to become champion': *Independent*, 25 February 1995.

'Tibbs was the man who might': *Daily Mirror*, 25 February 1995.

'Benn blitzed Barkley': *Independent on Sunday*, 19 February 1995.

p. 232 'However difficult Chris Eubank was': *Independent*, 21 February 1995.

'It seems like everyone wants Nigel Benn': *Daily Mirror*, 23 February 1995.

'He challenged me': *Daily Mirror*, 24 February 1995.

'If a fight's going to get me going': *Daily Record*, 25 February 1995.

'If Benn tries to have his famous': *Guardian*, 27 February 1995.

p. 233 'I lost the fight?': *Daily Telegraph*, 2 December 2011.

'His brain is quite swollen': *People*, 26 February 1995.

p. 235 'You got what you wanted': *Daily Telegraph*, 2 December 2011.

'It broke my heart': *Independent*, 27 February 1995.

p. 236 'He's not aware he's blind': *Los Angeles Times*, 14 January 1996.

Chapter Fifteen. Twit in a trance

p. 239 'Watch that little Arab': *Sunday Times*, 28 November 1993.

p. 240 'He's flash but we can forgive him': *People*, 9 August 1992.

'I will change British boxing': *Sunday Times*, 28 November 1993.

'He can develop into a bigger': *Daily Mirror*, 24 March 1994.

'I fight so brilliantly': ibid.

'Vincenzo does not understand': *Sunday Times*, 15 May 1994.

'Abolitionists who contend': ibid.

p. 241 'I have to apologise to Eubank': *Sunday Mail* (Glasgow), 21 August 1994.

'without doubt the most exciting': *Daily Record*, 14 October 1994.

p. 242 'I quoted him a small extract': Chris Eubank, *Eubank: The Autobiography* (Willow, 2003).

p. 243 'I have never been so insulted': *Daily Mirror*, 7 February 1995.

p. 244 'Eubank's OK, he's just not in touch': *Independent on Sunday*, 10 March 1995.

'Chris was on the verge': *Daily Mirror*, 18 March 1995.

p. 245 'ON EUR BIKE!': *People*, 19 March 1995.

'TWIT IN A TRANCE': *Sunday Mirror*, 19 March 1995.

'EU HAD IT COMING!': *Daily Record*, 20 March 1995.

'There are legions who are convinced': *Sunday Times*, 19 March 1995.

'Eubank gave his title away': *Sunday Mirror*, 19 March 1995.

'I didn't want what became of Watson': Eubank, *Eubank*.

p. 246 'I'm not annoyed with myself': *Sunday Mirror*, 21 May 1995.

'as soon as my family': *Daily Mirror*, 10 February 1995.

'Collins now says he wasn't': *People*, 21 May 1995.

'a little more ruthlessness': *Independent*, 27 May 1995.

p. 247 'a cheat, a sly creep, a gouger': *Daily Mirror*, 30 May 1995.

'Next time I face Collins': *People*, 30 July 1995.

p. 248 'My career is more important': *Daily Mirror*, 9 September 1995.

'Having beaten Eubank once': *Sunday Mirror*, 3 September 1995.

p. 249 'I don't know what he will do': *Sunday Mirror*, 9 September 1995.

'It's sadly the end': ibid.

p. 250 'I have invested wisely: *Daily Record*, 17 October 1995.

p. 251 'I was only trying to cheer that kid up': Eubank, *Eubank*.

'With my dress code': Eubank, *Eubank*.

'Chrome. Midnight blue. Beautiful': *Sunday Telegraph Magazine*, 11 February 1996.

p. 252 'The truck lifts people': Eubank, *Eubank*.
'The noise is driving me mad': *Daily Mirror*, 2 September 1995.

Chapter Sixteen. That's fucking it

p. 253 'worse than being hit': *Sunday Mirror*, 9 July 1995.
'put the animal back in me': ibid.
p. 254 'Same arena, different man': *Independent*, 24 July 1995.
'The taxman might be looking for him': *The Times*, 24 July 1995.
'We are going to travel down': ibid.
p. 255 'I don't think I am shot': *The Times*, 4 March 1996.
p. 257 'I feel naked without my belt': *The Times*, 29 March 1996.
'I was treated like a king': *Sun*, 1 August 1996.
'I honestly think this is it': *News of the World*, 7 July 1996.
'There is still a lot of fighting': ibid.
'The public who still flock': *Sun*, 10 July 1996.
p. 258 'It was looking more like': *Observer*, 6 October 1996.
'I am becoming more and more aware': *Daily Mirror*, 18 October 1996.
p. 259 'I've been in with Eubank': *Sunday Mirror*, 3 November 1996.
'What I see is a man under pressure': *Sun*, 8 November 1996.
p. 260 'I can't go on': *Sunday Mail* (Glasgow), 10 November 1996.
'Give him his due': *Sunday Times*, 10 November 1996.
'I would not have sat down': *Daily Mirror*, 11 November 1996.
'You've still got a lot to do': ibid.
'What have you come back for?': ibid.
p. 261 'I run my business': Chris Eubank, *Eubank: The Autobiography* (Willow, 2003).
'I shall always wear that big smile': *Sun*, 20 April 1996.
p. 262 'I love boxing': *The Times*, 23 September 1997.
p. 263 'I loved Chris to death': *Sun*, 8 October 1997.
p. 264 'No doubt many of the paying public': *Sun*, 11 October 1997.
p. 266 'If I had got out sooner': *The Argus* (Brighton), 16 November 2000.
p. 269 'Unfortunately, the nature of the modern game': Eubank, *Eubank*.
p. 270 'Naz was taunting and goading me': *Daily Mirror*, 23 October 1997.
'scientific social experiment': Eubank, *Eubank*.

p. 271 'The only way you get into the legendary ranks': *Sunday Mirror*, 5 April 1998.

'I've been to a film premiere': *Independent*, 16 April 1998.

'He's a phoney': *Daily Mirror*, 17 April 1998.

p. 272 'If I was a weaker man': *Daily Mirror*, 17 April 1998.

p. 273 'Have you ever seen such guts?': *Independent*, 20 April 1998.

'I would like to see Chris Eubank retire': *Daily Record*, 20 April 1998.

'If he does carry on': *Sun*, 21 April 1998.

'When I was winning': *The Argus* (Brighton), 13 November 1998.

p. 274 'You win some, you lose some': *Sunday Times*, 19 July 1998.

Chapter Seventeen. So bloody noisy

p. 275 'There exist certain generalised conditions': A. J. Liebling, *The Sweet Science* (Gollancz, 1956).

'Just when the sweet science': Kasia Boddy, *Boxing: A Cultural History* (Reaktion Books, 2008).

p. 277 'People should have been talking about me': BBC Sport website, 4 May 2011.

p. 278 'Now I think I could have fought': *Wales on Sunday*, 29 October 2007.

p. 282 'Boxing can be heartbreaking': BBC Sport website, 8 December 2010.

Chapter Eighteen. People still stare

p. 285 'willingly accepting a risk': *Daily Record*, 20 December 2000.

p. 287 'Michael has no business walking': *Independent on Sunday*, 13 April 2003.

'ashamed but at the same time inspired': *Observer*, 4 May 2003.

p. 288 'It's so difficult to be up in the spotlight': Herol Graham, *Bomber: Behind the Laughter* (T H Media, 2011).

p. 289 'That life, it's over with': *Des Moines Register*, 6 July 2008.

'I'm not coming back for a pay day': BBC Sport website, 11 April 2013.

p. 290 'almost as hard to hit as Will-o'-the-Wisp Willie Pep': Budd Schulberg, *Ringside: A Treasury of Boxing Reportage* (Ivan R. Dee Inc., 2006).

'He's not going to quit fighting': Yahoo! website, 23 April 2013.

'I was hanging out with Eddie Murphy': *Daily News* (New York), 16 April 2011.

p. 291 'I had never dealt with it': *News of the World*, 25 February 2007.

'When he said that he would change': *The Times*, 30 July 2011.

'I was Satan's right-hand man': *Independent*, 7 June 2011.

p. 295 'I had been given the opportunity': Chris Eubank, *Eubank: The Autobiography* (Willow, 2003).

'All I want is for people to say': *Guardian*, 13 March 2002.

p. 298 'I think my character has taken its toll': *Independent on Sunday*, 15 January 2006.

p. 299 'Hello, I am Christopher Livingstone Eubank': *Daily Telegraph*, 3 April 2013.

p. 300 'When Christopher told me': *Sunday Times*, 3 March 2013.

p. 302 'The athlete was inconsolable': *Independent*, 5 August 2012.

p. 307 'I went there to play a game': *Daily Express*, 29 August 2003.

'No way on God's green earth': *Daily Record*, 30 August 2003.

'He's not a talker, he's a brawler': *Evening Times* (Glasgow), 30 August 2003.

'I've moved on. He hasn't': ibid.

Index